H
61
B43

18574

DATE DUE

DEC 1 3 1982		
OCT 31 '83		

30 505 JOSTEN'S

CARLTON E. BECK
Associate Professor of Education
University of Wisconsin-Milwaukee

JIM A. BARAK
Project Assistant in Political Science
University of Wisconsin-Milwaukee

THE STUDY OF SOCIETY

INTERNATIONAL TEXTBOOK COMPANY
Scranton, Pennsylvania

Standard Book Number   7002   2186   7

Copyright ©, 1969, by International Textbook Company

All rights reserved. No part of the material protected by this copyright notice may be reproduced or utilized in any form or by any means, electronic or mechanical, including photocopying, recording, or by any informational storage and retrieval system, without written permission from the copyright owner. Printed in the United States of America by The Haddon Craftsmen, Inc., Scranton, Pennsylvania.
Library of Congress Catalog Card Number: 75-76415

To Helen and Jacqueline
with love
J.B.

It has been justly said that American positivist philosophy ... has achieved the rare feat of being both extremely boring and frivolous in its unconcern with human issues.
—V. Bertalanffy

PREFACE

We have attempted to develop a set of readings which not only will make clear the limitations of the now dominant trends in the methodology of social science, but also will outline a clear alternative. Approximately three-fourths of the readings, therefore, are devoted to the development of a model of social inquiry based on "sympathetic introspection" as a method. The approach developed is an outgrowth of the "symbolic interactionist" sociology developed over the years primarily by social scientists associated with the University of Chicago. This volume undertakes to make a constructive contribution to the debates over methodology and behaviorism by offering a constructive alternative to positivism in social science. The readings outline the methodological foundations and some of the techniques of a non-positivist approach to making the social studies "scientific" by building on what is known about the nature of the subject matter: man.

The starting point for most of the controversies which have raged in the last few years over method in the social sciences has been the desire of many social scientists to make their disciplines more "scientific." The reactions to these programmatic statements of behaviorism have been many and varied. Some have attacked "scientism" from the perspective of some sort of philosophical idealism. Others have been skeptical of some particular technique or project of quantification or operational definition. The critical approach to the so-called behavioral revolution offered in this book is somewhat more limited in scope than the first type and more basic than the latter. This book attempts to outline a critique of the present trends in philosophy of social science and methodology toward positivism and behaviorism, but from a perspective interested in the development of social science, and yet unwilling to ignore the complexities and nuances of the subject matter in a futile quest for rigor and certainty.

This volume is designed primarily for use in three types of courses. It is relevant to a general undergraduate introductory social science course, where it might serve as an introduction to the methods of the social sciences. Second, it is aimed at courses in the philosophy of the social sciences or in the methodologies of the substantive social science disciplines. Third, it should be of use to those concerned with the professional training of social scientists and teachers of the social studies. Its aim is a substantial reorientation of the sociological disciplines, toward a stance which will do justice to the status of the social sciences—the crossroads where science and humanism meet. The social sciences are, or ought to be, the "scientific humanities."

Debts of gratitude for suggestions, advice, possible readings, and bibliographies are necessarily incurred in an enterprise such as this. We therefore express our great appreciation to the authors and journals who have given us reprint permissions. It is our pleasure to thank Professors Earl S. Johnson, Robert Frogge, John McGovern and Thomas Grotelueschen for their help and encouragement. Michael Sullivan read the commentary, and, as a result, the text is far better than it would have been otherwise.

Carlton E. Beck
Jim A. Barak

Milwaukee, Wisconsin
March 1969

CONTRIBUTORS

CHARLES A. BEARD served as president of both the American Historical Association and the American Political Science Association. Among his many books are the monumental four-volume *Rise of American Civilization* (with Mary R. Beard), *An Economic Interpretation of the Constitution*, and *President Roosevelt and the Coming of the War, 1941*. He died in 1948.

HERBERT BLUMER is now Professor of Sociology at the University of California-Berkeley. He taught for many years at the University of Chicago and edited *The American Journal of Sociology*. Among his many publications are a classic study of *Movies and Conduct* and numerous articles on the methodology of the social sciences. A collection of his essays will be published by Prentice-Hall in 1969.

CHARLES H. COOLEY was a pioneer among American sociologists. His trilogy—*Human Nature and the Social Order, Social Organization*, and *Social Process*—has recently been reprinted. Cooley did much of the early thinking on the social genesis of the self. He died in 1929.

EARL S. JOHNSON is Emeritus Professor of the Social Sciences in the University of Chicago, and currently Visiting Professor of Secondary Education at the University of Wisconsin-Milwaukee. He wrote *The Theory and Practice of the Social Studies* and is now preparing for publication a volume on the school and society.

FRANK H. KNIGHT is M. D. Hull Distinguished Service Professor of the Social Sciences and Philosophy in the University of Chicago. His papers have been collected in *The Ethics of Competition, Freedom and Reform*, and *On the History and Method of Economics*. He is the author of some classic volumes on economic theory, as well as of innumerable journal articles.

ROBERT M. MACIVER taught for many years at Columbia University in New York City, as well as at many other institutions in the United States, Canada, and the United Kingdom. *The Web of Government, Power Transformed*, and *Society: A Textbook of*

Sociology are among his many contributions to the social sciences.

C. WRIGHT MILLS was, at his death in 1962, perhaps the best-known sociologist in the United States and had acquired a reputation in the Third World which is still growing. His books, such as *The Power Elite, The Sociological Imagination,* and *Listen Yankee!*, were hard-hitting critiques of current practices. A volume entitled *The New Sociology*, edited by I. L. Horowitz, appeared in memoriam in 1964.

ROBERT REDFIELD was Robert M. Hutchins Distinguished Service Professor of Anthropology in the University of Chicago and served also as Dean of the Division of the Social Sciences. Two volumes of studies edited by Margaret Park Redfield have appeared, entitled *Human Nature and the Study of Society* and *The Social Uses of Social Science*. Together they comprise an extraordinary series of essays on the foundations of the social sciences.

KURT RIEZLER was an exile from German Fascism. His articles on philosophy and social science appeared frequently in American sociological journals. His book, *Man: Mutable and Immutable,* appeared in 1951.

ALFRED SCHUTZ, who died in 1960, taught for many years at the New School for Social Research. His interests spanned philosophy and the social sciences, and he contributed as much in his phenomenological studies as he did in his pure sociology. His collected papers have been published in three volumes by Martinus Nijhoff at the Hague.

FRANCIS D. WORMUTH teaches political science at the University of Utah. His articles on political science have appeared in the professional journals. His essay, "Matched-Dependent Behavioralism," is a recent critique of the quantitative and "scientistic" trends in political science, which are similar to those in the other social studies since the last war.

CONTENTS

PART I Is Social Science a Natural Science? 1

R. M. MacIver
  "Is Sociology a Natural Science?" 9

Frank H. Knight
  "Social Science" 19

Charles A. Beard
  "Written History as an Act of Faith" 33

Earl S. Johnson
  "Ways of Knowing" 44

PART II Understanding in the Social Sciences 57

Kurt Riezler
  "Some Critical Remarks on Man's Science of Man" 64

Charles Horton Cooley
  "The Roots of Social Knowledge" 85

Herbert Blumer
  "Sociological Implications of the Thought of
  George Herbert Mead" 104

Alfred Schutz
  "The Social World and the Theory of Social Action" 120

Robert Redfield
  "Book Review of Social Research" 137

Francis D. Wormuth
  "Matched-Dependent Behavioralism: The Cargo Cult
  in Political Science" 139

PART III Reorientation of Social Science Teaching
  and Research 185

Herbert Blumer
  "What Is Wrong with Social Theory?" 193

C. Wright Mills
> "Two Styles of Research in Current Social Studies" 206

Robert Redfield
> "The Art of Social Science" 219

Earl S. Johnson
> "Humanism and Science in the Social Studies" 235

PART I

IS SOCIAL SCIENCE
       A NATURAL SCIENCE?

INTRODUCTION

It is often said that discussions of method are a mark of the infancy of a discipline. The seeming uselessness of much that passes for discussion of method in the social sciences might incline one to agree with the comment. Nevertheless, even if much of the disputation has been lacking in relevance, it is also true that the quarrels have highlighted some crucial problems. One need not subscribe to what Abraham Kaplan has dubbed the "myth of methodology"—the belief that if one can only devise a correct methodology, the progress of science is assured—to believe that a sensible and realistic account of the logic of social inquiry would be extremely useful in furthering the progress of empirical research.

The discussions about methodology have raised many significant questions. Is social science really a science after the fashion of the physical sciences? If it is, must concepts be made operational? Can social inquiry be value free? Is quantification a necessary part of empirical research in the social sciences? Do contemporary trends encourage a dangerous scientism? Are there laws of human behavior? Knowledge for what? Is sociology a behavioral science? Can science save us? What degree of rigor and precision is possible in concept and theory formation? The interesting point which may be noted about all these questions is that they are all consequences of a single demand: the positivist assertion that the social studies must be positive sciences concerned with the development of objective social knowledge. Because of this it should be worthwhile to inquire into the meaning of this "objectivity" which is demanded.

The meaning of objectivity has never been exactly clear, but the necessity for it has been the stick with which those critical of concern with attitudes and values have for some years beaten their opponents. The need for objectivity has been the *rationale* given for the use of quantitative techniques, the operational definition of concepts, and in general for the mathematical empiricism which has been so pervasive. This need for objectivity has been argued mostly, however, in a negative fashion, e.g., by citing counter-examples, rather than in any cogent formulation. Before introducing the readings on the scientific character of the social sciences, it might clarify things somewhat if we examine the meaning of this crucial notion of objectivity. The reason that the positivist case has often seemed compelling lies in the fact that there are four basic notions, separate and distinct, buried in the usage of the term. When attacked, positivists tend to shift imperceptibly from one usage to another in argument.

The first meaning associated with objectivity is simply "truth." This identification frequently recurs in the literature on method. Writers attempt to identify objective knowledge with truth *per se*, in the sense of "in accord with the facts." An objective or "scientific" approach is contrasted with other forms of knowledge or inquiry which, presumably, yield only opinion. Critics of the cult of objectivity are then accused of ignoring truth and, by implication, of distortion, bias, and perhaps outright falsification. The suggestion is that only those who are objective are concerned with truth.

Objectivity has been linked with truth in a manner something like this: Relativism, for example, argues that the origins of an idea are not irrelevant to its validity. In other words, our judgment of truth hinges to some degree upon the standards, values, and prior assumptions which we bring to bear. Positivists tend to compare any attempt to question the tenets of scientific empiricism (or the simple gathering of facts as a model of inquiry) to deliberate Nazi and Communist attempts to suppress scientific truth and evidence. The clear suggestion is that those who are critical of the positivist model of inquiry are not concerned with the truth.[1]

A second meaning often associated with the concept of objectivity is "neutrality." The usage here approximates the comment sometimes heard in an argument when someone suggests that a party not concerned in the dispute should be brought in because he will be more "objective." Neutrality is thus conceived of as detachment or dispassionate observation, simply "mirroring" in some sense the facts "out there." Passion, commitment, involvement, and concern must be avoided because they hinder disinterested contemplation of the facts. The implication which positivists draw from some instances of commitment leading to bias is that anyone who is not neutral is

---

[1]See Sidney Hook's essay in Hook, ed., *Philosophy and History* (New York: New York University Press, 1963).

INTRODUCTION 5

"unscientific," desiring or at least falling into biased research by way of letting prior commitments obscure the plain facts.[2]

The third connotation which objectivity has acquired links it with "externality," as contrasted with an "inside" or subjective point of view. The term subjective has a double meaning. It may refer to any data which are connected with human values or feelings, or it may refer simply to any findings which cannot be directly or observationally verified. The implicit assumption is that things which are not amenable to direct observation either don't exist or, fortunately, are so unimportant that it is all right to ignore them. Since values, attitudes, and feelings are important, however, even the positivists have had to take practical cognizance of them. Yet they have done this, not in terms of the requirements of the subject matter, but by attempting to ignore them. They have tried to substitute models or operational definitions for reality and then research or work out the implications of these. Thus, the concept of I.Q. supposedly takes the place of the subjective judgment of intelligence. These attempts have so far been somewhat less than completely successful.

The fourth positivist criterion for objectivity is a demand for measurement and quantification. Stuart Rice, for example, has written:[3]

> The quantitative expression of social fact is to be preferred for scientific purposes whenever it can be used. It reduces individual bias to a minimum, permits verification by other investigators, reduces and at the same time makes evident the margin of error, and replaces the less exact meanings of descriptive terms with the precision of mathematical notation.

Many positivists have gone further and virtually identify quantification and scientific method. Non-quantitative research is viewed as unreliable, subjective, and less worthy.

How are these criteria of objectivity to be appraised? In essence, these criteria formulate the positivist assumptions underlying the dominant position in the field of methodology today. The position which one takes in regard to them determines completely one's posi-

---

[2] For a critique of this view which owes something to James Harvey Robinson's remark that objective observation is observation without an object, see Carlton Beck and Jim Barak, "The Place of Values in the Study of Society," *School and Society*, February 18, 1967.

[3] Cited by Pauline V. Young, *Social Scientific Surveys and Research* (4th ed.); Englewood Cliffs, N.J.: Prentice-Hall, 1966, p. 274.

tion in regard to general questions of method. This entire book is really an extended critique of these assumptions and undertakes to offer an alternative set. But a preliminary evaluation may be undertaken at this point in summary of the limitations of the positivist point of view.

1. The identification of objectivity with truth rests upon an oversimple notion of what truth is and what facts are. The latter are seen as hard, specific, unambiguous bits of information which one goes out and collects after the fashion of a rock-hound strolling around a cavern. Whenever a problem arises, the first suggestion of a positivist usually involves "getting all the facts." This language is very interesting. We *find* the facts. But which facts? And how do we know that they are facts? How shall we know them when we find them? The answer is that we do not find them. We *make* facts. Facts are consequents of inquiry, not antecedent to it. The positivist position seems to assume that we have or can get the facts before we start. In truth, a fact is an established piece of information, a warranted assertion which has been validated by inquiry. *Data* are *prior* to an inquiry, *facts* are its *conclusions*. The positivist account of the logic of inquiry reverses the whole thing. Knowledge processes are still imperfectly understood, but it may be confidently asserted that we do not acquire knowledge simply by looking.

2. The truth is simply that the facts are not "out there" to be found. This suggests some limitations of the positivist notion that inquiry can and should be neutral in the sense of being undertaken without preconceptions. The main difficulty is that without prior assumptions, biases, or values we cannot define our objects of inquiry or know which data are relevant. We simply do not just look and see —and see anything! The distinction involved may be illustrated by suggesting that one ponder the difference between what a mechanic and a layman see beneath the hood of an automobile. What is seen is a function of prior knowledge, assumptions, and values. The one case involves looking at a functioning engine, the other gazing aimlessly at a pile of machinery. What we see in research is a function of our hypotheses.

These hypotheses are prior to inquiry. Human beings cannot in any sense simply "mirror" the facts, for there are no simple facts out there to mirror. One can only mirror the data, which is to say, mirror the problem and be confused. The old realist or empiricist account of the process of learning and knowing is far from adequate.

INTRODUCTION

The pragmatic account comes much closer to a description of what goes on in inquiry. There is a problem, which results from a situation as defined by our assumptions and values, and this sets the context of inquiry. The data are selected in terms of the problem. Relevance rests upon connection with the problem under scrutiny. Standards (values, if you will) are involved throughout the process of inquiry, and the researcher is never neutral.

3. The third assumption, that of externality, will be dealt with at some length in the commentary on the second set of readings, but a few comments may be offered here. First, one notices the positivist desire to limit the data of the social scientist to phenomena which are capable of direct observation or simple measurement. If this program were carried out successfully, nearly all of the subject matter of the social sciences and everything that makes human behavior distinct from that of other living organisms would be ruled out of social science. In the nature of the case, the program cannot be carried out, but a quest for certainty which ignores most of the subject matter is, to say the least, a positive inhibition to the progress of science. In fact, externality itself is no guarantee of certainty. The notion implies a consensus definition of truth—an idea which is in itself highly questionable.

4. The fourth assumption of a positivist philosophy of social science, that which demands quantification and measurement as the *sine qua non* of science, may also be criticized. No one denies that measurement is often a necessary tool or that quantification is often indispensable in studies, for example, which involve mass behavior; mathematical treatment sometimes does add rigor and precision. But much of human behavior is simply not amenable to fruitful quantitative treatment. Such techniques can be used, but they are less appropriate or productive than, for example, interviewing or participant observation. The underlying difficulty involves the fact that human beings are not interchangeable units, such as those required for mathematical calculation. Sociological inquiry, as Herbert Blumer has pointed out, is often centered on exactly the difference between one peasant and another or between one wife and another. Individuals in social science cannot be reduced to cases or instances of a type, and feelings, values, and attitudes are never exactly comparable.

To conclude, in the social sciences we are not dealing with inquiry after the model postulated by the positivist philosophy of social science. We do deal with warranted assertions and facts accumulated by inquiry, but not with truth conceived of as the simple gathering and manipulation of data. As William James once remarked, the mind is no "prolix gut to be stuffed." In sum, the social sciences are not limited to external observation, quantitative measurement, and a spectator theory of knowledge. To treat the social studies as positive sciences misconstrues the nature of science and the nature of man.

R. M. MacIVER

IS SOCIOLOGY A NATURAL SCIENCE?*

Sociologists are and have been much concerned with the question of their scientific standing. One is tempted to recommend that we students of sociology forget altogether for a time the very word "science," that we disregard altogether, for the present, the claims of our subject to be a science. But a better alternative would be that we reflect more thoroughly on scientific method, for such reflection would show that many of our ideas about science are not themselves scientific. Take for example our idea of induction. We are apt to set induction over against deduction, regarding the former as a simple, easily understood, all-sufficing, and alone legitimate process of passing from particulars to the general. It is safe to say that, so understood, induction is a chimera and is never the method by which scientific generalization is attained.

Sociology has been plagued all through its history by its tendency to seek for models in the fields of the other sciences. At one time the fashion was to think of a society as a kind of organism, to make sociology a pale reflection of biology. Now the attitude changes and the first article of the creed has become the formula that sociology is a "natural science." Unfortunately this claim may mean anything or nothing. Of all words, the word "natural" is the most equivocal. "Natural" in contradistinction to what? Assuredly not to unnatural or to supernatural, since there are no unnatural or supernatural sciences. Assuredly again it cannot be natural as opposed to social, because it is the social we are speaking of. I can, in fact, find no meaning in the assertion unless it be that the social sciences either use the same methods or deal with the same types of phenomena as do the sciences sometimes distinguished by the term "natural." One or other of these claims must be asserted under this dubious rubric and

*Reprinted by permission of *Proceedings of the American Sociological Society*, Vol. XXV, No. 2 (May 1931), pp 25-35.

that this position is taken the context usually shows. The implication is that sociology, like the physical sciences, is concerned with objects of perception, objects amenable to registration by means of instruments, objects divisible into units capable of summation and other quantitative processes.

Is this a dogma or is it a conclusion derived from reflection on the proper subject matter of sociology? It is implied in these "natural science" manifestoes that the subject matter of sociology is very similar to that of the physical sciences and that therefore the same tools of investigation should be employed. This position, I shall try to show, ignores or denies the very differentia of our subject matter. It ignores precisely the difference between a physical relationship and a social relationship.

It is easy to pass from extreme to extreme, from the bold generalizations of Spencer and Ward to the rejection of theory altogether in the name of the sacred fact. It is easy to pass from a social science saturated with theological and moralistic prepossessions to one animated by the revolutionary dogma of behaviorism. From a discredited conception of the nature of consciousness men revert to a conception which ignores its existence; from an outworn principle of values to a viewpoint which deals with social relationships as though they existed objectively apart from the values which created them.

The trouble is that the social sciences suffer from certain embarrassments from which the "natural sciences" are more or less free. They have to deal with phenomena which involve a kind of causation unknown in the purely physical world, since they are "motivated," in fact brought into being, by that elusive and complex, but undeniable, reality, the mentality of man. Not a single object which the social sciences study would exist at all were it not for the creative imagination of social beings. Consequently the social sciences have to deal with variable and indeterminate concept such as capital and labor, family and nation, state and sovereignty, crime and unemployment, folkways, institutions, social attitudes, and other intangibles. The social scientist has no "natural" classifications to guide him such as those with which nature is expected to accommodate the geologist or the entomologist. Under these circumstances every authority is free to define his concepts in his own way and treat them in his own way. Consequently it is easy to pose as an authority. In the resulting confusion men turn with longing eyes to the non-social sciences. Let us follow their example, they say, and all will be well. Let us ignore the differences between our subject matter and theirs. Let's have social physics and social mechanics and social engineering; let's talk of social organisms, of social osmosis, and of social symbiosis. Let's lay out attitudes along a line and construct a yardstick to measure opinions. Let's get a perceptual basis for all our distinctions. Let's find out what radicals and conservatives really are by setting down the percentage of accuracy with which those so-called can draw correctly an object seen through the looking glass. Let's reduce temperaments to glandular activities. Let's measure all the incommensurates and weigh all the imponderables. Thus shall we have vindicated the claim of the social sciences to be sciences indeed.

I confess that this kind of emulation makes little appeal to me. The aim of the sciences of society should not be to dress themselves in the garments of their elders and look so like them that the guardians of the halls of science will not perceive the difference. The object of science is to carry the light of understanding, to show us truth. If a piece of research aids us to understand better, more fully, some aspect of this so complex universe of man and nature, then is it worth while. If it does not, then no parade of figures will make it anything more than labor lost. Our methods should be adjusted to our materials and not our materials to our methods. There are some adherents of method who, like the extreme behaviorists, would even jettison their proper subject in order to claim the name of science for a beggarly residue. They would imitate at all costs the mathematicians and the physicists. Imitation, though always bearing the signs of the inferiority complex, may nevertheless succeed when, in following its original, it is applying like tools to like materials. But it is most apt to fail when it applies like tools to unlike materials, and this is just what the social scientist is in danger of doing. For his subject matter is very different, and it therefore craves a different mode of treatment. What we are seeking must always determine how we seek. We do not cut wood with a shears or cloth with a saw. We do not comprehend legal codes by measuring them or discover the origins of the World War by an index of culpabilities. There are fundamental methods common to all the sciences—though these are just the methods which our devotees of the "natural science approach" to society ignore—but each has its distinctive methods as well. The botanist cannot be content with the methods of the astronomer or the biologist with those of the physicist. Each must discover his own road to his truth. And first he must know what kind of truth he is out to find.

Unfortunately many of our social researchers go forth without stopping to ask what the object of their search may be. Armed with method all they ask is a field in which to hunt. Then they are sure to bring home a large bag of facts. A scholar once told me he was going to study unemployment. I asked him what aspect of the subject he was going to study, and he replied that he was going to gather all the facts first, and then decide. Now no one can gather all the facts "about" unemployment, even if he had endless time and infinite energy and all the resources of all the foundations. Facts do not lie around, like pebbles waiting for the picker, or even lie embedded, like precious stones to be dug for with patience. They become facts only as we learn how to treat them as facts, and therein lies another problem to which I shall return. But many of our young scholars are led to believe that there is an article called a hard fact, or sometimes a cold fact, that they lie around in plenty, and that when you have discovered a number of them they will "speak for themselves." Those who go out in this faith are apt to find that the so-called facts speak with a mighty small voice, and the wiser ones learn at length that, so far from the facts speaking for themselves, they have to act as ventriloquists for their facts. In plainer language they must become interpreters, for the facts come into being only with the work of interpretation, and they grow more numerous and more interesting and more complicated and more ordered and more simple as the interpreter brings his own intelligence into play. They will give him no answers except the answers he himself construes for his own questions. And he cannot ask questions unless he knows what he is in search of.

Our would-be imitators of the natural sciences—I call them "would-be," because, like other imitators, they generally have an antiquated conception of their live and changing model—are so engrossed in method that they have no questions to ask of their subject matter. The following seem to be the chief tenets of their creed. First, I believe in facts, and to be saved I must discover new ones. Second, when I have discovered them, I must if possible measure them, but, failing that consummation, I must count them. Third, while all facts are sacred, all theories are of the devil. Hence the next best thing, if one can't discover new facts, is to refute old theories. This can be done very simply by taking a few cold facts and applying them. But the process is so easy that not much merit is acquired that way. "The primary business of the scholar," says one exponent of the school, "is to deal with facts rather than theories." How you can "deal with" facts apart from theories remains a mystery of the faith. Since, as a profane outsider, I can see no way in which a fact can be apprehended, much less related to others, without a theory, I am inclined to think that the whole of the faith has not been divulged. I observe certain indications that among the elect it is permissible to hold theories in secret, the primary condition being that they shall never be disturbed, or even mentioned.

The spread of this faith from certain elders to the younger generation of scholars has been very remarkable. It is particularly in evidence at the preliminary stage when the candidate for a higher degree is looking around for a subject on which to operate. For example, his first requirement for a possible theme is this: Has it ever been "done" before? If someone has already staked his claim over it then he must go elsewhere in his search, even if, like other seekers after virgin soil, he must push on into less promising and less fertile regions. This vain idea that a subject is "done" once for all is part of the same doctrine that the researcher must go out to gather the hard facts and that once these are gathered the field is bare. That research may consist in the interpretation of data already known, in the critical analysis of materials already provided, in the illumination of a subject of interest that may come from the sheer use of the reflective judgment of the trained student—all this is alien to the code. One result is that the very idea of research tends to be narrowed to a kind of mechanical spade work—digging up the hard facts. It is interesting to observe, also, that the hard facts are only certain kinds of facts. Thus it is research to collect the ideas of primitive peoples or primitive parts of the population, such as the Plains Indians or the inhabitants of the Kentucky Mountains, or even of the lower economic classes; but it is not research to examine the social ideas of the well-to-do or the cultivated. It is research to collect all the doctrines of a particular author and set them in a chronological "pattern," but it is more dubious research to scrutinize and evaluate any of his deliverances. It is research to test radicals and conservatives by confronting them with mirror images, or to discover what percentage of them were made radicals by unhappy marriages or by bad harvests; but it is hardly research to inquire into the opposing ideals and antithetical schemes of life which may correspond to these terms. It is research to produce any new and valid row of figures, but it is not research to give meaning to the figures which someone else has produced. Is it because the latter is too easy a task—or too difficult?

I am not—far from it—arguing against what is called the quantitative method in the social sciences. The further it can go the better, the surer, our knowledge will become. I am arguing against the naive assumptions which accompany a too exclusive confidence in the use of statistics. I am suggesting that the quantitative method can by itself yield us nothing but quantities, and that in the social sciences quantities—averages, ratios, correlations, and so forth—are not the goals, but only the media, of our research. What we are really seeking to understand are systems of relationship, not series of quantities. With the quantitative method must go hand in hand the method of logical analysis and synthesis. This of course is true of every science. What would we think, to take a crude example (but one very suggestive of the practice of many social researchers), of the meteorologist who sought to discover the relationship between lightning, thunder, and rain-clouds solely by the statistical method; who collected as many instances as possible in which lightning was seen and no thunder heard, in which thunder was heard and no lightning seen, and in which both lightning and thunder were observed but no rain fell; who then computed percentages and let it go at that? Possibly he might discover some observer who, like the ancient Horace, declared he had heard thunder coming from a clear sky—a triumphant addition to his collection of "facts."

Again, I am not arguing against the necessity for the direct and thorough exploration of the field of study. Thoroughness is the hallmark of the true scholar. I am really protesting against a code which is content with the job half-done and omits the less mechanical, more exigent, and more rewarding part of it. It is not enough to muster those raw materials we call the facts. I am pleading for the finished product. We need more raw materials, but even now we are not using a tithe of the raw materials which we possess. Take, for instance, such a mine of wealth as the U.S. Census. Much of it remains unexploited. In the social field the task of providing the raw materials is proving too big for individual scholars and is becoming more and more the task of governments and co-operative agencies such as the foundations. This is as it should be. In our social utopia the individual scholar will no longer think it his job to go out with his spade and do in some corner what governments and foundations are doing with their steam shovels. He will do what these great agencies cannot do for him, but what they can vastly encourage him to do for himself—take up the expert and arduous task of interpretation. If, for example, he has before him sufficient data to show how the pressure of social conformism weighs down the life of the small American town, he will then investigate the theoretical question of why it should be so, or the practical question of what, if anything, can be done about it.

I am protesting against the code which mechanizes research. Many of our scholars have the notion that, for the complete researcher, all that is needed is to send out questionnaires, describe the process and the results, tot up the "yesses" and the "noes," and work out some correlations. I am protesting against the theory that a work of research must be dull. I believe that the danger of mechanized research in the social sciences is peculiarly great at the present time. In an age of general mechanization, highly desirable practically but too engrossing spiritually, we might well expect that danger. But it confronts us also for a special reason. Those who on the boards of foundations or universities dispense research funds have a very difficult task in adjudging the relative merits of the numerous projects laid before them. If they seek to do it at all they are almost bound to lay down certain standards to which a project must conform, and these standards are most likely to include such objective and measurable considerations as the novelty of the project, the definiteness of the results to be expected, and so forth. I submit that such standards, excellent in intention, are likely to encourage the one-sided idea of research which I am opposing. I believe it would be the wiser course for such bodies not to depend on such standards at all, to make their decisions not in terms of any expected results whatever, but almost solely in terms of the quality or competence or promise already exhibited by the respective claimants.

To make research mechanical, to make it safe, is to rob it of most of its meaning and all of its interest. Research is exploration of the yet unknown, and every explorer, to be worthy of the name, must take risks. By the use of quantitative methods, where they are admissible, he will avoid unnecessary risks—foolish risks—but do not deny him on that account the use of his intelligence and of his imagination, the precarious and exhilarating business of judicious speculation. In some important fields, such as law and history, he will probably not be able to use these methods at all. In others, particularly where we deal with natural units, as in population studies, or with conventional ones, as in economics, they are quite essential. But even in these latter fields they will carry the scholar only to the halfway house of correlation. Do not encourage him to stop there —it is still far from his goal. If theories without facts are empty, facts without theories are blind. I fully sympathize with the reaction against uncontrolled speculation, which is as bad in scholarship as in business. But neither business nor scholarship can prosper without some degree of speculation, and its absence is a sure sign of lean and meager times. In both spheres we must find ways to control it, not to abolish it. There was a time when the social sciences generalized overboldly, without adequate control over their materials. There were economists who found one simple law to explain everything, and there were sociologists who discovered a new law on every page. "The fathers have eaten sour grapes and the teeth of the children are set on edge." In revolt from their sometimes foolhardy fathers they vainly seek for foolproof methods of getting at new truth. But no great, perhaps no small, discovery even, is made without the aid of the imagination, disciplined and rendered critical by appropriate training. No facts ever speak for themselves, and no figures ever proclaim the truth behind them. Only he that has eyes to see can see. Without the spark of imagination no one is fitted to be a researcher, but this truth is unfortunately able to pass unnoticed under the influence of the prevailing code.

We may, perhaps, sum up the matter as follows: first, the aim and method of all science is broadly the same. Science is never concerned with facts as isolated facts; it is never merely empirical. It is concerned with phenomena as they reveal an order, a system of relationships. Science, therefore, begins with concepts which it seeks to refine, correct, and establish so that by their aid it may comprehend that consistency and coherence of reality, the belief in which is its first article of faith. Second, the specific methods of the various sciences vary with the specific subject matters with which they deal. These specific methods cannot be determined a priori nor derived by analogy. Only experience in dealing with our subject matter can teach us the appropriate methods to employ. Third, the subject matter of sociology—and of all the social sciences in so far as they

IS SOCIOLOGY A NATURAL SCIENCE? 17

are really social—differs in some highly important respects from that of the physical sciences.

Since this last point is crucial, we must deal with it further. Society presents us with a vast array of individual social situations, each in some respects unique, but science always seeks to pass beyond the concrete to the abstract. It cannot deal with any situation in all its concreteness. It is not as a concrete occurrence but as a system of phenomena revealing a present focus of relationships and a process of continuity, that science must deal with the individual situation. We shall not here consider the greater question of the general laws which is the further goal of science. We shall confine ourselves to the mode in which a given situation presents itself for scientific treatment.

The following summary statement is all that the limits of this paper permit me to put forward on this subject.

1. Every social situation consists in an adjustment of an inner to an outer system of reality. The inner system is a complex of desires and motivations; the outer is a complex of environmental factors, in so far as these constitute the means, opportunities, obstacles, and conditions to which the inner system is adjusted. It is this relationship between an inner and an outer which constitutes, in respect to the problem of causality, the essential difference between the social and the physical sciences. The latter are concerned with an outer order alone.

2. Each system, the inner and the outer, is coherent in itself and the two together form also a single coherence. In other words, for the social scientist, the outer is never, as in physics, a mere outer. A room is not a four-walled inclosure with apertures for light and air and with various objects of wood and metal and cloth strewn about it. A city block is not, for the sociologist, a peculiar configuration of stone, iron, and glass. The outer is always seen under an aspect. It is shot through with significance. It reflects human purposes and human limitations. For the sociologist, the outer is always an environment.

3. Each system has, in relation to any attribute of it which may be under sociological investigation, a specific character. To interpret the attribute, it is necessary to know its relation to a specific situation. If, for example, we are seeking to explain the prevalence of divorce in the United States, or in any portion of it, it is not enough to refer to such general characteristics as mobility of population,

degree of prosperity, economic opportunity for women, religious attitudes, modes of education. A peculiar conjuncture of these and other factors is present and unless we understand that peculiar conjuncture, we cannot hope to explain, for example, why the divorce rate is so much higher in Oregon than, say, in Massachusetts. Or again, it is not enough to explain a phenomenon like the gang as due to the desire of the adolescent for companionship and adventure, since these general desires, to bring the phenomenon into being, are directed, modified, and made specific by the ethos of the group and by the opportunities or hindrances of its expression. Nor, turning to the outer system, can we adequately explain the phenomenon as the consequence of poverty and deteriorated neighborhoods, since these factors may equally be adduced to explain other social phenomena such as ignorance, crime, desertion, alcoholism, drug addiction, prostitution, etc., and since, in any event, these factors may be present in a greater or less degree, without involving a greater or less development of the phenomenon. The specific phenomenon involves, in addition, specific opportunities, specific needs, specific stimulants, or precipitates.

4. The interpretation of a social phenomenon is never more than approximate. It depends on an understanding of the relation of inner to outer, an understanding which demands experience as well as knowledge, insight as well as calculation. There can be no complete explanation, just as there can be no mechanical method of discovering social causation. An explanation in this field is always a partially verified hypothesis and there is no such thing as complete verification. The idea of complete verification depends on an oversimple concept of induction. A negative instance does not necessarily disprove a conclusion, nor does any quantity of positive instances completely prove it. Because insight is necessary, hazard is always present.

I conclude that the great need of sociology is not ready-made methods nor ready-made models but the trained and disciplined imagination. Just as this capacity is needed in a treatment of practical problems, whether on the scale of the family, or of our international civilization, so it is needed in the building up of a science. Let us even forget that we are scientists, if only we remember that we are seekers after truth, that our aim is to understand and to convey to others the understanding of the intricate and often baffling web of social relationships, which, being created by man, must be understood by a similar creative capacity in ourselves.

FRANK H. KNIGHT

SOCIAL SCIENCE [1]

When we speak of social science we are reminded that originally and etymologically the word "science" is more or less a synonym for knowledge. Our inquiry has to do with what we know, and can know, and how, about society. The question inevitably runs into that of the meaning of knowledge itself and, as a part of its meaning, its function, or why we want it, and hence raises at the outset the ultimate problems of philosophy. In this field, as elsewhere, knowledge is wanted both for its own sake and for use. It is a serious reflection that the unsatisfactory state of affairs in social science has largely resulted from the very progress of science, the revolutionary development of techniques for acquiring knowledge, and applying knowledge, which is an outstanding feature and achievement of civilization in our own and recent time.

The primary function of a discussion such as this—at least such is the main point contended for in this paper—is to correct a fallacy which is particularly current in social-science circles. The fallacy is that social science is a science in the same sense as the natural sciences, in which the revolution has occurred, that its problems are to be solved by carrying over into the study of society the methods and techniques which have produced the celebrated triumphal march of science in the study of nature, and that this procedure will lead to a parallel triumph in our field, both in the yielding of knowledge and insight and in the transformation of life.

In this connection in particular—more or less characteristically for social problems in so far as they can be solved—it would seem that a clear statement of the issue ought to be sufficient to resolve it definitively. It ought to be obvious that the relation of knowledge to action cannot be the same or closely similar, nor can knowledge itself,

[1] A paper presented at a joint session of the American Philosophical Association and Section K of the American Association for the Advancement of Science, Philadelphia, December 28, 1940. Reprinted in *Ethics,* Vol. LI, No. 2 (January 1941), pp 127–143.

apart from the question of action, be at all the same where the knower and the known are identical as where they are external to each other. In a genetic-historical view the fundamental revolution in outlook which represents the real beginning of modern natural science was the discovery that the inert objects of nature are not like men, i.e., subject to persuasion, exhortation, coercion, deception, etc., but are "inexorable." The position which we have to combat seems to rest upon an inference, characteristically drawn by the "best minds" of our race, that since natural objects are not like men, men must be like natural objects. The history of British-American social thought in modern times is particularly interesting in this connection. In general, it has represented a combination of positivism and pragmatism— two philosophical positions with respect to the nature of man and his place in the cosmos and specifically with respect to social action, which are at once contradictory between themselves, and equally indefensible as a basis of social action. For man, conceived in positivistic terms, could not act at all; and conceived in pragmatic terms, he could not act upon himself.

So much for the negative view of the problem, which brings us to the point at which the discussion ought to begin. From an affirmative or constructive standpoint the case is far less simple. For, on the one hand, there certainly can be and are, within some limits, "positive" sciences of man and society—not one but many—and these are in widely varying degrees of like kind with the sciences of nature. And, unquestionably, these "natural" sciences of man not only yield genuine knowledge but are of genuine and profound relevance to action. In view of what has been said the possibility of such sciences becomes a mystery to be explained, as well as their necessary limitations.

As these statements imply, any truly rational attack upon the problems of knowledge and of action, in connection with human and social data, must at least provisionally rest upon a pluralistic conception of the object matter. It is an indisputable fact that man is a physical object and that man, as an object, and the phenomena into which he enters are in part to be explained by physical science. And man also is a biological organism and as such is in part to be explained, with the phenomena in which he plays a role, by biological science.[2]

[2]Of course this raises the issue whether biological phenomena might ultimately be explained as physical phenomena merely. The question cannot be argued here, beyond noting that biological science does use teleological categories, like struggle and adaptation, and that it is sheer dogmatism to assert that they could be reduced to purely physical or positive content.

Next, it is as indisputably a matter of fact, in the inclusive sense, that man and human phenomena present characteristics which any discussion must and does recognize as sharply different from those of nonhuman biology. Man is a being who thinks, and acts on the basis of thinking, in a way which sharply differentiates him from any other organic species and which, we have to assume, is not characteristic of inanimate nature at all. Other distinctions will be developed in the detail allowable, as we proceed. It should be clear that man is at the same time many different kinds of being or entity which are not reducible to any one kind. The urge to treat man scientifically in the sense of the natural, and specifically the physical, sciences can itself be readily explained. Man as an intellectual inquirer is characterized by a craving for intellectual simplification and unification, for monism as against pluralism. And since "he" cannot deny that "man" is a physical being, this craving leads him to deny that he is anything else. And of course the triumph of physical science and technology, in yielding intellectually satisfactory knowledge along with power to transform his environment and his own life, contributes largely to the strengthening of the prejudice. But why these considerations should actually lead man as inquirer to deny to man the characteristics of an inquirer (even the faculty of denying) must be allowed to remain in the status of mystery as far as the present essay or the present writer is concerned.

We enter upon the domain of social science with the naming of the next familiar distinguishing characteristic of man—that he is a "social animal." The statement does not of course have for us its original significance of a member of a *polis*. But it has a profusion of other meanings, at least three of which must be distinguished. In the first place, the sociality of man is in fact utterly different from that of any other species, and it is for the most part the differences which enter into the subject matter of social science. It is not as an animal that man is social, and the designation of a social animal is misleading and essentially untrue. In the subhuman animal kingdom there is no clear line between aggregates which consist of associated individuals and others which are to be viewed as individual organisms composed of units or cells. Human society is again pluralistic in that it presents both characteristics to a striking degree, but it presents both in a highly distinctive sense.

The important facts about human society, whether from the standpoint of knowledge and understanding for their own sake or for use in action, is that it is made up of units of the general character insisted upon in the next to the last paragraph, i.e., rationally purposive individuals. Man is an individual in a special and unique sense—a sense which goes infinitely beyond the meaning of the term in any other connection. Yet this particular kind of individual is also social, in a sense just as distinctive and unique. The kind of society which human society is presupposes such uniquely individualistic individuals, and at the same time the existence of such individuals presupposes the existence of such a society. This relationship is embarrassing to the analytical student in making it difficult to discuss either man as an individual or human society, prior to discussion of the other.

Man and society necessarily developed from animal life in a historical process of creative interaction of individuals upon each other and of interaction between individual and group, extending over a long geological epoch. The history of this development, which would no doubt help a great deal toward understanding and exposition, is almost completely and irrevocably lost. The biological strain which led to man must have branched off from the evolutionary tree at a point where life was not social in either of the main possible senses of the word. The most developed form of animal society is a termite colony. Its structural organization, its functioning, and all the phenomena which belong in it are (presumably) based upon instinct. But human society involves a widely different animal type, belonging to a branch the other orders and families of which are not truly social. It is not based on instinct, and it is more than doubtful whether this type of social life could have evolved out of instinctive social life. It would seem as if there had to be, as an intermediate link, society in a third meaning, based upon tradition or "institutions." Institutional life is a quasi-mechanical concept, involving habit in the individual and the transmission of the pattern of associative life by unconscious imitation, i.e., by social or cultural, in contrast with biological, inheritance. Traditional or institutional associative life was important in human evolution because it allowed for adaptive modification independent of biological and biologically inherited change, whether by natural selection of random variations or by mutation.[3]

[3] Cf. preceding note as to instinct and mechanism. It may be doubted whether purely institutional social order is conceivable, apart from a degree of individualism on the part of the units; and it is still more doubtful whether such a picture of human development is in harmony with the facts, such as are available as a basis for inference, in existing primitive societies and in the evident incipient rationality of the higher animals, and even more in their emotional makeup.

Because human society is an association of consciously purposive individuals rather than an organism to be viewed as a unit and analyzed into individual components (or while it is both, the former viewpoint is more fundamental) the individual is logically prior to society. A more decisive reason is that the study of society is, and cannot be kept from being, relative to social problems—problems of social action; and in a society which has the essential character of human society such problems arise out of the individual nature of the individual human being rather than out of his social nature. In a society based upon instinct or even in one based exclusively upon tradition and institutions there are no problems, either individual or social, for, or to, either the society itself or the individuals which compose it. Human social problems arise out of *conflicts of interest* between individual members. From this point of view a termite colony is in principle of the same kind as an animal organism, the individual members being in the position of cells. And the same would be true of a society which was purely a phenomenon of socially inherited patterns of associative life.

The argument so far shows that man must be described in terms of at least five fundamental kinds of entity or being. He is (*a*) a physical mechanism; (*b*) a biological organism, with characteristics extending from those of the lowest plant to the highest animal in the biological scale; (*c*) a social animal in the traditional-institutional sense; (*d*) a consciously, deliberatively purposive individual; and, concomitantly, (*e*) a social being in the unique sense of an association of such individuals. (He may also be to some extent a social animal in the proper instinctive sense; but, if so, it is to such a limited degree that for present purposes it may be left out of account.)

It is evident that at least the first three of these types of existence can each be the subject matter of a distinct positive science or group of such sciences. And these sciences have already been more or less extensively developed. We do have more or less distinctively human physics and chemistry, human biology, and institutional science, sociology, or culture anthropology. And of the last, in particular, there are many branches, including institutional economics. Each of these sciences deals descriptively with an aspect of human phenomena which is isolated and treated in the positive terms of "uniformities of coexistence and sequence," which is the general pattern of a natural science. At least one further distinction must be made—a fourth type of scientifically describable form of existence recognized. Consciousness is not necessarily or always active, deliberative, or problem-solving. And to the extent that it is not of this character but is phenomenal (or epiphenomenal), it is possible, in theory, and more or less so actually, to describe consciousness in positive categories. Such description is the task and subject matter of another highly developed science—that of psychology—in the meaning indicated by the statement, which is its original and proper meaning, in distinction from various special physical and biological sciences such as neurology, physiology, and "behaviorology."

It is also evident that all these sciences must in a sense take account of the social nature of man. Yet they are not social sciences, with the exception of culture anthropology. This is in a sense *the* science of society, if the word is restricted, as far as the subject matter allows, to the category of a natural or positive science. But it should hardly be necessary to emphasize that the content of culture anthropology as a positive science—namely, institutions—is not learned like natural science data through sense observation merely but primarily through intercommunication. And the science can have no direct significance for social action in the society of the scientist himself; for if it results in such action, its conclusions are no longer true. It does, however, need to be emphasized that culture anthropology may have for its subject matter a very large range of the phenomena characteristic of societies which do face and solve problems, which "act," on the basis of deliberation by the society as a unit. The phenomena of our own society are very largely of the traditional-institutional character, and this must be true of any society which is even intellectually conceivable, just as any real or possible society must involve human beings in all their "lower" aspects. The study of these phenomena may bring them above the threshold of social awareness and make them problems of social action.

The study of actual or possible society must involve a large congeries of special positive sciences, more or less effectively interrelated, co-ordinated, and unified, according to the actual possibilities of such an achievement, which are to be discovered only by trying. But such study must also involve other sciences not of the positive sort, or only partly so, but still sciences, bodies of knowledge. It must involve social science in a distinctive sense, the nature of which must be considered in the light of the nature of the human individual as the real unit.

The main distinctive characteristic of the human being has already been mentioned; he is individualistically and rationally purposive. But this concept calls for further analysis. One aspect of rationality appears in the use of means to achieve ends. And it goes without saying that any means used by an individual are used to realize ends which are individual (though they may also be social) and are at the same time individual means. The human individual, then, inherently involves two aspects—individual ends and individual possession or control over means or power. These two aspects, factors, or elements constitute the economic man—a concept methodologically analogous to the frictionless machine of theoretical mechanics and essential to analysis in the same way.

The notion of power in turn includes two factors: (*a*) possession or control of means in the narrow sense of actual things or instruments used in purposive activity and (*b*) knowledge of the use of means (with skill in an ambiguous position). The confusion between means in the concrete sense and procedures for using means, the content of knowledge in its economic aspects, under the inclusive term "means," is one of the serious confusions in our everyday terminology. A much more important confusion prevails with reference to the meaning of the end in economic behavior (the behavior of the economic man). The concept of economy clearly implies a *given* end and one which is measurable, or quantitatively comparable with other ends, in terms of the means to be employed. Economic behavior implies or is, in the degree in which it is economic, the use of means in such a way as to realize the maximum quantity of some general end or objective, embodied in specific wants and conditioned by the limited means available to an individual subject. The general end, now usually called "want satisfaction," is to be realized by correct apportionment of the given means among various modes of use, bound up in a "preference function" with intermediate specific ends or wants. Further analysis or discussion cannot be undertaken here. The essential point at the moment is that in economic behavior as a concept ends are given, defined by actual preferences on the part of the subject as an economic man as he stands at the moment of making any choice involving the disposal of means. A preference is a datum, whether it represents merely individual taste, or good taste, or the solution of a value problem reached in preceding "calm, cool hours" of deliberation.

Thus the notion of economic behavior defines a particular form of rational-deliberative or problem-solving activity or *conduct*, involving what may be referred to as economic rationality. Such behavior is the subject matter of several descriptive social sciences and of theoretical economics. Economic activity is to be sharply distinquished from other, and higher, forms of rationality or problem-solving, to be noticed presently. But economic rationality requires further discussion because it exemplifies problem-solving at the level of greatest simplicity, and the general features of problem-solving activity are crucial for our discussion as a whole. It is of the essence of such activity, and hence of distinctively human behavior (conduct), that, by virtue of being problematic, the course of events involved is not accurately predictable in advance, in terms of any possible knowledge. That is, it is conceptually distinct from mechanical cause-and-effect sequence and so cannot be made the subject matter of any positive science. A problem is not a problem unless the solution involves effort and is subject to *error,* features, or notions which are absolutely excluded from mechanical process or positive cause and effect.

But human behavior, in an essential part, element, or aspect, is problem-solving, and first in the limited sense of economic problem-solving. The human being does confront the problem of using given means to realize given ends and does solve this problem *more or less* correctly. To think of its always being solved correctly would be to deny that it is a problem and to deny an undeniable fact. Thus perfect economic rationality, while implied as a "limiting case" in the notion of varying degrees of it, is as a real concept self-contradictory. (It is exactly like the concept of universal causality in this respect.)

Another significant aspect of the notion of economy, which should not be overlooked in any discussion of methodology, is that as a quality of motivation it is a purely intuitive idea. Even the propositions of mathematics can be derived and verified inductively, to a degree of generality and accuracy to which there is hardly any limit except that of cost in time and effort; but no mere sense observation can give any indication as to whether any conduct is economic, or in what degree. Even the subject himself cannot know at all accurately, even afterward.

But economic rationality as a description of deliberative conduct is limited in two further respects, fully as important in principle as the fact that actual results of action diverge in all degrees from the intention of maximizing a given end. First, the end is rarely or never actually given in any strict sense of the word; rather, it is in some degree redefined in the course of the activity directed toward realizing it, and the interest in action centers in this definition and discovery of ends, as well as in their achievement. That is, the end is always itself more or less *problematic,* as well as the procedure (use of means) for realizing it. One of the most absurd items in the common folklore about human beings is the idea that they know what they want or that "there is no disputing about tastes." It may be seriously doubted whether there is any thinking at all about conduct which does not center on determining the end to be aimed at, or what end is "right" in various senses, as well as the type of activity which will realize some end. An actual problem may be to any extent that of the end or that of procedure—except the limiting case at either extreme. Deliberation about ends in turn takes many forms, but detailed exploration of these must be omitted here. The form most important in connection with social science in relation to action—which is necessarily one vital aspect of any science, though never the whole problem—is the selection of good or right ends. This is the problem of value—moral, aesthetic, or intellectual—to which we must return presently.

The second limitation to which the notion of given ends is subject—ultimately rather an aspect of the same fact that they are not given but problematic—is that to the extent to which an end is given, it is not really the end in the sense of finality. Given, concrete ends are means, or intermediate steps, in the achievement of *purposes,* which even more clearly are not and cannot be *data* in any definite sense. This would come out most sharply in a discussion of "non-serious" conduct. In play, it is obvious that the objective—what a player is trying to do—is a means, first to victory, and, beyond that, to a good game. Again, casual conversation is one of the most characteristic human activities, and it can hardly be said to have any end. This is one of the most seriously neglected aspects of conduct in general. Play, diversion, recreation—the "moral holiday"—is just as essential to human life as even nutritional activity.

A clear and adequate recognition of the nature of individual economic activity is essential as a prerequisite to social science, first, because all conduct whatever has this character in some degree, along with other aspects. The aesthetic, intellectual, moral, and even the religious, life involve the use and the economy of means, as well as what are usually thought of as sustenance activities. In fact, provision for these values makes up the greater part of the sustenance problem itself, as measured by cost, at any level of life which can be called civilized or properly human. In the second place, the ends of individual motivation, and even more the purposes to which they are essentially relative and instrumental, are also social, and in two senses. They are partly created by the unconscious cultural processes of society, and partly decided upon or chosen through intellectual activity, which is always fundamentally social in character. Finally, individual desires and purposes are largely realized through economic activity which is socially *organized;* and *conflicts* between individual ends and purposes, centering in the use of means or power, form the main source of the important social problems in our culture. It is primarily in connection with such problems of conflict between individuals wielding power that it is at once necessary to have and difficult to secure the agreement which is required to maintain the degree of peace and order requisite to rationally purposive life, individual and social.

These statements, especially in their excessive brevity, tend to overemphasize the importance of economics in the picture of social science and its conceptual-methodological problems. They must not be taken in this sense any more than economic interests and problems are to be dismissed as trivial or sordid. Man is not only a rational animal; his emotional nature is as real and important as his thinking (in a sense even more fundamental) and rationality also includes much more than economic rationality. It is difficult to strike a correct balance here. On the one hand, economic problems are relative to problems of ends and in that sense are subordinate. But, on the other hand, the correct use of means is not only a universal aspect of all problems of action but is an indispensable condition of their solution and of all achievement of purpose or creation of value. The fundamental category of economic activity is *power*. It is equally (because in both cases completely) essential to any good activity to have power and to direct its use "rightly"—and in particular not to treat the acquisition of power as an end or purpose on its own account.

The two main currents of social-ethical thinking in modern Western civilization—namely, Christianity and liberalism—respectively embody the two evils suggested by this last statement. The one is a naive, romantic-mystical voluntarism, the other a naive, instrumentalistic intellectualism. The central tenet of the Christian ethic is the repudiation of power, the denial of real value to goods dependent on the use of means. Virtue, defined as "love" of God and man, is left without content other than a feeling attitude and a vague "neighborly" helpfulness to persons in distress through some calamity. In particular the teachings of the Gospels enjoin indifference to political power and obedience to any established authority, which clearly seems to exclude the good Christian from any participation in political activity as well as from wealth-getting or wealth-using. On the other hand, modern utilitarian liberalism, including pragmatism as its most recent phase, has tended to see the whole problem of life in terms of the acquisition of power and efficiency in its use. It virtually ignores the problem of values to which concrete ends are usually, if not always in some degree, instrumental. And the social ethic of liberalism has emphasized individual liberty and, specifically, the economic freedom of the individual. Its conception of social policy is, or was, the maintenance of such freedom. This logically and necessarily means that the individual is to be left free to use power in his possession in practically any way he pleases—including its use to acquire more power, indefinitely—subject to the important restriction that he does not act in such a way to infringe the equal freedom of others.

It will be seen that while the ideals of Christianity and liberalism for the individual life are antithetic, their conceptions of social ethics are not so far apart. Christianity repudiates any concern with politics, while (the older) liberalism was chiefly concerned to restrict the functions of law and the state to the negative field of preventing interference by individuals with one another's freedom of action (though sweeping exceptions were made by Adam Smith and other advocates of laisser faire). Christian nonresistance is closely akin to liberalist nonintervention. In both systems the main substance of social life is left to unconscious processes—to an "invisible hand"—whether this is interpreted in theological terms or those of historical-cultural mechanics. And neither system has any place for social science with any relevance for social action.

Social science must, on the one hand, strive to tell the whole truth, to recognize all the facts, in the large sense of the word, about society and about man as a member of human society. It must not stultify itself by oversimplification, by stressing a particular set of facts or a particular aspect of the facts, in response to an intellectualistic prejudice on the part of the scientist. This is just what it has largely tended to do in the past. And the absurdity is especially egregious because it involves ignoring in, or denying to, man in general the very characteristics of individual and social interests and activity which are distinctive of the scientist himself as a human being. For science itself is problem-solving, both in the economic sense and in the higher sense of exploration and creation in the realm of values. Scientific activity is the pursuit of truth. And truth is essentially a value, not merely a want; and still less is it merely an effect in a causal sequence.

The contrast between (*a*) fact (interpreted in positive terms of cause and effect), (*b*) end (as given, the object of desire or wish), and (*c*) value (or purpose) is of the essence of the meaning of all three. And all three are inseparably involved in any true description of man and/or of society. Man as an individual acts to achieve ends, and these, in turn, are instrumental to purposes, and to rational purposes or values. And no description of him and his behavior makes sense if it ignores this fact. Among the kinds of value pursued is truth, which is a value as well as instrumental to the achievement of ends in the narrower sense. In a sense, truth includes all other values, however classified. It is typical of all value in that men want it without knowing concretely what it is, but as the solution of a problem, and especially in being desired *because* it is a value. The thing that men most characteristically want is to be right. Truth is at once a social and an ethical category. All truth, even as fact, or as instrumental, or as a value, is arrived at by co-operation among individuals acting freely and in a spirit of ethical, even religious, integrity. Such co-operation in its ideal form is equalitarian, or democratic in the ideal sense of that concept; it excludes any exercise of power or wish to exercise power, over other participants in the quest, on the part of any individual. The pursuit of truth or of value in any form is the ideal-type of ethical association, which is to say of all true society; it represents the type of life-activity properly described as social in social science itself.

Furthermore, any genuine science must, even as science, be relevant to action. But natural science itself, in its relevance to action, must certainly recognize that the action to which it is relevant is not merely action upon natural objects, which are inert and passive, but is also action by a subject who does act and who consequently has a fundamental nature categorically opposed to that of the object matter of action. Social science must also be relevant to action and to the kind of action to which it is relevant. But this is not action upon an inert, passive object matter. To some extent men do indeed act upon other men. Indeed, they also must do so in the actual world, or in any possible world, as in enforcing law and in education. But, on the one hand, it is clearly of the essence of that ideal human social life which men as men strive to realize that no individual ought to use any other as a means. Action of man upon man is necessary or defensible only to the extent that the man acted upon is not a moral person in the ideal or complete sense. And it must be one of the basic ideals of social policy to reduce to a minimum both the fact and the need of such action, to treat all men as free and equal persons, as far as obviously greater evils are not involved. When any individual does act upon another, the relationship is not truly social. And, incidentally, the technique and concepts involved in such action are sharply different from what is involved in the action of men upon inert objects. Action upon men takes such forms as coercion and deception, which have no meaning in the relations of man to physical nature—in addition to being universally recognized as intrinsically immoral.[4]

Social action, in the essential and proper sense, is group self-determination. The content or process is rational discussion, of which science itself—the pursuit and establishment of truth—is the primary type, for truth is a value, established by criticism, and a social category. Discussion is social problem-solving, and all problem-solving includes (social) discussion. As directive of social action, discussion has for its objective the solution of (i.e., the truth about) *ethical* problems, eht establishment of agreement upon ethical ideals or values, for the reconciliation of conflicting interests. Ethical ideals have for their content right or ideal relations between given individuals and also, and more fundamentally, ideal individuals, to be created by ideal social institutions, which form the immediate objective of social action.

In their social, superindividual, normative character, values are objective. No discussion can be carried on in propositions beginning with the words "I want." Everyone—when not momentarily defending a theory to the contrary—recognizes a difference between individual preference and what ought to be, between personal taste and good taste, between personal opinion or wish and truth. Thus values belong to a value-cosmos which has the same kind of validity, or reality, for our thinking as the external physical world.[5]

[4]Competitive social play calls for discussion in this connection, and also the vital problem of leadership.
[5]The only significant difference is in the possibility of measurement, in various senses, in physical phenomena, whereas values, like preferences, are quantitatively compared by estimation only. The prior claim to validity made for data of sense-observation is untenable, for the reason that objectivity in this field is established only by verification by other observers, which depends on intercommunication and also on the competence and integrity of the observers.

Social action consists, concretely and for the most part, in making, which is to say changing, the law, including public and constitutional law, which is the main repository of social institutions as subject to socially voluntary and deliberate change. In practice, social policy is discussed chiefly in connection with the selection of individuals who are to act as agents of society in carrying into effect the policies decided upon, or who in varying degrees are intrusted with the concrete formulation of the policies themselves. The social problem in the strict sense, however, is purely intellectual-moral. All physical activity involved in social-legal process is carried out by individuals who act as the agents of society, in so far as they are true to the trust confided to them. Social action, which is social decision, uses as data both facts and cause-and-effect relations, pertaining both to nature and to man. But the social problem is not one of fact—except as values are also facts—nor is it one of means and end. It is a problem of values. And the content of social science must correspond with the problem of action in character and scope.

CHARLES A. BEARD

WRITTEN HISTORY AS AN ACT OF FAITH[1]

History has been called a science, an art, an illustration of theology, a phase of philosophy, a branch of literature. It is none of these things, nor all of them combined. On the contrary, science, art, theology, and literature are themselves merely phases of history as past actuality and their particular forms at given periods and places are to be explained, if explained at all, by history as knowledge and thought. The philosopher, possessing little or no acquaintance with history, sometimes pretends to expound the inner secret of history,[2] but the historian turns upon him and expounds the secret of the philosopher, as far as it may be expounded at all, by placing him in relation to the movement of ideas and interests in which he stands or floats, by giving to his scheme of thought its appropriate relativity. So it is with systems of science, art, theology, and literature. All the light on these subjects that can be discovered by the human mind comes from history as past actuality.

What, then, is this manifestation of omniscience called history? It is, as Croce says, contemporary thought about the past. History as past actuality includes, to be sure, all that has been done, said, felt, and thought by human beings on this planet since humanity began its long career. History as record embraces the monuments, documents, and symbols which provide such knowledge as we have or can find respecting past actuality. But it is history as thought, not as actuality, record, or specific knowledge, that is really meant when the term history is used in its widest and most general significance. It is thought about past actuality, instructed and delimited by history as record and knowledge—record and knowledge authenticated by

[1] Presidential Address delivered before the American Historical Association at Urbana, December 28, 1933. *Reprinted by permission of *American Historical Review*, Vol. XXXIX, No. 2, (January 1934).
[2] For a beautiful example, see the passages on America in the introduction to Hegel's *Philosophy of History*.

criticism and ordered with the help of the scientific method. This is the final, positive, inescapable definition. It contains all the exactness that is possible and all the bewildering problems inherent in the nature of thought and the relation of the thinker to the thing thought about.

Although this definition of history may appear, at first glance, distressing to those who have been writing lightly about "the science of history" and "the scientific method" in historical research and construction, it is in fact in accordance with the most profound contemporary thought about history, represented by Croce, Riezler, Karl Mannheim, Mueller-Armack, and Heussi, for example. It is in keeping also with the obvious and commonplace. Has it not been said for a century or more that each historian who writes history is a product of his age, and that his work reflects the spirit of the times, of a nation, race, group, class, or section? No contemporary student of history really believes that Bossuet, Gibbon, Mommsen, or Bancroft could be duplicated to-day. Every student of history knows that his colleagues have been influenced in their selection and ordering of materials by their biases, prejudices, beliefs, affections, general upbringing, and experience, particularly social and economic; and if he has a sense of propriety, to say nothing of humor, he applies the canon to himself, leaving no exceptions to the rule. The pallor of waning time, if not of death, rests upon the latest volume of history, fresh from the roaring press.

Why do we believe this to be true? The answer is that every written history—of a village, town, county, state, nation, race, group, class, idea, or the wide world—is a selection and arrangement of facts, of recorded fragments of past actuality. And the selection and arrangement of facts—a combined and complex intellectual operation—is an act of choice, conviction, and interpretation respecting values, is an act of thought. Facts, multitudinous and beyond calculation, are known, but they do not select themselves or force themselves automatically into any fixed scheme of arrangement in the mind of the historian. They are selected and ordered by him as he thinks. True enough, where the records pertaining to a small segment of history are few and presumably all known, the historian may produce a fragment having an aspect of completeness, as, for example, some pieces by Fustel de Coulanges; but the completeness is one of documentation, not of history. True enough also, many historians are pleased to say of their writings that their facts

WRITTEN HISTORY AS AN ACT OF FAITH

are selected and ordered only with reference to inner necessities, but none who takes this position will allow the same exactitude and certainty to the works of others, except when the predilections of the latter conform to his own pattern.

Contemporary thought about history, therefore, repudiates the conception dominant among the schoolmen during the latter part of the nineteenth century and the opening years of the twentieth century —the conception that it is possible to describe the past as it actually was, somewhat as the engineer describes a single machine. The formula itself was a passing phase of thought about the past. Its author, Ranke, a German conservative, writing after the storm and stress of the French Revolution, was weary of history written for, or permeated by, the purposes of revolutionary propaganda. He wanted peace. The ruling classes in Germany, with which he was affiliated, having secured a breathing spell in the settlement of 1815, wanted peace to consolidate their position. Written history that was cold, factual, and apparently undisturbed by the passions of the time served best the cause of those who did not want to be disturbed. Later the formula was fitted into the great conception of natural science—cold neutrality over against the materials and forces of the physical world. Truths of nature, ran the theory, are to be discovered by maintaining the most severe objectivity; therefore the truth of history may be revealed by the same spirit and method. The reasoning seemed perfect to those for whom it was satisfactory. But the movement of ideas and interests continued, and bondage to conservative and scientific thought was broken by criticism and events. As Croce and Heussi have demonstrated, so-called neutral or scientific history reached a crisis in its thought before the twentieth century had advanced far on the way.

This crisis in historical thought sprang from internal criticism— from conflicts of thought within historiography itself—and from the movement of history as actuality; for historians are always engaged, more or less, in thinking about their own work and are disturbed, like their fellow citizens, by crises and revolutions occurring in the world about them. As an outcome of this crisis in historiography, the assumption that the actuality of history is identical with or closely akin to that of the physical world, and the assumption that any historian can be a disembodied spirit as coldly neutral to human affairs as the engineer to an automobile have both been challenged and rejected. Thus, owing to internal criticism and the movement of external events, the Ranke formula of history has been discarded and laid away in the museum of antiquities. It has ceased to satisfy the human spirit in its historical needs. Once more, historians recognize formally the obvious, long known informally, namely, that any written history inevitably reflects the thought of the author in his time and cultural setting.

That this crisis in thought presents a distressing dilemma to many historians is beyond question. It is almost a confession of inexpiable sin to admit in academic circles that one is not a man of science working in a scientific manner with things open to deterministic and inexorable treatment, to admit that one is more or less a guesser in this vale of tears. But the only escape from the dust and storm of the present conflict, and from the hazards of taking thought, now before the historian, is silence or refuge in some minute particularity of history as actuality. He may edit documents, although there are perils in the choice of documents to be edited, and in any case the choice of documents will bear some reference to an interpretation of values and importance—subjective considerations. To avoid this difficulty, the historian may confine his attention to some very remote and microscopic area of time and place, such as the price of cotton in Alabama between 1850 to 1860, or the length of wigs in the reign of Charles II., on the pleasing but false assumption that he is really describing an isolated particularity as it actually was, an isolated area having no wide-reaching ramifications of relations. But even then the historian would be a strange creature if he never asked himself why he regarded these matters as worthy of his labor and love, or why society provides a living for him during his excursions and explorations.

The other alternative before the student of history as immense actuality is to face boldly, in the spirit of Cato's soliloquy, the wreck of matter and the crush of worlds—the dissolution of that solid assurance which rested on the formula bequeathed by Ranke and embroidered by a thousand hands during the intervening years. And when he confronts without avoidance contemporary thought about the nature of written history, what commands does he hear?

The supreme command is that he must cast off his servitude to the assumptions of natural science and return to his own subject matter—to history as actuality. The hour for this final declaration of independence has arrived: the contingency is here and thought resolves it. Natural science is only one small subdivision of history as actuality with which history as thought is concerned. Its dominance in the thought of the Western World for a brief period can be explained, if at all, by history; perhaps in part by reference to the great conflict that raged between the theologians and scientists after the dawn of the sixteenth century—an intellectual conflict associated with the economic conflict between landed aristocracies, lay and clerical, on the one side, and the rising bourgeois on the other.

The intellectual formulas borrowed from natural science, which have cramped and distorted the operations of history as thought, have taken two forms: physical and biological. The first of these rests upon what may be called, for convenience, the assumption of causation: everything that happens in the world of human affairs is determined by antecedent occurrences, and events of history are the illustrations or data of laws to be discovered, laws such as are found in hydraulics. It is true that no historian has ever been able to array the fullness of history as actuality in any such deterministic order; Karl Marx has gone further than any other. But under the hypothesis that it is possible, historians have been arranging events in neat little chains of causation which explain, to their satisfaction, why suceeding events happen; and they have attributed any shortcomings in result to the inadequacy of their known data, not to the falsity of the assumption on which they have been operating. Undiscouraged by their inability to bring all history within a single law, such as the law of gravitation, they have gone on working in the belief that the Newtonian trick will be turned some time, if the scientific method is applied long and rigorously enough and facts are heaped up high enough, as the succeeding grists of doctors of philosophy are ground out by the universities, turned loose on "research projects," and amply supplied by funds.

Growing rightly suspicious of this procedure in physico-historiography, a number of historians, still bent on servitude to natural science, turned from physics to biology. The difficulties and failures involved in all efforts to arrange the occurrences of history in a neat system of historical mechanics were evident to them. But on the other side, the achievements of the Darwinians were impressive. If the totality of history could not be brought into a deterministic system without doing violence to historical knowledge, perhaps the biological analogy of the organism could be applied. And this was done, apparently without any realization of the fact that thinking by analogy is a form of primitive animism. So under the biological analogy, history was conceived as a succession of cultural organisms rising, growing, competing, and declining. To this fantastic morphological assumption Spengler chained his powerful mind. Thus freed from self-imposed slavery to physics, the historian passed to self-imposed subservience to biology. Painfully aware of the perplexities encountered as long as he stuck to his own business, the historian sought escape by employing the method and thought of others whose operations he did not understand and could not control, on the simple, almost childlike, faith that the biologist, if not the physicist, really knew what he was about and could furnish the clue to the mystery.

But the shadow of the organismic conception of history had scarcely fallen on the turbulent actuality of history when it was scrutinized by historians who were thinking in terms of their own subject as distinguished from the terms of a mere subdivision of history. By an inescapable demonstration Kurt Riezler has made it clear that the organismic theory of history is really the old determinism of physics covered with murky words. The rise, growth, competition, and decline of cultural organisms is meaningless unless fitted into some overarching hypothesis—either the hypothesis of the divine drama or the hypothesis of causation in the deterministic sense. Is each cultural organism in history, each national or racial culture, an isolated particularity governed by its own mystical or physical laws? Knowledge of history as actuality forbids any such conclusion. If, in sheer desperation, the historian clings to the biological analogy, which school is he to follow—the mechanistic or the vitalistic? In either case he is caught in the deterministic sequence, if he thinks long enough and hard enough.

Hence the fate of the scientific school of historiography turns finally upon the applicability of the deterministic sequence to the totality of history as actuality. Natural science in a strict sense, as distinguished from mere knowledge of facts, can discover system and law only where occurrences are in reality arranged objectively in deterministic sequences. It can describe these sequences and draw from them laws, so-called. From a given number of the occurrences in any such sequence, science can predict what will happen when the remainder appear.

With respect to certain areas of human occurrences, something akin to deterministic sequences is found by the historian, but the perdurance of any sequence depends upon the perdurance in time of

WRITTEN HISTORY AS AN ACT OF FAITH

surrounding circumstances which cannot be brought within any scheme of deterministic relevancies. Certainly all the occurrences of history as actuality cannot be so ordered; most of them are unknown and owing to the paucity of records must forever remain unknown. If a science of history were achieved, it would, like the science of celestial mechanics, make possible the calculable prediction of the future in history. It would bring the totality of historical occurrences within a single field and reveal the unfolding future to its last end, including all the apparent choices made and to be made. It would be omniscience. The creator of it would possess the attributes ascribed by the theologians to God. The future once revealed, humanity would have nothing to do except to await its doom.

To state the case is to dispose of it. The occurrences of history—the unfolding of ideas and interests in time-motion—are not identical in nature with the data of physics, and hence in their totality they are beyond the reach of that necessary instrument of natural science —mathematics—which cannot assign meaningful values to the imponderables, immeasurables, and contingencies of history as actuality.

Having broken the tyranny of physics and biology, contemporary thought in historiography turns its engines of verification upon the formula of historical relativity—the formula that makes all written history merely relative to time and circumstance, a passing shadow, an illusion. Contemporary criticism shows that the apostle of relativity is destined to be destroyed by the child of his own brain. If all historical conceptions are merely relative to passing events, to transitory phases of ideas and interests, then the conception of relativity is itself relative. When absolutes in history are rejected the absolutism of relativity is also rejected. So we must inquire: To what spirit of the times, to the ideas and interests of what class, group, nation, race, or region does the conception of relativity correspond? As the actuality of history moves forward into the future, the conception of relativity will also pass, as previous conceptions and interpretations of events have passed. Hence, according to the very doctrine of relativity, the skeptic of relativity will disappear in due course, beneath the ever-tossing waves of changing relativities. If he does not suffer this fate soon, the apostle of relativity will surely be executed by his own logic. Every conception of history, he says, is relative to time and circumstances. But by his own reasoning he is then compelled to ask: To what are these particular times and circumstances relative? And he must go on with receding sets of times and circumstances until he confronts an absolute: the totality of history as actuality which embraces all times and circumstances and all relativities.

Contemporary historical thought is, accordingly, returning upon itself and its subject matter. The historian is casting off his servitude to physics and biology, as he formerly cast off the shackles of theology and its metaphysics. He likewise sees the doctrine of relativity crumble in the cold light of historical knowledge. When he accepts none of the assumptions made by theology, physics, and biology, as applied to history, when he passes out from under the fleeting shadow of relativity, he confronts the absolute in his field—the absolute totality of all historical occurrences past, present, and becoming to the end of all things. Then he finds it necessary to bring the occurrences of history as actuality under one or another of three broad conceptions.

The first is that history as total actuality is chaos, perhaps with little islands of congruous relativities floating on the surface, and that the human mind cannot bring them objectively into any all-embracing order or subjectively into any consistent system. The second is that history as actuality is a part of some order of nature and revolves in cycles eternally—spring, summer, autumn, and winter, democracy, aristocracy, and monarchy, or their variants, as imagined by Spengler. The third is that history as actuality is moving in some direction away from the low level of primitive beginnings, on an upward gradient toward a more ideal order—as imagined by Condorcet, Adam Smith, Karl Marx, or Herbert Spencer.

Abundant evidence can be marshaled, has been marshaled, in support of each of these conceptions of history as actuality, but all the available evidence will not fit any one of them. The hypothesis of chaos admits of no ordering at all; hence those who operate under it cannot write history, although they may comment *on* history. The second admits of an ordering of events only by arbitrarily leaving out of account all the contradictions in the evidence. The third admits of an ordering of events, also by leaving contradictions out of consideration. The historian who writes history, therefore, consciously or unconsciously performs an act of faith, as to order and movement, for certainty as to order and movement is denied to him by knowledge of the actuality with which he is concerned. He is

WRITTEN HISTORY AS AN ACT OF FAITH

thus in the position of a statesman dealing with public affairs; in writing he acts and in acting he makes choices, large or small, timid or bold, with respect to some conception of the nature of things. And the degree of his influence and immortality will depend upon the length and correctness of his forecast—upon the verdict of history yet to come. His faith is at bottom a conviction that something true can be known about the movement of history and his conviction is a subjective decision, not a purely objective discovery.

But members of the passing generation will ask: Has our work done in the scientific spirit been useless? Must we abandon the scientific method? The answer is an emphatic nagative. During the past fifty years historical scholarship, carried on with judicial calm, has wrought achievements of value beyond calculation. Particular phases of history once dark and confused have been illuminated by research, authentication, scrutiny, and the ordering of immediate relevancies. Nor is the empirical or scientific method to be abandoned. It is the only method that can be employed in obtaining accurate knowledge of historical facts, personalities, situations, and movements. It alone can disclose conditions that made possible what happened. It has a value in itself—a value high in the hierarchy of values indispensable to the life of a democracy. The inquiring spirit of science, using the scientific method, is the chief safeguard against the tyranny of authority, bureaucracy, and brute power. It can reveal by investigation necessities and possibilities in any social scene and also offerings with respect to desirabilities to be achieved within the limits of the possible.

The scientific method is, therefore, a precious and indispensable instrument of the human mind; without it society would sink down into primitive animism and barbarism. It is when this method, a child of the human brain, is exalted into a master and a tyrant that historical thought must enter a caveat. So the historian is bound by his craft to recognize the nature and limitations of the scientific method and to dispel the illusion that it can produce a science of history embracing the fullness of history, or of any large phase, as past actuality.

This means no abandonment of the tireless inquiry into objective realities, especially economic realities and relations; not enough emphasis has been laid upon the conditioning and determining influences of biological and economic necessities or upon researches designed to disclose them in their deepest and widest ramifications. This means no abandonment of the inquiry into the forms and development of ideas as conditioning and determining influences; not enough emphasis has been laid on this phase of history by American scholars.

But the upshot to which this argument is directed is more fundamental than any aspect of historical method.

It is that any selection and arrangement of facts pertaining to any large area of history, either local or world, race or class, is controlled inexorably by the frame of reference in the mind of the selector and arranger. This frame of reference includes things deemed necessary, things deemed possible, and things deemed desirable. It may be large, informed by deep knowledge, and illuminated by wide experience; or it may be small, uninformed, and unilluminated. It may be a grand conception of history or a mere aggregation of confusions. But it is there in the mind, inexorably. To borrow from Croce, when grand philosophy is ostentatiously put out at the front door of the mind, then narrow, class, provincial, and regional prejudices come in at the back door and dominate, perhaps only half-consciously, the thinking of the historian.

The supreme issue before the historian now is the determination of his attitude to the disclosures of contemporary thought. He may deliberately evade them for reasons pertaining to personal, economic, and intellectual comfort, thus joining the innumerable throng of those who might have been but were not. Or he may proceed to examine his own frame of reference, clarify it, enlarge it by acquiring knowledge of greater areas of thought and events, and give it consistency of structure by a deliberate conjecture respecting the nature or direction of the vast movements of ideas and interests called world history.

This operation will cause discomfort to individual historians but all, according to the vows of their office, are under obligation to perform it, as Henry Adams warned the members of this Association in his letter of 1894. And as Adams then said, it will have to be carried out under the scrutiny of four great tribunals for the suppression of unwelcome knowledge and opinion: the church, the state, property, and labor. Does the world move and, if so, in what direction? If he believes that the world does not move, the historian must offer the pessimism of chaos to the inquiring spirit of mankind. If it does move, does it move backward toward some old arrangement, let us say, of 1928, 1896, 1815, 1789, or 1295? Or does it move forward to some other arrangement which can be only dimly divined

—a capitalist dictatorship, a proletarian dictatorship, or a collectivist democracy? The last of these is my own guess, founded on a study of long trends and on a faith in the indomitable spirit of mankind. In any case, if the historian cannot know or explain, history as actuality, he helps to make history, petty or grand.

To sum up contemporary thought in historiography, any written history involves the selection of a topic and an arbitrary delimitation of its borders—cutting off connections with the universal. Within the borders arbitrarily established, there is a selection and organization of facts by the processes of thought. This selection and organization —a single act—will be controlled by the historian's frame of reference composed of things deemed necessary and of things deemed desirable. The frame may be a narrow class, sectional, national, or group conception of history, clear and frank or confused and half conscious, or it may be a large, generous conception, clarified by association with the great spirits of all ages. Whatever its nature the frame is inexorably there, in the mind. And in the frame only three broad conceptions of all history as actuality are possible. History is chaos and every attempt to interpret it otherwise is an illusion. History moves around in a kind of cycle. History moves in a line, straight or spiral, and in some direction. The historian may seek to escape these issues by silence or by a confession of avoidance or he may face them boldly, aware of the intellectual and moral perils inherent in any decision—in his act of faith.

EARL S. JOHNSON

WAYS OF KNOWING°

It is my thesis that the ways of knowing are the ways with which man, even mankind, is endowed. They are the way of facts, the way of method or logic, by which man orders his facts, and the way of imagination, by which he becomes sensitive to the value of his facts.

Let me now change the terms of my thesis in order to clarify it. Man is a knowing animal, hence he uses facts. Man is an ordering or systematizing animal, hence his wont to discipline his facts. Man is a passionate animal, hence his use of imagination.

Again I change the terms of my thesis in order to relate it to man, here and now. He is beset by ignorance, by muddle-headedness, and by crassness or lack of imagination. Thus the judgment that he needs facts, that he needs logical structures for ordering the relations between his facts so they may make reliable knowledge possible, and that he needs imagination in order to overcome his crassness.

I now combine facts and structured facts as ways of knowing and associate them with *rational* men. There remains imagination or sensitivity as a way of knowing which I associate with *passionate* man. Thus, taken generally, I identify the sciences and the arts. These, in turn, symbolize Truth and Beauty which man is capable of knowing.

In these restatements or reinterpretations of my thesis I have sought to remove from the more to the less abstract. I suspect, however, that my statement about man's capacity to know Truth and Beauty stands in needs of simplification. Let Truth symbolize *homo sapiens*, man the wise. Let Beauty symbolize *homo faber*, man the creator. Thus I identify man's bivalent nature—his ability to think and his ability to create values, pre-eminent among which is love.

*Published in *The Nature of Knowledge*, the School of Education, University of Wisconsin-Milwaukee, 1961, and *Social Education*, January, 1963. Reprinted by permission of the School of Education, University of Wisconsin-Milwaukee.

I have sought thus far to say that the act or art of knowing admits of three perspectives and that these correspond to man's nature. These are the perspectives of fact, ordered fact, and imagination. In my reference to Truth and Beauty I have reduced the perspectives to two and, correlatively, the ways of knowing to two—namely, the rational and the emotional. Doing so, I simplify and falsify in order to clarify.

I shall examine my thesis from the perspectives of the following questions: (a) are these ways of knowing to be practiced according to a fixed order? That is, does each occupy an unchanging place in a hierarchy from least to greatest? (b) are they operable across the full continuum of man's concerns? That is, with poetry, politics and physics—in sum, in all the arts and sciences? (c) are these ways of knowing separate and discrete or are they, in a manner near to inscrutable, inter-twined and interdependent? and (d) what injury to man's fullest knowing attends his failure to practice all these ways?

We are prone, at least in common sense, to arrange these ways of knowing in the order in which I have stated them: facts, logic, and imagination. But a great man tells us that imagination favors the informed mind, equipped not only with facts but ordered facts. Santayana expresses quite the same meaning in his remark that "the growth of what is known increases the scope of what may be imagined and hoped for." Furthermore, imagination is the way in which insight is spent and insight requires knowledge. Imagination also has a good deal of intuition in it, if indeed they are not quite the same thing. A columnist has lately said that intuition is nothing but "reason in a hurry," a view which disturbs the assumption that the ways of knowing are separate and discrete. We also know that imagination is deeply implicated in the ordering of facts. Let an eminent scientist, Gilbert N. Lewis, tell us how he sees the matter.

> I take it that the scientific method, of which so much has been heard, is hardly more than the native method of solving problems, a little clarified from prejudice and a little cultivated by training. A detective with his murder mystery; a chemist seeking the structure of a new compound, uses little of the formal and logical modes of reasoning. Through a series of intuitions, surmises, fancies, they stumble upon the right explanation, and have a knack of seizing it when it once comes within reach.

In light of this view, could it be that we have mistaken the apparatus of the laboratory for the essence and spirit of science?

Now let us ask a philosopher how facts are ordered to the end that reliable knowledge may be created. William E. Hocking writes:

> Now a powerful induction is no result of following logical rules—*pace* the textbooks that is, by their leave there are no rules! It comes as a stroke of insight, after long mulling over the data, which—under new light from God knows where, probably an intimation of necessity—reconceives those data.

Here is no hint of fixed order or hierarchy.

There are many whose testimony in this matter might be shared with you, but I must choose from among them. John Dewey tells us that "There is no thought unless it be enkindled by an emotion" which is quite a different view from that given in his characterization of the layman's mind which holds that "the intellect is pure light; the emotions are a disturbing heat." I recall Robert Redfield's view given in these words, "I think now that what I see men do and understand as something that human beings do, is seen often with a valuing of it." From this comes his term, "feeling-knowing." This same way of knowing is reported in Lear's encounter with Glouchester when, to the king's question, "Doest thou not see how the world goes?," the blind duke replies, "Yes, I see it feelingly."

There is Darwin's axiom that "all observation must be for or against some view, if it is to be of any service," and Goethe's belief that "we see what we know." Morris Cohen tells us that the positivist does not escape judgments of value but only hides them or, having dismissed them at the front door of his mind, finds that they entered his workshop by the back stairs.

J. Bronowski's view is that "science is not an impersonal construction." Karl Jaspers writes that "science left to itself as mere science is homeless," and Michael Polanyi's revolutionary book, *Personal Knowledge*, is dedicated to the view that we must reject the notion of detachment in all science. We have William James's faith that "whenever there is a conflict of opinion and difference of vision, we are bound to believe that the truer side is the side that feels the more, and not the side that feels the less." Lin Yutang writes that "feelings are facts also. They are in you." And Dewey, once again in good counsel, tells us that "rationality is not a force to evoke against impulse and habit. It is the attainment of a working harmony among diverse desires."

From such evidences as these it is my judgment that we err when we let ourselves believe that man's attempt to know can transcend the anthropocentric. Archimedes may have dreamed of a point outside his world but modern man can afford no such extravagant imagery.

Likewise, from such evidences, I come to the belief that the scientific attitude is not passionless but the function of man's whole being and not merely the so-called intellectual part of him. Here too is ground for my view that if there is no emotion or affection for reason to discipline and direct, then we must believe that the mind can be engaged only in doing something with the greatest exactness, the most faultless reliability, and the neatest precision about matters which are not at all important.

If, perchance, this recitation has revealed a personal bias, I feel no guilt on that account. Thus, far too briefly to do justice to the question of hierarchy, I find that no case can be made for it.

Let me now postpone consideration of the second question, namely whether the ways of knowing are operable across the full continuum of man's concerns, in favor of some attention to the nature of fact and imagination, even though some comments on the latter have already been made. The nature and function of various logics by which man orders his facts will be included in the discussion of the continuum of his concerns, as well as in the section following it.

In my remarks about fact and imagination I shall, in all likelihood, cover some ground quite familiar to you as well as some already trod. Nevertheless, I think it appropriate to carry the discussion along the lines indicated.

Respecting the nature of facts I am disturbed by the conception implied by Thomas Huxley, which is held almost as sacred writ by layman and scientists alike. I refer to his classic remark about the necessity to "sit down before a fact as a little child, be prepared to give up every preconceived notion, follow wherever nature leads, or you will learn nothing."

With Huxley's general sentiment I am in accord, but my understanding is that facts are not the result of random observation, the dismissal of all preconceptions, or of the mere accumulation of data. On the contrary, they imply a theoretical, which is to say, a symbolic element and most, if not all of them, began as hypotheses. They are, as I understand them, the result of man-made judgments. In this view they are the fruit of the perceptive sets of given perceivers and bear the hall-mark of their fashioners. If they are objective, as Huxley's language implies, they are also subjectives.

I have lately come across a remark by George Macauley Trevelyan, the eminent British historian, which reports a quite similar conception of the nature of facts. The remark is this: "Let the science and research of the historian find the fact and let his imagination and art make clear its significance." How such a separation of thing and meaning can be achieved is unclear to me. Facts are, as I view them, not found but made and in this interpretation I am happy to learn that Crane Brinton takes the same position. The stark divorce of objective and subjective which I find in Trevelyan's remark is, for me at least, inconceivable. My criticism, in fine, is that he seems to separate the significance of the historian's facts from their identification in the first instance, through what I choose to call the artful use—is there any other?—of his imagination. That he may reflect imaginatively on them later is not thereby gainsaid.

The concerns of the scientist, whether he be historian or physicist, are, furthermore, greatly affected by the kinds of problems which are before the scholarly or civil community, or both. I mean that the scientist's interests reflect what might be called the run-of-attention of the culture of his time and place; one might even call it the passion of his culture. This accounts for the fact that history is being continually re-written not because, to use an innocent but ridiculous expression, "the facts are not yet all in" (they never will be), but because the interests and concerns of scholars shift with the times and thus new issues, new problems and new facts come to view.

This phenomenon of the run-of-attention goes far to explain why the work of Grimaldi on light waves in the mid-seventeenth century went unnoticed for more than 150 years. Grimaldi's work did not come into the direct focus of concern of the scholarly community; and hence not into its own full flower, until 1927 when Heisenberg elaborated the principle of indeterminacy in quantum mechanics. I forbear any remarks on the pseudoscience of Lysenko in the field of genetics for here the determinant is not the run-of-attention of the culture, but the fiat of the state.

I must conclude that the making of facts and their intelligent ordering by the logic appropriate to the field in which they are made, be it history or physics, are not culture-free and, by that token, are not value-free. If Emile Zola's observation be true that art is nature seen through the medium of temperament, it appears that much of what we know as science gives us its view through the same medium.

Certain it is that science is a tool and a guide but that which it 'tools' and that toward which it guides is provided not by science but by human passion and concern. Even the making of taxonomies, a concern as internal to science as can be imagined, involves the making of judgments. It is clear, then, that knowing cannot be settled or ended at the level of facts as the lay mind conceives them. This does not render them impotent or unimportant; it only affirms that they are dependent on the interests of the observer and the logic by which he orders them.

If one were adequately to delineate the properties, the scope and the work of imagination, he would need more of it than I possess. Hence I enter upon my discussion of it with genuine misgivings.

Despite my protestations to the contrary, I seem to have given imagination top priority which, in principle, I would deny to any of the constituents in the act or art of knowing. Perhaps its dynamic quality and its ubiquity—its everywhereness—will serve to deliver me from complete error in this matter. This view does not conceive imagination as a separate entity but rather as something that enters into any complete knowing through the sense of fact and the operation of reason and logic. In this view it is not a mere catalytic agent, for such an agent remains constant in its acceleration or retardation of a process.

It is my feeling, or more accurately, my feeling-knowing, that the power and ability to imagine is the attribute of man which most characteristically differentiates him from lower animal forms, for without imagination there could be no intimation of "something better," in which plight the concept of morality would be impossible and meaningless. It is in this sense that imagination gives us "possible things," things not given in the concrete situation. But they are not, by that circumstance, unreal, but rather to be realized. Imagination is the starting point for poet and scientist alike—a feeling, a hunch, an intimation of something which is not, but could be, even *ought* to be. How each shall clothe or structure what he imagines is resolved quite differently by each in his own tongue, but for each what is imagined is the passionate component of his work.

When Galileo founded his new science of dynamics he had to begin with the conception of an entirely isolated body which moves without the influence of any external force. Such a body had, of course, never been observed and could never be observed. I am told that the "square root of minus one" is a 'difficult' number but I also understand that until its riddle was solved there could be no such thing as the wireless telegraph. Thus the role of imagination in the so-called exact sciences is confirmed. Its role in the labors of the historian whose place, so to speak, is in both the humanities and the much less exact social sciences, has already been noted.

To tell us of the place of imagination in poetry let us call upon Sir Philip Sydney, sixteenth century poet, soldier and courtier. In an idiom which we would now consider ungrammatical he wrote that,

> . . . for everie understanding knoweth the skill of ech artificer standeth in that *Idea* . . . and that the Poet hath that *Idea*, is manifest by delivering them foorth in such excellence as he had imagined them.

We call now upon Archibald MacLeish who, I suppose, comes closer than any one of our time to filling a post which we have not created, that of poet laureate. He tells us that,

> there exists in our society the strange and ignorant belief that the life of the imagination lies at an opposite pole from the life of the enquiring mind . . . that man can live and know and master their experience of this darkling earth by accumulating information and no more. Men who believe that have, in effect, surrendered their responsibilities as men.

And finally in this brief and all too inadequate discussion on imagination let us share the wisdom of Hoyt Hudson, late professor of humane letters at Stanford whose book, *Educating Liberally*, from which I quote, is a classic though little known treatise on the kind of education of which the American college stands in such dire need.

> If what I call the imaginative way of knowing is actually not a way of knowing at all, but only another name for illusion, then the world of matter and sense is ultimate, the God of things is the one true God and Everyman is as the beasts that perish—only worse off, for he is bedeviled by his dreams, hopes, loyalties, and troublesome sympathies and appreciations.

I am now obligated to speak to the question as to whether or not the ways of knowing I have identified are operable across the full continuum of man's concerns.

By the phrase "the full continuum of man's concerns," I refer to the symbol systems or structures which man has elaborated as media for meeting his world and coming to terms with it.

These symbol systems are, as we know, two in number: the discursive and the presentational. With the former we associate the sciences: physical, life and the so-called social sciences. With the latter we associate the humanities: language, art, religion, myth and magic. The logics and structures which we designate as sciences, those named above, give us *understanding*; the logics and structures which we designate as disciplines, namely the humanistic studies just noted, give us *appreciation*.

As a convenient and I hope, proper heuristic device, I choose to relate these symbol systems—the two great branches of the tree of knowledge—to each other through a polar construct whose termini I name, *science* and *art*. To these let us add, respectively, the subscriptions, rational and non-rational. The intention is to treat these polar terms as quite different, even antithetical bodies of knowledge. I shall also consider them as having a great deal in common and hence far less polar than I originally supposed them to be. My emphasis, as well as the moral of my account, will be on what they have in common and manifest in their respective involvements in the discourse of reason through facts, a scheme of ordering them, and the meaning or value of the facts so ordered.

I now wish to share with you a number of such polar constructs each of which is offered to represent a continuum. Each continuum symbolizes the same progression. This is a progression *from* man's confrontation with his world through a minimum of emotional-personal involvement *to* a maximum of his emotional-personal involvement. Each set of polar terms and the continua which they enclose are named in the order of "most rational" to "least rational."

The polar terms and the continua are these: William James' "knowledge about" to his "acquaintance with"; Pascal's "spirit of geometry" to his "spirit of finesse"; Wilhelm Dilthey's *Anschauen*, literally looking at us from the outside, to his *Nacherleben*, literally re-living the experience of another; Robert MacIver's "spatial knowledge" to his "social knowledge" which gives us respectively, statistical and consensual man; Galton's numerical-statistical method to Cooley's method of "sympathetic introspection," and Michael Polanyi's "detached observation" to his "pure indwelling."

Along each continuum lie the sciences and disciplines noted above: the physical, life and so-called social sciences, and the humanities conceived to include language, art, religion, myth and magic. It hardly need be remarked that the sciences tend to bunch, so to speak, toward the rational pole although as we move from physics and chemistry to biology and physiology and on to history and sociology, bunching at that pole becomes less marked. This is due, of course, to the fact that the data of these sciences lend themselves more to the observer's personal identification with them as the progression moves from physics to sociology.

The nature of the humanistic disciplines requires that we find them bunched toward the non-rational pole and this by virtue of the fact that the humanistic quality enters when we admit that man's nature, seen from their perspectives and logics, cannot be deduced from any number of principles. The novelist, the poet and the painter depict characters and situations; they do not generalize about them. But I undertake here no neat placement of the humanities along these continua. If time permitted and my knowledge were sufficient, I might make some representative placements of, at least, some phases of each of the humanistic studies. Language, for example, makes rigorous structural demands through grammar and rhetoric, thus requiring that it be placed—in these respects—closer to the rational pole than, say, the painter's highly individualized and unique ways of structuring form and color.

Each of these polar constructs may be viewed from the perspective of its complete "either-orness," that is, as ways of knowing which are purely rational or purely non-rational. Such a view must, of course, be abandoned by reason of what we know about the relation between facts and imagination. But this view does not prevent my viewing scientific and artistic ways of knowing as different ways, but still having much in common. It must, however, be affirmed that each gives a partial knowledge—that which its treatment of the objects of its concern permits through the logic and structure proper to it. Each, by reason of this fact, creates different kinds of facts, ideas and values. Correlatively, each engenders different qualities of attitudes.

I wish now to illustrate a difference in structure as between the scientific and artistic approach to the same object. Whether I shall use a structure and logic which admits of a maximum of what I have called impersonal-rational involvement or one which admits of a maximum of personal-emotional involvement with my world depends on my idosyncracies and the purposes for which I seek different kinds of knowledge.

I can, if I choose, treat the moon in its quarter-phase as an astral body. In this view of it I would employ the intensely rational logic of astronomy whose chief tool is mathematics. I can, however, if I am in the mood of the poet, try to treat it as Vachel Lindsay does in these lines: "the moon is the North Wind's cookie"—thus non-rationally. The rational or scientific logic and the structure through which it operates give me a rational command over or *understanding* of the moon. The emotional or poetic logic and the structure through which it operates give me a non-rational command or *appreciation* of the moon. Which logic or which moon, as different kinds of facts I choose depends, as I say, on my idiosyncracies and the purposes for which I seek different kinds of knowledge.

> Emotions must be dammed back to the wit-mill, not just turned loose in exclamation. No force will express far which isn't shut in by discipline at all pores to jet at one outlet only. Emotion has been known to ooze off.

Admitting, as Sir Francis Bacon importuned us to do, that the subtlety of nature is far beyond that of sense or understanding, I make no claim, in what I have shared with you, to have completely or thoroughly treated the ways of knowing as I sense them in man's scientific and artistic confrontations with his world as it may be conceived to lie along the continua which I have noted. I do profess, however, that they are man's ways of knowing, whatever his calling and that teachers ought to do what lies within their province and powers to teach all of them.

These observations bring me to discuss, very briefly, what injury attends one's failure to practice the full complement of the ways of knowing.

Without competence in all, one cannot participate fully in the discourse of reason which it is the business of education to advance and perfect. That competence, however, must be manifest by due regard for the balance and choice required by situations which differ greatly respecting the logic and structure appropriate to them.

Such a range of competences is all the more mandated by the fact that no longer can the objectives of an education, at any level of formal schooling, be expressed only or chiefly in terms of mere information, the facts one should know, for their fund is now so enormous that it cannot be known. Our emphases must now, increasingly, fall on the means and modes of knowing, that is on skill in manipulating structures, and knowing which one belongs, so to speak, to a given needs-situation.

This view does not deny that students ought to know some facts, indeed a great many. It is, rather, to affirm that they ought to know how to make, test, confirm, relate, understand and appreciate them and, perhaps most important of all, to assimilate facts, logic and meanings to their conduct. This is the ultimate test of the transfer of learning.

It is my belief that we do less than we ought to nourish our students' intuitive and imaginative powers, for they are the mid-wives to new forms of thought and conduct, new vistas and even new social institutions and systems. These powers are sorely needed in a time when the capacity to feel with and be deeply moved by the life and labors of people in far-flung places may well be the deciding factors in world comity and peace.

We must insure the most rigorous and rewarding competition to what seems to be the eternal bane of teaching, rote learning— "that frost of fact by which our wisdom gives correctly stated death to all that lives." We must teach our students how to transmute facts into knowledge through mastery of the logics and structures appropriate to various situations. The truth or falsity of statements of fact are important only in their ultimate bearing on the making of judgments about matters of better or worse.

Emphases such as these will, one may devoutly hope, rescue the teaching profession from the deadening effects of excess emphasis on the didactic; the inevitable consequence of which is docility and the death of the imagination and mental and spiritual spontaneity. A tranquil world in which the docile might at least survive is with us no more.

These observations report my deepest concern, even alarm. I believe that we tend, even tragically, to deny the worth of artistic structures for confronting and dealing with a confused and tangled world. Lionel Trilling states well what I have in mind:

> It is a truism of contemporary thought that the whole nature of man stands in danger of being brutalized by the intellect, or at least by some one of its apparently accredited surrogates. A specter haunts our culture—it is that people will eventually be unable to say, 'they fall in love and married,' let alone understand the language of *Romeo and Juliet*, but will, as a matter of course say, 'Their libidinal impulses being reciprocal they activated their individual erotic drives and integrated them within the same frame of reference.'

Thrilling then adds,

> Now this is not the language of abstract thought, or any kind of thought. It is the language of non-thought. But it is the language which is developing from the peculiar status we in our culture have given to abstract thought. There can be no doubt that it constitutes a threat to the emotions and thus to life itself.

But, for fear that I have unduly disturbed the balance for which I have pled and argued throughout this discussion I turn again to the wisdom of a philosopher. In his near to classic essay, "What Man Can Make of Man," William E. Hocking observes that,

> ... the new conscience is finding its courage, because man's soul is recovering the sight of both its eyes! It is taking the scientific conscience into the house, not as master but as partner.

I come thus to affirm again the dual nature of man and the two great and transcendent ways by which he knows, the way of Truth and the way of Beauty. Through them, as I am disposed to see the matter, man may come to know and do the Good.

BIBLIOGRAPHY

Beard, Charles A. "That Noble Dream," *American Historical Review*, XLI, No. 1 (October 1935), pp. 74–87.

Becker, Carl L. "The Function of the Social Sciences," in Ruth Anshen ed., *Science and Man*. New York: Harcourt, Brace, 1942, pp. 243–269.

Blumer, Herbert. "Sociological Analysis and the Variable," *American Sociological Review*, XXI, No. 6 (December 1956), pp. 683–690.

Bolton, Charles D. "Is Sociology a Behavioral Science?" *Pacific Sociological Review*, VI, No. 2 (Spring 1963), pp. 3–9.

Bruyn, Severyn T. *The Humanistic Perspective in Sociology*. Englewood Cliffs, N.J.: Prentice-Hall, 1966.

Cohen, Morris R. "The Social and the Natural Sciences," *Reason and Nature*. Glencoe, Ill.: The Free Press, 1964, pp. 333–368.

Crick, Bernard. *The American Science of Politics*. Berkeley, Calif.: University of California Press, 1959.

Dewey, John. *Logic: The Theory of Inquiry*. New York: Henry Holt, 1938.

Kim, K. W. "The Limits of Behavioural Explanation in Politics," *Canadian Journal of Economics and Political Science*, XXXI, No. 3 (August 1965), pp. 315–327.

Matson, Floyd W. *The Broken Image: Man, Science and Society*. New York: Anchor Books, 1966.

Park, Robert E. "Physics and Society," *Canadian Journal of Economics and Political Science*, VI, No. 2 (May 1940), pp. 135–152. Reproduced in Robert E. Park, *Society*. Glencoe, Ill.: The Free Press, 1955, pp. 301–321.

Stein, Maurice, and Arthur Vidich, eds. *Sociology on Trial*. Englewood Cliffs, New Jersey: Prentice-Hall Spectrum Books, 1963.

Walsh, W. H. "The Limits of Scientific History," *Historical Studies*, III (London: Bowes & Bowes, 1961), pp. 45–57.

PART II

UNDERSTANDING
IN THE
SOCIAL SCIENCES

INTRODUCTION

The nature of explanation and understanding is the central question around which most of the disputes over concept and method in the study of human development have revolved. Positivism assumes that reality consists of hard, determinate, interchangeable units, or at least that the objects of social study can be analyzed realistically in such basic units. The techniques of study envisaged are those of causal analysis, which aims at specification of the factors or variables involved in any given situation. The underlying assumption is that it is possible to know reality from the outside by external measurement and observation. Those traits of an object which are distinctive can legitimately be ignored in favor of the common elements which it shares with other objects in the same class. The aim of science on this view is the collection of facts about individual units; that is, of data, which later are to be correlated so as to arrive at generalizations and, eventually, laws which formulate the regularities in the behavior of the object. The lawful regularities embodied in the causal laws are eventually to be linked in a hierarchical structure of theory. It is this model of inquiry, borrowed from the philosophy of the natural sciences, which contemporary positivism in the social sciences utilizes as the standard or norm by which to judge the methodological purity of social scientific investigation.

Recent changes in the positivist model, such as the acceptance and utilization of the so-called hypothetico-deductive model of explanation, do not really alter the nature of positivism or necessitate changes in the portrait sketched above. The emphases are still upon externality, measurement, data collection, quantitative verification, and lawful regularities. The hypothetico-deductive model, which stresses freedom of discovery in theory formation, is certainly a step forward from the purely inductive logic of proceeding from fact to fact toward generalization, but the positivist philosophy of science is still far from providing a cogent account of explanation.[1]

[1] See Michael Scriven, "Explanations, Predictions and Laws," *Minnesota Studies in the Philosophy of Science*, Vol. III (1962), pp. 172–230.

The difficulties which the positivist account raises revolve around the fact that its criteria have little realistic relevance either to human characteristics or to the study of human behavior. While it may be possible to ignore the differentiating aspects of natural phenomena for purposes of research, e.g., rocks or meteorites, this is unprofitable in the study of human beings. That which is distinctive is often exactly that which is important. To use another example, meaning cannot be understood from an external or objective perspective alone; in fact, it cannot be understood *at all* from a purely objective or behavioral point of view. If an illustration of what is meant by this statement is desired, we suggest that one attempt a purely behavioral description of a football game. This would mean that all words referring to meaning, purpose, aim, desire, or intention must be ruthlessly eliminated. Only physical movements may be described. The results should indicate what is meant by the impossibility of conveying understanding of meaning from an external point of view. A third point: regularities are in most cases accidental in a philosophical sense. Cause does not equal causal conjunction, and the Humean view that it does has long been discredited in philosophy and natural science. But variable analysis in social science rests upon exactly this foundation. If cause does not equal constant conjunction, what is the point of the extraordinary significance attached to high statistical correlation? In sum, the criteria for good methodology projected by the positivist model of inquiry are simply not applicable to sociological research.

Understanding in the social sciences depends upon the ability to comprehend the meaning of human action; that is, upon the intelligibility of essentially subjective phenomena. The social sciences are, to be sure, concerned with more than specification of meaning, but this is, on the other hand, an aspect of social action which must invariably be taken into account. The readings in the group which follows are basically concerned with the methodological implications of that fact.

The understanding of a human action is primarily a matter of placing it in context, of making clear the purposes, execution, and consequences of an act. The quality which seems to make human behavior distinctive from that of other living organisms is the ability to make self-indications, to attach meaning and define objects by way of the manipulation of symbols. The conditions of action are an important aspect of the act, but any study which limits itself to the study

INTRODUCTION 61

of conditions while ignoring or minimizing the import of the act itself is thoroughly inadequate. The continuum of self-indication, symbolic construction of meaning, and purposive behavior is crucial to the subject matter of the social sciences. Yet such a recognition does not, contrary to positivist fears, land us in a bog of total subjectivity. The resolution of this problem represents one of the many contributions George Herbert Mead to empirical philosophy and social science. Mead was the first to place the subjective aspects of experience in explicit behavioral context as the preliminary stages of the act.[2] Mead conceived of the act as a continuum which begins with impulse, which is mediated or transformed by symbolic interaction, and which eventually issues in overt behavior. The subjective side of culture, to borrow a phrase from Ellsworth Faris, is thus placed in context, and a clue is supplied as to how to undertake the study of such phenomena. The suggestion which may be drawn from Mead's analysis also supplies a clue to the resolution of the controversy over sympathetic introspection, or *verstehen,* as a technique in social research. The process of *verstehen* really gives us hypotheses or working assumptions drawn from empathetic identification. These may be tested by specification of the probable consequences which could follow if the hypotheses were correct.

The structure of understanding in the social sciences does not consist of laws which simply formulate statistical regularities in behavior, even though social scientists often do make use of such generalizations. The structure of understanding involves the over-lapping of patterns or *gestalts* which explain particular situations. This is far from being a simple additive matter. Configurations do not necessarily arrange themselves into a hierarchical structure. They may even in some cases be plainly incompatible, reflecting the ineluctable diversity of the empirical world. The aim of the social sciences, therefore, cannot be to resolve these patterns of meaning into a small set of master generalizations which would explain all social reality. The true aim of the social sciences must be to develop as many configurations or gestalts as possible, which can then be utilized whenever or wherever appropriate. The psychological mechanism involved in social understanding may be suggested by way of comparison with the flash of insight which often seems to occur when in reading a novel or

---

[2] See George H. Mead, *Mind, Self and Society* (Chicago: University of Chicago Press, 1934), *passim;* and Mead, *The Philosophy of the Act* (Chicago: University of Chicago Press, 1938), Part I.

a short story we come upon a passage which brilliantly illumines some aspect of our own experience.

The pattern or gestalt is not exactly comparable to a causal web. Naturally, there are some relations among the phenomena involved which might be called "causal" in nature; but not all the relations need be causal, and nomothetic generalizations may be rare. For instance, we may explain the meaning of a gesture or greeting by simple translation or by placing the gesture in an appropriate class of signs which we call "greetings." No causal links whatever are involved, yet meaning hinges on placing the gesture in context. It would be extremely arbitrary to limit the term "explanation" to cases in which causal explanation *per se* is involved, let alone only to situations where we can use nomothetic generalizations.[3]

Understanding in the social sciences, then, is not primarily a matter of the simple accumulation of facts, of developing a hierarchy of laws, or of enveloping the empirical world in a web of causal laws which would make prediction invariably successful because of total determinism. Understanding as an aim in the social studies does involve concern with human beliefs, purposes, and values and with the consequences of social action. The latter involves studies of social organization, the province of the various special empirical social sciences, such as political science and economics. Political science deals with the study of relationships involving power and authority. Economics is concerned with exchange, bargaining, and resource allocation. Anthropology is concerned with the social organization of primitive tribes and human groupings. Sociology is the basic social science concerned with a general understanding of human action.

Sociology is interested in specification of the basic *forms* of sociation or social interaction.[4] It is interested in the classification of types of human relationships and in the understanding of the basic mechanisms at work in social interaction. The other social sciences are really interested in the specific *contents* of various episodes or classes of social action. Thus, to repeat, economics is concerned with bargaining, exchange, and resource allocation. Economics studies specific transactions and elements of social structure concerned

---

[3]See John Passmore's paper on "Explanation in Everday Life, in Science and in History," in G. H. Nadel (Editor), *Studies in the Philosophy of History* (New York: Harper Torchbooks, 1965), pp. 16–34.

[4]See Nicholas Spykman, *The Social Theory of Georg Simmel* (Chicago: University of Chicago Press, 1925), pp. 26–89.

with these aims. The relation of economic processes to human behavior in general is the province of general sociology. The form is essential, the content accidental. This is why it is possible, for instance, to study exchange relationships or bargaining in dating and courtship,[5] or to study the politics of a corporation.[6] The form is universal, the content or occasion unpredictable.

These, then, are the social sciences and their infinitely complex subject matter—man in society. The essays which follow undertake to explicate human nature and the ways in which the nature of man must shape the contours of social scientific investigation. This is the central message of this book: the necessity of developing a position on method in the human sciences on the basis of what we know about the nature of human beings. In the last section, we turn to a consideration of the practical reorientation of the social sciences in line with the conclusions about human nature set forth in the readings which follow.

[5] See Peter Blau, *Exchange and Power in Social Life* (New York: Wiley, 1964).
[6] Walton Hamilton, *The Politics of Industry* (New York: Knopf, 1957).

KURT RIEZLER

SOME CRITICAL REMARKS ON MAN'S SCIENCE OF MAN*

I

Though many sciences deal with man, there is no science of man. Man has been cut into pieces and distributed among different departments of research. The number of pieces increases as the quantity of our knowledge increases. Yet man goes on being one.

The many sciences apply different methods and conceptual schemes. They look at their different pieces under different aspects. Only a butcher who knows the animal can find the right joints. Hence the philosopher, as Plato demands, should be a good butcher. The butcher of man does not know man. Even if a perfect butcher could find the right joints, the pieces would not fit into one another, as divergent conceptual schemes took a hand in shaping the pieces. The scholars in charge of the pieces speak different languages, which the student of man cannot translate into one another. In despair he turns to philosophy for a universal grammar. But the professors of philosophy disagree on the alphabet.

Still man goes on being one.

Man, a compound of physical chemical events in the department of physiology, grows in the divinity school into a soul to be saved, and sinks in the department of psychology into a mechanism of stimuli and responses. The economist confronts his construct of pure theory with the reality of a changing economic life, and sees rational man upset the mechanism of the market by acting even collectively, as a romantic fool. The anthropologist collects the material data of different cultures only to realize that the core of his problem is a "system of meanings." He tries to classify and compare cultures. On what basis, if each culture is unique? The sociologist aims at the laws of

*Reprinted by permission of *Social Research*, Vol. 12 (1945), pp. 481–505.

CRITICAL REMARKS ON MAN'S SCIENCE OF MAN

social change. But his variables are at best the variables of a particular genus of society. They desert him as the society changes. He tries to classify in order to get at least at the variables of a class, but looks in vain for a principle of classification. Whatever age, country or culture the historian describes as unique, he will be suspected of describing it only in the light of his own age, which is equally unique. Yet he finds analogies between different ages and countries, and finally confesses that man, the eternally mutable being, is what he has always been and ever will be. But he does not say what man is and when at his best describes a particular time as an ephemeral manifestation of an eternal though unknown man.

The various sciences are eager to draw lines that demarcate areas in a system of sciences. These divides, however, merely divide professors. We learn that psychology deals with the individual qua individual, social psychology with the individual as a member of a group, sociology with groups. But it is as individual that man is a member of a group; as a member of a group that he is an individual. It is through individuals that groups behave. Yet areas of research must be differentiated. Certainly, if only the theories, the conceptual schemes developed in one area, did not forget that they must cover or be compatible with the phenomena of another area. The subject matter remains a unity. Conceptual schemes do not create the subject matter. They create aspects, a mirror, and the properties of the mirror share in shaping the image.

Biology, we learn, deals with nature; sociology with the social order. The one is supposed to stand still while the other moves. But biology and sociology speak different languages. Textbooks of sociology start with a description of human nature in terms of both biology and individual psychology, and proceed in another language to inquire into a social world that changes. But the laws of the social order are laws of nature. Biology does not exhaust nature. One nature embraces the changing and the changeless.

Man is not an aggregate of data to be set down side by side. Mere distinctions do not help; we must state how the "realms," "areas," "levels" we distinguish are related to one another. Whenever we absolutize any set of concepts used for one of these realms we stabilize a doubtful distinction, succumb to a master of our own making, deprive ourselves of any possibility of inquiring into these relations, and must finally acquiesce in the split between man and nature, mind and body, physical and mental experience.

We would do better to treat all our dividing lines and specific sets of concepts, those of biochemistry included, as merely preliminary results of tentative points of view. The question remains: what is man? Not only the answers differ. The little word "is" contained in the question itself has many senses. Yet man "is."

Social scientists never weary of discussing methodology—a sign of weakness, not of strength. Were they sure of their results, they would not quarrel over methods. The model of the "scientific method" is borrowed from the natural sciences and lives on their prestige. Its formulation is largely defective. Not a few fancy they could share in this prestige simply by accepting as "scientific" only facts that are "verifiable" by anybody, and by demanding that these facts be ordered and correlated in constant relations between measurable quantities.

The results of this method as applied by the social sciences are meager. Facts are amassed far beyond possible use. Some are not even facts; others are of dubious relevance. Correlations of data do not establish laws of social change. The variables chosen for the sake of easy and reliable verification are not universal, their relations not constant. We have not yet a system of variables whose claim to articulate the social reality is uncontested.

Does not the spirit of science demand that the subject matter determine the method? Does not the preconceived method circumscribe our interest, mutilate our capacity to observe, distort the subject matter? Maybe the social scientist would better heed his own counsel.

In the social sciences the facts are not given as isolated items. When isolated, these items are no longer the "facts." Moreover, granting that facts must be verifiable, demands for a specific verification are bound to lead to a preference for, or a selection of, a particular sort of facts. But these may not be the pertinent ones. We may prefer the clearly to the obscurely given; we cannot preassume that the clearly given explain or hold the key to the obscurely given. We may cherish the hope but should not deem the assumption scientific. Empiricists must be impartial. Science does not demand that we exclude facts; it demands that we refine and enlarge our capacity to observe.

It is obvious that in social life even such facts or items as can be isolated, observed and measured by instruments are what they are by virtue of their roles, functions, meanings in a dynamic context, the context of life. This is not only the first of all facts; it is the criterion of relevance: things are relevant with respect to it.

Our procedure of isolating items contains a great many hidden preassumptions. Many "facts" are not raw material, but the product of an initial, though unconscious, process of prefabrication. Though we must isolate, the social sciences cannot start with the product of isolation. Their facts are given in a living context.

The specific difficulties of the social scientist culminate in the demand for an "objective" description, on the one hand, and the necessity to recognize the relevance of "subjective" factors, on the other. In this apparent contradiction "subjective" and "objective" are used in different senses. The demand for an objective description is directed against the subjective bias of deficiency of the observer and holds for all science.

The subjective factors, whose relevance is recognized, belong to the thing observed, not to the observer. This thing, in the social sciences, is man. Man, a "subject," deals with objects. Objects have uses, functions, meanings for subjects. Subjects have attitudes toward objects. If the sociologist distinguishes subjective from objective factors, he thinks of meanings, attitudes that belong to a subject matter in which the objective object cannot be separated from the subject whose object it is. Their "subjectivity" is the subject-character of the subject—the object to be observed—not the subjectivity of the observer. The ambiguous use of "subjective" and "objective" blurs two senses and feeds an endless confusion.

A scientist who, aiming at objectivity whatever the cost, excludes not merely his own subjectivity but also the subjective factors of his subject matter, deprives himself of the greater part of his facts, and his subject matter of its specific nature. He puts a ban on any kind of interpretation, restricts himself to registering "overt actions," and finally prefers the behavior of rats to that of the human soul, since the latter but not the former might suggest an interpretation that could be deemed subjective.

He may have good reasons and the best of excuses. The subjective factors, though they belong to the object observed, are phenomena for which verification and any check on the subjective bias or error of the observer are difficult. He can point to volumes of obvious misinterpretation, since the philosophers or other theorists of the human soul would rather press their theories into the phenomena than look at the phenomena and patiently read their tale.

However good such reasons and excuses may be, the awkward situation remains. Overt actions are what they "mean." Two objectively identical actions may mean, and thus be, two different things.

All items of the material content of a culture may be reported "objectively"—the system of meanings remains the core of the problem.

Seemingly, the more reliable our observation, the less relevant our facts; the more relevant our facts, the less reliable our observation. What is *proteron pros hemas*—prior relatively to us—need not be *proteron physei*—prior by its nature.

While, guided by the practical problems the manipulation of our own complex society poses, the science of society piles fact upon fact, inquires into trends, and establishes correlations, which, however useful, coordinate merely average values of ephermeral variables of our own society, social theory—aiming at a science of man—is not sure of the questions to ask, the concepts to apply, the language to use, the bearing of the answers it gets.

There is only one way: whether we are scientists or philosophers, we must refine and develop our capacity to observe, even if that takes us beyond the boundaries of easy verifiability by anybody. Unless we achieve an "objective" treatment of the "subjective" factors, we shall continue to move hither and yon between meaningless facts and doubtful meanings.

II

Science aims at a system of permanences. In a world of change these permanences are assumed to be constant relations between variables, which as "laws" govern the change. But is social life not indefinitely mutable?

When looking at social life as it unfolds around the globe and through the ages we see societies grow and decay, cultures follow one another, groups within groups wrestle with the world, change their gods, their ways of life and the interpretations of their existence, more or less slowly or quickly, yet without rest or respite, amid some knowledge and much ignorance, much misery and some happiness. An enormous pageant reaches from a forgotten past into an unknown future through a confused present.

It seems to be a strange kind of drama. There is no audience. The actors are its sole observers. No actor, however, stays through the play from beginning to end. Even any hero drops out after hardly more than half a scene. Most of us are poor actors, playing merely ourselves. There are no rehearsals, no script. We do not even know our lines, though we have only one or two to speak. We must be satisfied if the two lines we improvise seem to make sense to our-

CRITICAL REMARKS ON MAN'S SCIENCE OF MAN

selves or to our nearest co-actors for some time, or are worth being remembered.

It may not be a play at all; before it is enacted it may lack the unity of a plot or a meaning as a whole. If there is a meaning the actors provide it during the play. This seems to be part of their acting. Nevertheless, man likes to pose as a divine observer outside the play. The philosopher of history pretends that every scene is what it is by virtue of its role in the play as a whole—the "meaning" of the whole to be interpreted by the philosopher of history. An insolent animal usurps God's throne. Such a philosophy of history, or any interpretation of the plot or meaning of the whole as expanded in space and time—even the philosopher's need for such an interpretation, his insistence that there must be such a meaning which justifies the parts—may be but a more or less ephemeral line in the play. The philosopher of history shapes his interpretation of the plot to fit the lines that he wants to say.

Yet there are "laws," invariants of history, a system of permanences. They are not, however, laws of any of the historical "worlds" that in time come to be and perish. They are rules that govern the acting of any possible actor in any possible play. They are to be searched for in the heart of the actor, and no interpretation of an historical cosmos can guide the search.

The philosopher of history will not find them in his imaginary meaning of the plot as a whole. Nor will a divine physicist find them in the mirror of his conceptual scheme. The physicist as observer would not even recognize himself in the description of himself as an object of his physics.

Each civilization, society, culture, builds up a "world," an order of a whole in which man lives. As the society changes, this world changes. We no longer live in our grandfathers' world. It seems to be our destiny as historical beings to move in a space that moves while we move. We try to escape this situation and stabilize our image of the world. The world should not move. We seek the system of permanences in the order of a stabilized cosmos. Yet this world changes, though we never intended it should. Again we try to escape and set up behind the changing world the image of a wider world in which this change of our world is thought to occur. We do so of necessity: it is one of the rules that govern our acting.

Yet every such cosmic image, the wider as well as the narrower, is a product of time, shoved aside by time. So far as we interpret human existence in terms of such cosmic images, the changes of the world involve our interpretation of man.

The system of permanences is not to be found in any cosmic scheme. The permanences reside in the structure of the dynamic context in which these cosmic schemes come to be and perish. This context is not a whole of history extended in time. It is the context of life as life, in any possible world. Its laws are the rules that govern any actor in any possible play, as, in improvising his lines, he builds up an image of a world in which his lines make sense, and wrestles with the passions of his heart and the stubbornness of things.

There are countless variables. Any social or cultural change involves a multitude of transformations. These transformations pervade one another and interact in innumerable ways. Some are easy, others difficult, to verify. We cannot assume that their verifiability is a test of their relevance. The data that undergo transformation cannot be put side by side in a list of traits and properties. The variables belong to different groups and are of different orders. They have more or less bearing on the concrete life of the society we study. What is their order? Which are universal?

There is only one way to search for an answer. All life, be it the life of a hermit in the woods or of the chairman of the Middle-town Women's Club, occurs as life in a dynamic context which, however general, has a definite structure. This dynamic context is omnipresent—implied in every fact, so far as it is a fact, of social life. Every question and every answer in a questionnaire presupposes it. The scheme of this context must contain in itself the principle of its differentiation, provide places for its variables, and thereby articulate its possible variations. If it does, it can claim to constitute a theory. Without such a scheme, the science of man will never be a science.

III

Sociologists, psychologists, anthropologists speak of the pattern of a society, of a culture, of life in a rural, urban, suburban community or in a primitive tribe. The term "pattern" is assumed to mean a kind of order that constitutes the unity of a system. These patterns change. What is the pattern of all patterns within which these changes occur?

There is open or tacit agreement on one answer to this question. Man and environment, linked to each other in such terms as "adjustment," "maladjustment," "effective" or "ineffective" relationship, are thought to constitute a system of variables and to serve as the "pattern of all patterns."

In speaking of a good or bad adjustment, an effective or ineffective relationship, we assume that man's relation to his environment moves between good and bad, effective and ineffective; we even imply a kind of vector, tendencies toward a better adjustment or a greater effectiveness, forces within the system that tend to change the system in a certain way. However meager, this scheme is meant to be universal.

Yet little has been done to articulate and enrich the scheme. It may be that whenever a human being of any kind faces an environment much more is universal and given. But even the inarticulate scheme poses a great number of embarrassing questions.

Its variables are of two kinds. Man and environment are presumed to be indefinitely variable. The term "adjustment" suggests a variability between 0 and 1. Expressed as a formula: $M _o^1 R - E_n$. Different men can live in an equally effective relationship or an equally perfect adjustment to different environments, and thus be compared in terms of their adjustment. Actually this does not mean much, yet it implies a great deal. It contains a hint: the universal variables may be relations. Of course, the different variables must be described independently of one another before we can trust any correlation we may be able to observe. But here we encounter another difficulty.

Since the correlations we are looking for presuppose an independent description of their relata, we treat man and his environment as different sets of items in the environment of the observer, to be identified by independent observations. This is, of course, perfectly legitimate and harmless whenever the observer and the human beings observed happen to live in the same environment. When we deal with an alien society and culture, the case is different. An anthropologist reports that the Andaman Islanders collect (empty) tin cans. He can be said to describe the life of the Andaman Islanders in terms of his own envirronment. But these are tin cans, "objectively"; they are manufactured in Philadelphia, as tin cans. Yes, but this kind of objectivity is irrelevant. They are what they are in the environment of the Andaman Islanders—rare, round, shiny objects—by virtue of the role they play in Andaman life. Thus the observer would do better to treat man and environment not as two separate sets of data but as the unity of a system whose inherent relations he should carefully respect.

"Environment" is obviously a relational term. An environment is someone's environment. Man is forever man in an environment. Both man and environment undergo change. Their changes change their relation to each other. This unity of a system can be said to be a dynamic context. It is full of tensions. So much everyone will be willing, or if not willing, can be compelled to grant.

I go a step further. The concrete reality of man and environment in relation to each other at any given moment is not merely what a man or his environment actually is or does here and now. It includes what a man or his environment can or could be or do, whether they actually are or do it. Our attitude toward other beings, human or not depends both on what they actually are, here and now, and on what we think they could be and do. Thus the "is" and "is not" have two senses, differentiated by the terms "actually" and "potentially."

In concrete life the reality of a being, human or not, includes its potentialities; they are part of the reality itself. I face an environment; I, as a being that is or does this, and can be or can do that, face an environment that is or does or yields this, but can or might be or do or yield that. Not only actualities but potentialities faced one another as the Pilgrim Fathers arrived in Plymough Bay. The customary way of recognizing potentialities in the sciences dealing with man is to talk about "faculties," "capacities," "dispositions" of men or things.

Men differ from one another in their actualities and in the range of their potentialities. The same holds true for environments. Some environments have many answers for man's demands; others, such as the Arctic areas, have scarcely one. Man has no choice; getting a "No" to all except one question he may ask, he has to accept the one "Yes" and live an Eskimo's life.

Mere potentialities are not yet "tendencies" or "forces." Tendencies or forces presuppose potentialities. Man strives, desires, wants. He puts demands on his environment, meets desires and wants of other beings; the environment puts demands on him. Man and environment may or may not yield to their mutual demands. The man-environment system is full of tensions between different tendencies and forces. Their possible concords and discords are present in each other as possibilities of the system. Man, when miserable, is still a being that could be happy.

The pattern of all patterns implies tensions between "is," "can be," "tends to be," "should be." I use "should" here in the innocuous sense of a response to demands, without moral connotations. Man and his environment may or may not be what they could, tend to, or should, be. Sometimes they do not tend to be what they should be. We move forever to and fro between the possible concords and discords of "is," "can be," "wants to be," and "should be." Their tensions are our life.

The pattern of all patterns is a dynamic context: a "could" and "should" inhere in the "is." "Facts" of an observer are what they are in their dynamic context. Isolation alters the "facts."

I return to the term environment. We have not yet faced the main difficulty. Environment must be someone's environment. A wood as such is not environment. It may be the environment of a hunter or a snake; it is not the same environment for the hunter as for the snake. Lots of things happen to the snake in his environment that do not and cannot happen to the hunter in his. Yet the environment is one and the same.

Psychologists distinguish between two meanings of the term "environment." The first is the geographical or physical; the second, the behavioral or functional. The difference seems obvious: the first is "absolute," the second, "relative."

The "absolute" environment could not be environment at all if it were no one's environment. And if it is someone's environment it is not absolute. The term can mean only that we regard the wood as the possible environment of an undefined multitude of possible beings. Only because there is such a thing that can become the environment of both a hunter and a snake can the hunter meet the snake.

The functional environment of the hunter does not become the functional environment of the snake. There is no common functional environment for the hunter and the snake. An I and You, able to talk with each other, can have a common functional environment—the functional environment of the group.

The geographer or the physicist pretends to describe the wood "objectively." By this he should mean merely that he describes it intersubjectively, without regard for any particular concrete observer but in relation to an anonymous observer whose data no possible observer can contest.

In the sciences dealing with man, environment means environment in relation to man. Here things are what they are in relation to man. Man, however, is concrete only as this or that man or group of men.

If an anthropologist describes the formation of an island in the South Pacific, its plants, animals and the like, in terms of geography, botany, zoology, he does not describe the environment of the tribe, which is the subject matter of his studies. What he describes and calls the objective environment is the potential environment of any possible tribe.

From there the anthropologist proceeds to the functional environment of the tribe: the functions, uses, meanings, interpretations of the things in this geographical or physical environment. He describes or should describe the environment no longer relatively to the anonymous observer, but to the tribe itself. This is a different story. The functional environment can be both narrower and wider than the geographical or physical. An infinity of things that belong to the physical environment may be no part of the functional. Things that do not belong to the geographical or physical environment may play an important role in the functional environment: spirits in trees and rivers, and the souls of the dead. Though the functional and physical environment can be distinguished, they cannot be separated.

As man knows himself to be not man but this or that man, he does not conceive of an environment as being merely a functional environment; nor does he think of a functional environment as being merely his own. Any ego-centered psychology misses at its very outset the road to social life. We have only to look at what really happens. Though the human being may never be able to characterize or describe his environment except as functional environment, that is, in terms of uses, functions, meanings, direct or indirect, relatively to himself, he forever posits it and all the things in it as absolute, that is, as having a being of their own beyond any function or meaning to him. The environment is not a psychological or phenomenal "field" whose center the individual is assumed to be. Man may put himself into the center of a psychological field; he never is and need not think of himself as the center of his environment. The environment is and is thought to be both the actual and the potential environment of other beings.

Man, as this or that man, refers his functional environment not merely to himself. He refers it as well to other beings whose functional environment it is or could be or become. The hunter posits the wood as something that has a nature of its own, independent from him. Even before the snake he steps on chances to become an item of his functional environment, he thinks of the wood as the potential environment of other beings, known or unknown to him.

We should be very careful not to forget that the "functional" character of our environment implies two references: to ourselves, and to an "absolute" character by virtue of which our environment is the potential environment of other beings. Friends and foes are not merely items of their respective functional environments. They are beings who refer their functional environments to each other. Thus only can they be friends and foes.

Here the man-environment scheme comes up against its crucial test, and falters. It cannot serve as pattern of all patterns. It cannot articulate the social situation. Hence sociologists limit its usefulness to the personality research of an individual psychology. But the personality problems of individual psychology arise in social situations. The single ego is an abstraction.

IV

What is this generalized man of the man-environment scheme? We assume that "man" stands for every possible individual ego, whoever it may be. In this assumption we are wrong, though in thinking in terms of classes and members of classes we have the best conscience in being wrong.

No man is born with a capital M, but as this or that being, male or female, Chinese or American, of a mother to whom he was something ere he could be alone with himself. He is not born merely as a member of a class "man." Man with a capital M is not the generalized Ego. Every Ego is an I to a You within a We, and only as such can it be generalized and writ large. It could not harm even individual psychology never to forget that every Ego, before being born, was an It; no one knew whether it would be a He or a She. It became first a He or a She, then a tentative Tu, and only as Tu an Ego. Indeed, it keeps on being a potential and actual Tue, He, or She, a member of a We, You, and They. Only as an Ego can it be all the others, and only as all the others can it be an Ego. Dying, it dies as an Ego and yet does whatever it can to outlive the Ego as a Tu, a He, or a She.

Individual psychology is a branch of social psychology by the nature of its subject matter. Though, in order of time, our social psychology developed as a branch of individual psychology, it still bears the imprint of its origin. In most of our talk about the "social field" the Ego still stands in the center of a psychological field. Like any other object in the field, the Alter Ego is referred to the Ego. This way of thinking, deeply ingrained in the habits of the psychologist, in the setting of his experiments, and in the questions he asks, seems to be, but is not, a matter of course. The child, though he refers the mother to himself, may perchance refer himself and some of his objects to the mother who enters his room. The social field is not the field of the Ego.

Thus we might do better to realize that the diverse entities in our environment are of two kinds: some are "objects" or things; others are "subjects" or living beings. In using these terms, however, we should remove the connotation they have in the theory of knowledge. Here the subject is the perceiver; the object, the perceived. Theory of knowledge asks: how does the subject come to perceive, to know, to think the object? There is only one subject, the perceiver; everything else, including the Alter Ego, is object. No one need, and psychology should not, yield to the pressure of a theory of knowledge that confronts a generalized subject with a generalized object of experience.

Some beings in our environment are subjects, though, to the theory of knowledge, they are merely objects, things perceived. What do or should we mean?

Subjects "live"; objects have no "life." We distinguish between organic and inorganic nature. These, however, are classifications within the objective world of a scientific observer outside his world—or within an "absolute" or physical environment that is no one's environment and therefore no environment at all.

If we remain within the dynamic context of man's relation to his environment we find ourselves still using and needing the distinction, though in a different sense. What we distinguish are relations between a man and the beings of his environment. We treat one being as a subject, another being as an object. The distinction need not coincide with the distinction between living beings and dead things in an "objective" world or an "absolute" environment. We can treat living beings as if they were dead objects, and often do so. We can even treat, at least within certain limits and for a while, dead things as if they were living beings.

Here are a man and a stone. The stone is something to be thrown, to stumble over, to be used for a house. Whatever it may be, it is treated, described, characterized relatively to a living being. This living being may be ourself or our tribe or the lizard that hides under the stone, or the scientific observer or a fusion of all possible beings, to whom the stone could be whatever it may be. The stone is an object. Objects have a relative being. They are of use or of no use, good or bad, healthy or poisonous to somebody. They are what they are *pros allo ti*, with respect to something else, yet they are posited as having a nature of their own, and thus an absolute and not only a relative being, independent of what they are to any other being. This absoluteness concerns merely *that* they are—not our knowledge of *what* they are.

The stone needs another being who has the power to bestow on it a being relative to himself. This other being—by virtue of so strange a power—is a subject. A cow has the power to let grass be food. A lizard has the power to let a stone be a hiding place, in the functional environment of the lizard. The poor stone has no such power. It is an object. Subjects have a kind of being in themselves, *en heautois*; objects have a being only *pros allo ti*. The stone can be something to us; we can be nothing to the stone. This marks the difference.

Fortunately, a man's functional environment consists not merely of objects that can have only a being relatively to himself. He is not the sole being in his functional environment that has the power to bestow on things such a relative being. Some beings in his environment are subjects—living beings—some of them human and his kin; they, too, have the power to bestow on things, even on him, a being relative to themselves.

Here are a man and his dog. A man can be something to his dog, and care; he can be a master, friend, companion, foe. From his dog he receives at least a tiny part of what he is to himself. He even meets and recognizes in things the power of the dog to let things be something relative to itself. He may continue to refer the dog to himself. He begins to refer himself to the dog. This is the fundamental fact, from which social life starts, though it has escaped many a philosopher and the greater part of presentday psychology.

Man is bound to encounter the power of his fellowmen over things and himself. He may or may not acknowledge this power. He may even try, successfully or not, to treat another human being as an object, a tool, or slave. He may or may not learn that this or that other being resists being treated as an object. His slave may not compel him to listen to his demands. His children will, or his wife—and he need not even be compelled. He can enjoy discovering in himself a being relatively to others.

Referring the environment to himself, man refers himself to his environment. He returns the reference. "Environment" suggests a one-way reference. The double reference reveals the limitations of the term. To psychologists who start as a matter of course with the man-environment dichotomy, man with a capital M becomes an isolated ego that "responds" to the "stimuli" of an environment. But this environment contains subjects: beings in themselves, to which man is or can be something. The line between the ego and all other things is not the only demarcation line between man and his environment. There are many possible lines. The cave man may not draw the line between his ego and the environment. His wife and children are not environment in the same sense as the stones and trees around his cave. He may draw the line between his family and the things around his cave. The I does not face merely the It. The I faces a You; the You is not an It. The I and You together face the It.

If we insisted on remaining within the man-environment scheme we would at least be compelled to go beyond the one-way sense in which we use it. It is not only that the environment is something in relation to man; man is what he is in relation to his environment as well as to himself. It is even true that what he is to his environment plays some role in whatever he is to himself.

By nature and of necessity man needs not only beings that he can treat as objects and refer to himself as food or shelter, as means of satisfying desires, or as instruments of procreation. He is in need of other beings—subjects—to which he can refer himself. The lonely man may even be inclined to treat an animal, a flower or a tree as subject, and "care" for it. He lets dead things take the place of the living beings he lacks and "objects" be "subjects." Man prefers man to animals and flowers. Man "responds."

In mutual response human beings bestow on one another a being relative to one another. What I am to You or to a We becomes part of what I am to myself. Even what the things are to You or to the group "in" which I live is part of what they are and can be to me.

V

Whenever we take pains to inquire into the meaning of this little word "in," a host of awkward questions come to the fore. The man-

CRITICAL REMARKS ON MAN'S SCIENCE OF MAN

environment dichotomy seems to set up man against his environment. Man "faces" his environment. We may ask where this "facing" occurs, and answer, indignant at so silly a question, that it occurs in the "objective" world. Quite frequently, however, this objective world turns out to be the functional environment of the observer. It should be at least the environment of the generalized observer of science, whom I call the anonymous observer. But the awkward question remains.

The Andaman Islander faces his tin cans neither in the functional environment of an American observer, to whom tin cans are defined by their use, nor in the "objective" world of an anonymous scientific observer, to whom tin cans are defined in terms of physics and chemistry, but in his own, the Andaman Islander's world, in which tin cans may have a kind of magic power. As the behavior of the Andaman Islander toward tin cans or other items of his environment depends upon the structure of the world "in" which he lives, we cannot disregard this world of his and treat the man and his environment as different and separate sets of items in the environment of a particular or a generalized observer. They constitute a system—together. This system is the legitimate subject matter of an observer, whose first obligation is to the nature of his subject matter. Things are what they are within this system. If we split them into two separate sets of items we destroy the relations in which the relata are what they are.

It may be doubted that this system of which man is a part should be called environment. The term is misleading. Man is not a part of his environment. He is well or badly adjusted, in an effective or ineffective relationship to it. We need a term that stresses not "against" but "in"—a small word, yet the most difficult in social theory.

Sociologists and psychologists recognize this need, and they resort to such terms as "atmosphere," "mental climate," "mental space," "life space"; or they borrow from physics the term "field." Each has some descriptive value. Following the lead of the word "in," we may say, using an ancient but now forgotten distinction, that man as subject is "in himself"—*en heauto*—though as a finite being among other beings he is in something else—*en allo*—which is not himself though it embraces him as a part. This all-embracing thing is the unity of an order as a whole. Whatever it may be or may be thought to be, it is unity of an order pervading both man and all the things of his environment. It is not an aggregate, the sum total of all the things in the environment plus one—man. It is this unity of an order that we call "world"; man and his environment are in the same "world." The world in which they are is man's world.

But the term "world," used in many different senses in scientific, religious, metaphorical language, is hardly less ambiguous than "environment." Moreover, it suggests problems of a philosophical nature which the term environment conveniently hides. The scientist shuns philosophy; he readily scorns it, except the rather anaemic one he need not be aware of, which is implied in the preassumptions of his "scientific method." For shunning philosophical implications he pays an enormous price in the emptiness of such terms as "adjustment" or "effective relationship to the forces of the environment," or of such definitions of culture as "the sum total of man's conditioned responses to his environment."

The advantage of the term "world" is that it exposes the ambiguities "environment" hides.

Since the rise of Gestalt psychology, psychologists can be supposed to be familiar with the logical distinction between a whole and an aggregate. The aggregate is a "many," a multitude of elements. It can be complete: no element belonging to it is lacking. It can be incomplete: one or some elements are lacking. A complete aggregate is not yet a whole. The multitude of all existing elephants, though no elephant is lacking, is not a whole. Whenever "world" is thought of as *omnitude rerum*, the totality of all things (meaning completeness), it is thought of as an aggregate.

"Whole" means a unity. Unity does not mean uniformity. It can be a diversity. But the diversity is not a composite of elements that are prior to the unity. It is the unity of a structure. So far as the whole has parts, every part sumbits to and contains this structure. The whole, as the unity of a structure, not as completeness of all parts, is present in every part.

The distinction between whole and aggregate, though difficult, is necessary. Man's behavior toward whatever we call his environment cannot be understood as the sum of his behavior to the sum of the things that constitute the environment as an aggregate. Man behaves toward the whole in which he thinks he lives as well as toward single things. Man's relation to this whole and his conception of its structure permeates his relations to single things; it not only orders his actual but predetermines his potential experience.

There is always a preformed scheme—preliminary or hypothetical, explicit or implicit, having some structure, however faint—which provides a possible place for what an item is or can be, and guides its interpretation. Without such a scheme, no experinece would be or could ever become experience. We do not simply meet and collect items; we locate and identify them, and say what they are by referring them to the unity of an order that encompasses both ourselves and our environment. Man facing the environment presupposes that man and environment are "in" the unity of a world.

The ambiguities of the term world correspond to the ambiguities of the term environment. As the environment of the man-environment scheme is the functional, not the geographical environment, so the world in which we think we live is our "subjective" world, not the objective world of a scientific observer outside the world. As our functional environment is not merely ours but includes the reference to a potential environment of other beings, so is our subjective world not merely subjective but referred to an objective world, which we posit as absolute but qualify relatively to us. Our world is not the world; the world is not ours. We call our valley, our village, our country "our world," though we know it is not the world. We may call the universe of the astronomer, the stars and spiral nebulae, the world, though it is not "our" world. It is not the world in which we live, care and act.

We say my world, his world, "the" world—meaning *le monde*, fashionable society—the diplomatic world, the gothic or baroque world, Goethe's or Shakespeare's world, the Greek or the Christian world, or everyone's world, our common world, world as the universe of all possible worlds. In all cases we have in mind a kind of whole "in" which the being whose world it is constitutes a part.

This whole in which we live is both a *mundus hominum*, the "group," and a *mundus rerum*, the world of things interpreted by the group, the one referred to the other. According to an ancient definition of space, but by no means the worst one, space, embraced by us, embraces us. Whenever we feel something like that double embrace of an order "in" which we are, we call it our world, and may mean our Bostonian society, our Massachusetts Bay, or our intellectual climate, or all three together as a unity. We feel pretty well "adjusted" to our environment whenever we can say "our world" and mean all three together—though we may not say it unless certain conditions are fulfilled concerning our relations to single things and to other human beings, the ones with respect to the others, and both with respect to this "world." Such expressions as "perfect adjustment" or "effective relationship to the forces of the environ- can be said to constitute a universal answer, cautious enough to pass as "scientific," to the old philosophical question of the "happy life" —a legitimate question and an empty answer.

The few distinctions, introduced here in the course, and for the purpose of a critical analysis of the man-environment scheme, may be used to articulate "perfect adjustment" or "effective relationship" in terms of mere relations between the constituents of a universal pattern, and may thus give the legitimate question an answer still universal and not quite so empty.

VI

The few distinctions I propose may be found helpful in articulating the psychological content of some general concepts used in sociology, whose lack of precision is admitted and deplored: integration, disintegration, growth and decay. Their further development may finally help to give such famous questions as the reasons for the lower suicide rate of Catholic populations a more accurate and specific answer than Durkheim's greater "social cohesion" which supports man in the "anxieties"—the maid of all work in modern psychology—of which suicide rates are said to be functions. The proposed distinctions may be useful for liberating social psychology from the pressure of an ego-oriented individual psychology. A certain though still modest enrichment of the man-environment scheme may provide the inquirer with some principles of possible differentiations and some tools for ordering the variations.

A mere revision of the man–environment dichotomy is not the suggestion to which this study is intended to lead. Much more is needed than to replace that scheme by another, more elaborate one. The man-environment scheme, however enriched, can hardly lose its fundamental ambiguity. It interrelates items in the environment of the observer which, as given relata, antecede their relations. This study suggests that the "fundamental pattern" the sciences of man are in want of should be conceived of as a dynamic context, implied in every fact of human life, individual or social, of whatever age and society. That dynamic context should not interrelate already given facts, but should articulate the variable interrelation of possible roles or functions of possible facts. This suggestion goes far

CRITICAL REMARKS ON MAN'S SCIENCE OF MAN 83

beyond any mere enrichment of the man-environment scheme. It sets a difficult task. It merely points in a direction; in this direction alone can we hope to find the way to the "universal variables."

Many a scientist will scorn a request to resort to what he calls arbitrary metaphysics or the empty void of philosophical speculation. He is requested to do nothing of the sort, even if along this way he should stumble upon some of the oldest and most stubborn problems of philosophy proper.

His task presupposes that he distrusts not merely any philosophy not his own, but his own as well, however conveniently hidden. It may demand that he refrain from absolutizing, as the reality of nature herself, the picture of human nature reflected in the conceptual mirror of biology and physiology. He is not required to shove the picture aside; he must accept the fact that in this particular conceptual mirror, in this particular light, his subject matter shows this particular order—an astonishing fact, to be wondered at no end. He must remain aware that, whatever order he himself assumes or discovers in his own mirror, this astonishing fact remains to be accounted for, as an aspect of the same yet unknown order in another conceptual mirror. But such acceptance does not compel him to submit to physiology and to "explain" emotions in terms of chemistry as a disturbance of glandular equilibrium.

The search for such a dynamic context may demand further that he resist the temptation to restrict his subject matter, under the excuse of a heuristic principle, to a certain type of order he would like to find. The scientific spirit by no means requires that the hidden nature of the subject matter correspond to a specific order which our practical interest in reliable predictions or in certain procedures of organized research would prefer.

This does not mean that the scientist should turn from observation to philosophical speculation. He may go on distrusting a philosophy in which he sees nothing but a body of traditional quarrels, perpetuated in changing terminologies by the professors of philosophy. It means only that he should patiently observe the phenomena as they are given in concrete life, and know what he does when he presses them into a mill in which, minced to facts, severed from their context, sifted according to verifiability, cumulated and correlated, they can no longer either tell the story of man's happy and miserable life or lead to laws of social change that social change cannot change.

Any such conceptual scheme of a "universal pattern" is not to be deduced from a preconceived metaphysical system and imposed upon the interpretation of the phenomena. It can only be an hypothesis and, like any hypothesis, a point of departure. It is to be corrected and refined, confirmed or rejected with respect to the power it may have or lack to order the diversity and to spell the concreteness of life. An analysis of the phenomenon in its living context, guided by the hunger for concreteness, and going many times to and fro from the most general to the most particular, may have some chance to order the variables in tentative groups of transformation, and finally to arrive, in many experiments of both thought and observation, at a working hypothesis of a system of universal variables that can outlive the change of material data, social institutions, and even of those cosmic images in which restless man interprets and reinterprets his own existence.

CHARLES HORTON COOLEY[*]

THE ROOTS OF SOCIAL KNOWLEDGE[1]

If we are to gain a large view of knowledge we should, it seems to me, consider it genetically by tracing it to its sources in human nature and human history. Knowledge is, after all, a phase of higher organic evolution, and has apparently been developed for the sake of its function in giving us adjustment to, and power over, the conditions under which we live. If these conditions present any fundamental division in kind we should expect that the capacities of the human mind and the knowledge based upon these capacities would show a corresponding division.

In fact, the conditions with which the mind has to deal, and has had to deal ever since life began to be human, divide themselves rather sharply into two kinds: the material, on the one hand, and the human or social, on the other. We have always needed to understand both things and persons, and the most primitive savage, though he may occasionally confuse them, is quite aware that they are different and must be understood in different ways.

This division lies as deep as anything in our experience, and it corresponds to a like division in our mental apparatus. For the external contacts we have our various senses, and also, in recent times, the extension and refinement of these through aptly named "instruments of precision" which have made the exact sciences possible. For the internal contacts we have a vast and obscure outfit of human susceptibilities, known as instincts, sentiments, emotions, drives, and the like, quite as firmly grounded in the evolutionary process as the senses, capable of extension and refinement in ways of their own, and giving rise to a kind of knowledge that we recognize as peculiarly human and social.

[1]Presidential address read before the Michigan Academy of Science, Arts, and Letters, March 31, 1926.
[*]Reprinted by permission of American Journal of Sociology, Vol. 32 (1926–7), pp. 59–79.

You will say, perhaps, that all knowledge, whether of things or of men, comes to us by the aid of the senses, and that the division I assert is therefore imaginary. It is true that all knowledge calls for sense activity of some sort or degree, but the function of this activity in material or spatial knowledge, on the one hand, and in human or social knowledge, on the other, is quite different. In dealing with things sensation is the main source of the raw material which the mind works up into knowledge; in dealing with men it serves chiefly as a means of communication, as an inlet for symbols which awaken a complex inner life not primarily sensuous at all. In the one case it is our principal instrument; in the other only ancillary. When I meet a stranger and judge by his face, bearing, and voice that he is a kindly and cultured man, and by his words perceive, in a measure, the working of his mind, the sensuous images are like the starting mechanism of an automobile; they set at work processes more complicated and potent than themselves, of which, mainly, the resulting knowledge consists.

For our present purpose we may, then, distinguish two sorts of knowledge: one, the development of sense contacts into knowledge of things, including its refinement into mensurative science. This I call spatial or material knowledge. The second is developed from contact with the minds of other men, through communication, which sets going a process of thought and sentiment similar to theirs and enables us to understand them by sharing their states of mind. This I call personal or social knowledge. It might also be described as sympathetic, or, in its more active forms, as dramatic, since it is apt to consist of a visualization of behavior accompanied by imagination of corresponding mental processes.

There is nothing mysterious or unfamiliar about social knowledge, except as we may be unaccustomed to recognize and think about it. It is quite as early to appear in the child and in the race as is material knowledge, quite as useful in the everyday affairs of life, and quite as universally accepted as real by common sense. If there are men of science who do not see that it is something distinct in kind, but are inclined to regard it as spatial knowledge in an imperfect state, destined in time to be perfected by more delicate measurements, this is doubtless because they approach the matter with the a priori conceptions appropriate to physical research. In relation to social phenomena the merely spatial conception of knowledge indicates an abstract way of thinking that does not envisage the facts.

It is not, in this field, in accord with common sense. All of us know that the essential things in our relation to other men are not subject to numerical measurement.

I trust it will not be supposed that I am advocating any metaphysical dualism between mind and matter. It is not necessary, for my present purpose, to take a side on that question, but I have myself no doubt that all the phenomena connected with social knowledge, including introspection, have physical concomitants in the brain and nervous system. In theory these physical facts are capable of physical measurement, but when we consider their minuteness and inaccessibility, the likelihood of their being measured in a spatial sense seems quite remote. We must get at them, in practice, through consciousness and through overt behavior.

Spatial knowledge, we know, has been extended and refined by processes of measurement, calculation, and inference, and has given rise to exact science. It is generally agreed that knowledge of this sort is verifiable and cumulative, making possible that ever growing structure of ascertained fact which is among the proudest of human achievements. It may be worth while to consider for a moment to what this peculiarly verifiable character is owing.

It is owing, I take it, to the fact that this sort of knowledge consists essentially in the measurement of one material thing in terms of another, man, with his senses and his reason, serving only as a mediator between them. If, then, a group of investigators can agree upon a technique of measurement they may go ahead, achieving results and passing them on from man to man and from generation to generation, without concerning themselves with the vagaries of human nature and social life. This technical agreement is found possible, and the accumulation of knowledge goes on. But we must, of course, discriminate between the immediate results of measurement and the body of hypothesis and theory which is constantly arising out of them. Science gives us fact out of which the intellect endeavors to build truth. And what we judge to be true, even in the spatial sciences, is largely a social matter dependent upon the general movement of thought. A group of scientific men, familiar with previous investigation in a given field and armed with a sound technique, is the best instrument we have for the pursuit of truth, and is one of the most remarkable products of our social system; yet it is, of course, far from infallible. All groups have a body of beliefs which are taken for granted merely because no one disputes them, and which often turn out to be illusions. Assent is induced by conforming influences not wholly different from those operating in religion or politics. In short, no group is a trustworthy critic of its own conclusions, and only the test of time and of exacting criticism from wholly different points of view can determine the value of its contribution. There have been many groups, made up of very intelligent men working devotedly and in full assurance of being on the right track, who are now seen to have been astray. And although scientific methods are no doubt improved, it would be fatuous to suppose that they are a guaranty against group error. Some of the teachings of science are permanent truth, but only time reveals which they are.

The practical success of spatial science in enabling us to predict, and even to control, the behavior of the material world about us has given it vast prestige and brought about a feeling that the more all our mental processes are like it the more perfect they will become. A conception of what social science ought to be has accordingly grown up and gained wide vogue which is based rather upon analogy than upon scrutiny of the conditions with which we have to deal. Let us return, then, to the sources of our knowledge of mankind, and consider for a moment the development of this sort of knowledge in a child. He comes into the human world already provided with a vast complex of innate capacity for life peculiar to the human race and embracing in its potential content those processes of social emotion, sentiment, and intelligence in which men find their chief interests and motives. All this is an outcome of evolution, highly practical, the very stuff that has made man the most puissant of animals, and it has, no doubt, the same physical reality as any other nervous or mental processes. Regarding the exact content of this inborn raw material of personal and social life there has been much discussion, into which, fortunately, we need not enter. Some say that it includes quite definitely organized mechanisms, similar to the instincts of the lower animals; other, that the inborn mechanisms of man are small and indeterminate, taking on organization only under the stimulus of a particular kind of life. However this may be, no one can doubt that we are born with an inchoate world of mental capacity, existing physically as a mass of brain and nerve complexes, which requires as the main condition of its growth an interchange of stimulation with similar complexes existing in other personal organisms.

The process by which a distinctively human or social mind and a corresponding type of knowledge grows up within us was first expounded at some length in 1895 by James Mark Baldwin, who called it "the dialectic of personal growth." It resembles a game of tennis in that no one can play it alone; you must have another on the opposite side of the net to return the ball. From earliest infancy our life is passed in eager response to incitements that reach us through the expressive behavior of other people, through facial expression, gesture, spoken words, writing, printing, painting, sculpture, the symbols of science, and the mechanic arts. Every response we make is a step in our education, teaching us to act, to think, and to feel a little more humanly. Our brain and nerve complexes develop in the sense of our social surroundings. And at the same time our consciousness takes account of this inward experience and proceeds to ascribe it to other people in similar conditions. Thus by a single process we increase our understanding of persons, of society, and of ourselves. When you play golf you not only acquire spatial knowledge in the shape of a certain muscular skill, but also social knowledge through learning the pride one feels when he makes a long drive, or the humiliation when he tops the ball and gets into the creek. As you see another man do these things you repeat, sympathetically, your own inner response on former occasions and ascribe it to him. A new reach of human experience is opened to you and you enlarge your understanding of men. And you extend your knowledge of domestic life, of letters, arts, and sciences in much the same way. Consider scientific work in the laboratory and in the field. Does it give only material knowledge of the behavior of *things* in test tubes, of the look and feel of strata, of the habits of fishes, or does it also teach you to understand chemists, geologists, and zoölogists as *men*, to participate in a phase of human life, share its ideals, and learn its social methods? And is not the latter knowledge quite as important to the man of science as the former? Able men in every field excel, as a rule, in human as well as technical knowledge, because both are the fruit of a richly developed mind, and both must also be cultivated as instruments of success.

If the distinctive trait of spatial knowledge is that it is mensurative, that of social knowledge is, perhaps, that it is dramatic. As the former may be resolved into distinctions among our sensations, and hence among the material objects that condition those sensations, so the latter is based ultimately on perceptions of the intercommunicating behavior of men, and experience of the processes of mind that go with it. What you know about a man consists, in part, of flashes of vision as to what he would do in particular situations, how he would look, speak and move; it is by such flashes that you judge whether he is brave or a coward, hasty or deliberate, honest or false, kind or cruel, and so on. It also consists of inner sentiments which you yourself feel in some degree when you think of him in these situations, ascribing them to him. It is these latter sympathetic elements which make the difference between our knowledge of a man and our knowledge of a horse or a dog. The latter is almost wholly external or behavioristic, although those who associate intimately with them may acquire some measure of true sympathy. We know animals mostly as a peculiarly lively kind of thing. On the other hand, although our knowledge of people is likewise behavioristic, it has no penetration, no distinctively human insight, unless it is sympathetic also.

There is, no doubt, a way of knowing people with whom we do not sympathize which is essentially external or animal in character. An example of this is the practical but wholly behavioristic knowledge that men of much sexual experience sometimes have of women, or women of men—something that involves no true participation in thought and feeling. The more behavior in the other sex is instinctively sexual, the more our understanding of it is apt to be external rather than sympathetic. Or, to put it rather coarsely, a man sometimes understands a woman as he does a horse; not by sharing her psychic processes, but by watching what she does. There is, in fact, a complete series in our knowledge of persons, from the purely external, like our knowledge of babies, of idiots, of the widly insane, up through all grades to the completely internal or sympathetic, as when, in reading a meditative writer like Marcus Aurelius, we know his consciousness and nothing else. For the most part, however, human knowledge is both behavioristic and sympathetic: the perception or imagination of the external trait is accompanied by sympathy with the feeling, sentiment, or idea that goes with it.

This is also the process by which we come to understand the meaning of a word, and through such understanding make ourselves at home in that vast realm of meanings to which words are the key. We may know words as mere behavior, as when a man speaks to us in a strange tongue, but in that case they do not admit us to the realm of meanings. To have human value the word and the inner experience that interprets it must go together.

In short, we learn to know human life outwardly and inwardly at the same time and by a single process continuous from infancy.

Adopting a convenient and popular term, I will call the individual human mind, including all these socially developed sentiments and understandings, the *mental-social complex.* I hope by the use of this colorless expression to escape from the traditional implications that obscure such terms as mind, consciousness, spirit, and soul.[2] About this, whatever we call it, the question of the nature and possibilities of social knowledge centers. It is our supreme gift; but for that very reason, because all the deep things of life are in it, it is the part of us about which we know least, and is least amenable to precise treatment. Can it be made available for science, or shall we try in some way to dodge it, or cancel it out, as the physical scientist does when he requires that the ideas about nature which come from it shall be verified by nature herself through physical measurement? The trouble with any such plan would seem to be that in human life the mental-social complex *is* nature. It is the very heart of what we seek to describe and make intelligible. It cannot be dodged without dodging life itself.

Suppose, for example, you secure, by a series of mental tests, detailed knowledge of what a certain person does in various situations. This may be of great value; I expect important results from such studies; but after all they cannot enable you to know the person as a living whole. The social man is something more than the sum of standardized acts, no matter how many or how well chosen. You can grasp him only by the understanding and synthetic power of your own mental complex, without which any knowledge you may gain from behavior tests must remain superficial and unintelligent. Is it not a somewhat equivocal use of terms when we talk of measuring intelligence or personality? What we measure is the performance of standardized operations. To pass from these to the organic whole of intelligence or personality is always a difficult and fallible work of the constructive imagination.

Many people, agreeing perhaps with what I have said about the ultimate difference in kind between spatial and social knowledge, will hold that just because of this difference anything like social science is impossible. While spatial knowledge is precise and communi-

---

[2] In a similar way the "group mind," that is, a collective view of individual complexes communicating with, and influencing, one another, might be called the social-mental complex.

cable, and hence cumulative, the dramatic and intuitive perceptions that underlie social knowledge are so individual, so subjective, that we cannot expect that men will be able to agree upon them or to build them up into an increasing structure of ascertained truth.

This is, in fact, a formidable difficulty which enthusiasts for exact social science are apt to ignore. I may say at once that I do not look for any rapid growth of science that is profound, as regards its penetration into human life, and at the same time exact and indisputable. There is a difference in kind here which it would be fatuous to overlook.

Regarding subjectivity, I may say that all knowledge is subjective in one sense: in the sense, namely, that it is mental, not the external thing, but a construct of the mind. Even the simplest perceptions of form or extent, much more the exact perceptions of science, far from being mere physical data, are the outcome of an extended process of education, interpretation, and social evolution. Your so-called physical sciences are, after all, part of the social heritage and creatures of the mental-social complex. In so far, then, spatial knowledge and social knowledge are on the same footing.

The question of more or less subjectivity, as among different kinds of knowledge, I take to be one of more or less agreement in the elementary perceptions. If the phenomena can be observed and described in such a way as to command the assent of all intelligent men, without regard to theory or to bias of any sort, then the factual basis of knowledge acquires that independence of particular minds which we call objectivity. A yardstick is objective because it provides an undisputed method of reaching agreement as to certain spatial relations. Professor Einstein has shown, I believe, that this objectivity is not absolute, but it suffices for most purposes of spatial science. Strictly speaking, there are no yardsticks in social knowledge, no elementary perceptions of distinctively social facts that are so alike in all men, and can be so precisely communicated, that they supply an unquestionable means of description and measurement. I say distinctively social facts, because there are many facts commonly regarded as social which are also material events, like marriages, and as such can be precisely observed and enumerated. But the distinctively social phenomena connected with marriage are inward and mental, such as the affection and desire of the parties, pecuniary considerations, their plans for setting up a household, and so on. These also can be known and communicated, but not with such precise agreement among observers as to make decisive measurement possible.

You may say that while it is true that the mental-social phenomena cannot be observed directly with much precision, they express themselves in behavior, which is tangible and which we may hope eventually to record and measure with great exactness. Even our inmost thoughts and feelings take form in the symbols of communication, in gesture, voice, words, and the written symbols which are preserved unchanged for ages. All this is true and much to the point: I am a behaviorist as far as I think I can be without being a fanatic. But we must not forget, as behaviorists sometimes appear to do, that the symbol is nothing in itself, but only a convenient means of developing, imparting, and recording a meaning, and that meanings are a product of the mental-social complex and known to us only through consciousness. Reliance upon symbols, therefore, in no way releases us from the difficulty arising from the unmeasurable nature of our elementary social perceptions. We can record behavior and handle the record by statistics, but I see no way of avoiding the ultimate question, What does it mean?

And how about introspection? Does not the kind of perception which I inculcate involve this disreputable practice, and if so, is it not thereby hopelessly vitiated?

The word "introspection," as commonly used, suggests a philosopher exploring his inner consciousness in more or less complete abstraction from the ordinary functions of life. While this method may have its uses it is thought to have been more relied upon in the past then it deserves. Let us observe men under more normal conditions, and preferably, it is urged, through their actions rather than through their supposed thoughts.

But just what, after all, is introspection? It is not merely the philosophic introversion I have indicated, but takes various forms, some of which, in everyday use by all of us, are indispensable to any real knowledge of the minds of other men.

That whole process of the social growth of the mind which I have mentioned involves elements introspective in character. We come to know about other people and about ourselves by watching not only the interplay of action, but also that of thought and feeling. As we perceive and remember sensuous images of gesture, voice, and facial expression, so, at the same time, we record the movements of thought and feeling in our consciousness, ascribe similar movements to others, and so gain an insight into their minds. We are not, for the most part, reflectively aware of this, but we do it and the result is social knowledge. This process is stimulated and organized by language and—indirectly, through language—by the social heritage from the past. Under the leading of words we interpret our observation, both external and introspective, according to patterns that have been found helpful by our predecessors. When we have come to use understandingly such words as "kindly," "resolute," "proud," "humble," "angry," "fearful," "lonesome," "sad," and the like, words recalling motions of the mind as well as of the body, it shows that we have not only kept a record of our inner life, but have worked up the data into definite conceptions which we can pass on to others by aid of the common symbol.

Much of our social knowledge, especially that acquired from reading, involves a process more consciously introspective. One can hardly read a play or a novel intelligently, I should say, without recalling ideas and emotions from his own past for comparison with those of the people described. The hero, as we conceive him, is fashioned out of material from our own lives. Is it not rather absurd for scientific men to repudiate introspection? Does anyone prepare a scientific report or article without first turning an inward eye upon the contents of his mind in order to see what he has to offer and how he can arrange and present it? In short, introspection, however abused by philosophers, is a normal and common process, without which we could know very little about life.

Introspection, if critical, is more objective than the usual practice of floating upon social currents without attempting to become aware of them. How can you be objective with regard to your motives unless you hold them off and look at them? I have in mind a recent book, a good book, too, in which the writer, who deprecates introspection, advances a series of opinions on social questions of the day so obviously those of his race, country, and social class that one can only smile at his naïveté. Surely a little introspection would not be out of place here: one's subjectivity needs to be understood, if only to avoid it.

It seems, then, that outside and inside in human life, consciousness and behavior, mutually complement and explain each other, and that the study of external behavior as a thing by itself must, in the human field, be as barren as mere introspection, and for much the same reason, namely, that it isolates one aspect of a natural process

THE ROOTS OF SOCIAL KNOWLEDGE

from another. Nature has joined these things together, and I do not think that we gain anything by putting them asunder. Records of behavior without introspective interpretation are like a library of books in a strange tongue. They came from minds, and mean nothing until they find their goal in other minds.

However, I see no reason for quarreling with those extreme behaviorists who hold that we should observe men merely from the outside, as we do other animals. Let them work on this theory, if they find it helpful, and show what they can do. Even if it is wrong it may give rise to a valuable technique, as wrong theories have done in the past. It is fair to judge behaviorists by their behavior. I suspect that they will be found in practice to make use of introspection when they need it, much like the rest of us.[3]

At the opposite pole, it would seem, from behaviorism we have the method, or rather various methods, of mental analysis through the probing of consciousness and memory. These all rest in great part upon sympathetic introspection, or the understanding of another's consciousness by the aid of your own, and give full play to the mental-social complex. They may be used in sociology as well as in psychitry, and, in fact, do not differ in principle from the personal interviews widely employed in the study of social situations. Indeed, I take it that the psychoanalytic psychology owes its vogue to its boldness in disregarding the rather narrowly spatial methods within which laboratory psychologists were confining themselves, and venturing, by the light of clinical interviews and introspective interpretation, to explore the weird caverns of the human mind. Men saw that the sequent revelations resembled what they knew of their own egos. The method is quite separable from the extravagant theories associated with it and will no doubt be largely used.

I have conceded that social observation is, on the whole, less precise and verifiable, and hence less surely cumulative, than spatial observation, not only because the conditions can seldom be reproduced by experiment, but because the perceptions themselves are less alike in different persons, and so less easy to agree upon. Experience shows, however, that these difficulties are by no means sufficient to prevent

---

[3] I need hardly say that the scientific study of behavior has no necessary connection with the group of men who call themselves "behaviorists." Their extreme doctrine of the rejection of consciousness is best understood as a reaction against a former extreme, in psychology, of purely introspective study. Social studies have always been mainly behavioristic.

objective and co-operative study of social phenomena, and a cumulation of knowledge which, though not so tangible as in experimental science, is capable in time of yielding vast results.

The basis of common social perceptions, and hence of cumulation, is in the general similarity of mental-social complexes throughout the human race, and the much closer similarity among those formed by a common language and culture. We become aware of this similarity by watching the behavior of other men, including their language, and finding that this behavior can be interpreted successfully by ascribing to them thoughts and sentiments similar to our own. The idea that they are like us is practically true; it works. It was generated in the experience of our earliest childhood, and we have gone upon it all our lives. This fundamental agreement upon meanings can be made more precise by the careful use of language and other communicative signs, something as sense-perceptions are refined by the use of instruments of precision (though probably to nothing like the same degree), and thus allows a transmission and cumulation exact enough for practical use.

All history, all news, all social investigation, is a record of what men did—of such visible acts as are thought to be significant, and also of their symbolic acts, their speech, and their works of art. But what makes the record interesting is that through our likeness to them it becomes also a record of what they were, of their meanings, of their inner life, the semblance of which is awakened in us by the acts recorded.

I open Herodotus at random and find an account of how the Carthaginians, having captured many Phoceans from disabled ships, landed them and stoned them to death. But after this the sheep, oxen, or men who passed the spot were stricken with palsy. So they consulted the Delphic Oracle, who required them to institute a custom of honoring the dead Phoceans with funeral rites. Here is a record of behavior which we interpret by sympathy. We feel the cruelty of the Carthaginians, their wonder and alarm at the strange conduct of the stricken men and animals, their anxious resort to Delphi, their awed obedience to the oracle. Of the grounds for criticizing this narrative from the standpoint of a wider study of human ideas and human behavior I need not now speak. Like all social observation that comes down from the past, it must be interpreted in view of the difference in mental complexes between the men who made the records and us who read them. We must, as we say, get their background and point

THE ROOTS OF SOCIAL KNOWLEDGE

of view. But men are, after all, so much alike that an imagination trained by comparative study can usually make out fairly well what the records mean. The true reason why we must, in sociology, rely mainly upon contemporary rather than historical facts is the inadequacy of the record. History does not tell what we want to know, and we must look in the world about us for answers to questions which the men of old never thought of putting.

At any rate we actually have accumulations of social knowledge. Aristotle and many other early writers collected facts which are still held to be trustworthy, and interpreted them by generalizations which still command respect. In modern times the process has gone on developing in volume, diversity, and precision, and has given rise to technical groups of specially trained men. We have many kinds of history, we have social anthropology, political science, law, economics, sociology, comparative religion, comparative literature and art, and other departments, each with its own archives of recorded fact.

Indeed, as regards cumulation the study of mankind has a great advantage in that its subject matter is uniquely self-recording. Even the records of geology and paleontology do not compare in richness with those that man hands down about himself through language and the several arts. And the more he approaches and enters a civilized state, the more extensive these records become. The dinosaur may leave his skeleton and even his (or her) eggs, but man deposits a fossil mind. We know infinitely more about him than we do about any other animal, and the difficulty of accumulating knowledge, so far as primary facts are concerned, is quite imaginary. Dispute, as in other fields, is mainly about interpretation. The selection and explanation of facts has heretofore proved provisional; it has to be done over again with every change in the general current of thought. But is not this true of all science? At this moment the whole theoretical trunk of physics has been torn up by the roots and seems likely to be thrown upon the rubbish pile. A lasting structure of knowledge is hardly to be expected, except as regards the primary facts and their simpler relations, and this much we may expect in social science as well as in spatial.

It is high time that I referred to that body of knowledge and practice known as statistics. Statistics is an exact method, and it is enabled to be such precisely because it is not in itself social but mathematical. It does not directly *perceive* social facts, or any other kind of facts, but it takes standard units of some sort, which may be perceived social facts, and compiles, arranges, manipulates, and presents them in a way intended to make them yield illumination. The statistician operates between the primary observer, on the one hand, and, on the other, the theorist who demands light on certain hypotheses. Perhaps I may without offense liken him to a cook, who neither supplies the food nor consumes it, but is a specialist upon the intervening processes.

Evidently it would not be good sense to assume any antagonism between the exact methods of statistics and the more fallible procedure of sympathetic observation and interpretation. They are complementary and do not or should not overlap. The only opposition likely to arise is one due to the bias of the practitioner. A statistician, if he lacks breadth of mind, is apt to be so fond of his exact processes that he avoids and depreciates anything else, while the sympathetic observer is apt to be impatient of statistics. This difference of tastes would not do much harm if the functions were kept separate, but when a man who is fit for only one assumes both the result is unfortunate. Much statistical work, especially that based upon questionnaires or interviews, is vitiated by a lack of dramatic insight into the states of mind of the people who supply the information. A questionnaire is an instrument of social perception, and if its use is to have any scientific character, the first duty of the user is to dramatize the play of thought and feeling that takes place between the person that puts the question and the person that answers it. What was the actual state of mind of the latter, and what the human significance of his reply? Not every investigator has the insight and the conscience to perceive and report this real fact, commonly so different from the apparent fact, upon which the value of his work depends.

And so with the questions or problems used in mental tests. If they aim only to test the power to perform standardized operations they are objective, but, socially speaking, superficial; if they go beyond this and attempt to discover social or moral attitudes they are subjective, and of no value for science without sympathetic interpretation.

It is not the case that social science is becoming exact through the substitution of statistics for social sympathy and imagination. What is taking place is, rather, that the use of sympathy and imagination is becoming more competent, while statistics is being substituted for guesswork in the manipulation of data.

Another impression which I take to be erroneous is that statistics is revealing uniformities or regularities in social phenomena which indicate that these phenomena may in time prove to be subject to exact prediction in quite the same way as those of physics. It is true that statistics is revealing sequence, order, and a remarkable degree of predictability in certain social processes. By analysis of what has taken place during the past ten years, especially in the economic field, where the facts are largely material, it may be possible to forecast what will take place in the next five; and no one can say how far we may go in this direction. The whole basis of this, however, seems to be the prevalence of inertia and the rarity and slowness of the more originative processes. The greater part of human phenomena are so far routinized as to be more or less subject to calculation. Wherever men, under the impetus of habit and suggestion, are moving ahead in a mechanical manner, or where their intelligence is merely repeating what is essentially an old synthesis of motives—as, for example, in deciding whether to marry or not—exact methods are in place. The complex of human events can, to a great extent, be resolved into currents of tendency moving on definite lines at ascertainable speeds. If we can measure these lines and speeds it may be possible to predict their combined operation, much as the motion of a comet is predicted by calculating the resultant of the gravity, tangential momentum, and other forces acting upon it. The whole basis of prediction in such fields as that of the business cycle is the belief that the underlying motivation is essentially standardized or repetitive.

Probably no exact science could have forseen the sudden rise of the automotive industry and the genius of Henry Ford, although now that this industry is developed and institutionalized we may perhaps calculate with some precision what it will bring forth in the near future.

There is no good reason to think that such statistical methods can anticipate that which, after all, chiefly distinguishes human life from physical processes, namely, originative mental synthesis, whether by outstanding individuals or by groups. The kind of mechanistic theory which would exclude the unique function of human consciousness and will is not only highly speculative and unverifiable, but seems, as a speculation, to be losing ground. Recent philosophic writers (for example, our colleague Professor Sellars[4]), in so far as they accept mechanism or determinism, interpret them in such a way as to leave

---

[4] R. W. Sellars, *Evolutionary Naturalism, passim.*

intact our human power of reorganizing and redirecting life in a manner that no exact science can hope to foresee.

There is indeed one way in which physical and social science may be assimilated. We may find that atoms and electrons are not so uniform and reliable as has been believed, that the supposed physical laws are only statistical, covering diversity in the phenomena somewhat as social statistics cover the diversities of individual men. Indeed, we are told by men apparently competent that "the present state of physics lends no support whatever to the belief that there is a causality in physical nature which is founded on rigorously exact laws."[5] In some such way this the gulf may be bridged, but never, I think, by reducing the human will to zero.

Having dealt so far with observation, wither direct or mediated by technique, I come now to the interpretive use of the data, to the attempt to build a structure of social truth. This is, in all sciences, a work of the imagination, and a work which has always in the past proved to be provisional and to require renewal to meet the general advance of thought. I see no reason to expect anything else in the future.

At the present time all the sciences of life are, I suppose, controlled by the idea of organic development. Darwin gave these studies their orientation by making them studies of process rather than state, of what is going on rather than what is, of a drama rather than a picutre. For many years, however, evolutionary ideas were applied to social phenomena chiefly in an external and analogical way; they were imposed artificially, not allowed to grow naturally out of social processes themselves. The result was a vast body of social theory and propaganda, all claiming to be evolutionary and scientific, but none of it the work of a technical group devoted primarily and disinterestedly to the study of social facts. Even at the present time specialists in contiguous evolutionary fields contribute profusely to social literature and by no means hide their belief that they know more about what is important to society than do the so-called "sociologists." Whether they do or not, it is a fact that some of these extraneous doctrines, like the pseudo-Darwinism of Nietzsche or the hereditary determinism of the more extreme followers of Galton, have had, and still have, a wide influence.

I shall assume, however, that, after all, social phenomena are

---

[5]Hermann Weyl, quoted by J. W. N. Sullivan, *Aspects of Science*, p. 158.

most likely to be understood by those who make the study of them their main business, and that the application of evolutionary ideas in this sphere is the task mainly of history, anthropology, ethnology, political science, economics, social psychology, sociology, and kindred disciplines. All of these studies have, in fact, a decidedly evolutionary trend, and several of them may be said to have been created by the evolutionary movement. All of them aim at the understanding of personal and social wholes in the actual process of living. All make increasing use of social psychology. They do not aim to resolve social phenomena into elements which are not social, but rather to investigate the simpler and more general social processes and use the knowledge thus gained in synthetic interpretation of larger social wholes. This may be done by the use of well-chosen samples, as in studies of individual persons, of typical local or institutional conditions, and the like.

In general, the insights of sociology, if I may take that subject as representative, are imaginative reconstructions of life whose truth depends upon the competence of the mind that makes them to embrace the chief factors of the process studied and reproduce or anticipate their operation. This requires native ability, factual knowledge, social culture, and training in a particular technique.

It is sometimes supposed that pre-Darwinian studies in history, literature, art, and social theory were essentially unscientific and futile; in fact, mere rubbish needing to be swept aside by the advancing forces of science. On the contrary, many of these studies were based on common sense, had a sound empirical basis, and are even now of more value than hurried, dogmatical, and mostly analogical efforts to supplant them by something having the appearance of natural science. Such efforts have given rise to a variety of pseudo-sciences, some of which are flourishing at the present time, but they have not broken the real continuity of contemporary social knowledge with the solid work of earlier generations. Sociology, at least, recognizes whole-heartedly the value of pre-evolutionary research, and expects that its students shall know something of the great currents of historical, literary, and artistic tradition; shall have, indeed, as broad a culture in the humanities as possible. This culture affords the only access to great stores of facts with which we cannot dispense. It also affords a perspective of the development of social interpretation. Most of the generalizations now being defined, explored, tested, and developed into systematic knowledge were foreshadowed by penetrating minds of the past. How much of modern social psychology is implicit in the maxims of La Rochefoucauld, what insight into social processes had Gibbon! Sainte-Beuve, who saw literature as an organic human whole, observing the individual writer and the current of literary tendency with equal understanding, was a real sociologist in the field of criticism. Goethe was one in an even larger sense. An honest and competent student will be deferent to the achievements of the past and will lend no countenance to those shallow spirits who see scientific method as a sort of trick of laboratories and schedules by which they may avoid the slow approaches of actual social knowledge.

As to prediction, I have already pointed out that in the more mechanized processes of the social system it may be remarkably exact. We have no ground, however, to expect any such exactness in foretelling the multitudinous fluctuations of human life in general. Prediction, in any science, requires that the mind embrace the process, as the physicist, in his formula, embraces the process of a falling body, and so, through participation, foresee the outcome. Even in natural science this can usually be done with precision only when the process is artificially simplified, as in the laboratory. The social processes of actual life can be embraced only by a mind working at large, participating through intellect and sympathy with many currents of human force, and bringing them to an imaginative synthesis. This can hardly be done with much precision, nor done at all except by infusing technical methods with a total and creative spirit.

The human mind participates in social processes in a way that it does not in any other processes. It is itself a sample, a phase, of those processes, and is capable, under favorable circumstances, of so far identifying itself with the general movement of a group as to achieve a remarkably just anticipation of what the group will do. Prediction of this sort is largely intuitive rather than intellectual; it is like that of the man with a genius for business as contrasted with that of the statistician; it is not science, but it is the very process by which many of the great generalizations of science have first been perceived.

Predictions of any sort, however, are most likely to be sound when they are made by those who have the most precise familiarity with the observable processes, and it is the increase of this familiarity on the part of social observers, along with their greater insight into principles, that should make them better guessers of what is to happen than they have been in the past.

THE ROOTS OF SOCIAL KNOWLEDGE

What, then, is there new in contemporary social science, what, if anything, that promises a more rapid and secure accumulation of knowledge than in the past? Mainly, I should say, the following:

1. Liberation from outworn theological and metaphysical assumptions and reorganization on the basis of factual study and an evolutionary outlook.

2. The rise of a technical group of adequately trained scholars, with those traditions and standards, that expert criticism and exacting group atmosphere, indispensable to all higher achievement.

3. The development, since 1860, and especially since 1900, of a network of factual theory, by which I mean theory springing from observation and capable of being verified or refuted by the closer study of fact. Such theory is to be distinguished from much of the older speculation, which was largely metaphysical, unverifiable, and for that reason of no use in stimulating research.

There is nothing startling in the present movement. It shows no break with the past, does not promise any phenomenal power of prediction, and is, in fact, chiefly occupied with the ascertainment of what is actually going on and with the development of technique. We are trying to describe and interpret human life in the same spirit that the life of animals and plants has been described and interpreted, but with due regard to the different character of the problem. The human material is peculiar not only in its enormous abundance and variety, but in requiring, to deal with it, a radically different theoretical and technical equipment.

HERBERT BLUMER

SOCIOLOGICAL IMPLICATIONS OF THE THOUGHT OF GEORGE HERBERT MEAD*

My purpose is to depict the nature of human society when seen from the point of view of George Herbert Mead. While Mead gave human society a position of paramount importance in his scheme of thought he did little to outline its character. His central concern was with cardinal problems of philosophy. The development of his ideas of human society was largely limited to handling these problems. His treatment took the form of showing that human group life was the essential condition for the emergence of consciousness, the mind, a world of objects, human beings as organisms possessing selves, and human conduct in the form of constructed acts. He reversed the traditional assumptions underlying philosophical, psychological, and sociological thought to the effect that human beings possess minds and consciousness as original "givens," that they live in worlds of pre-existing and self-constituted objects, that their behavior consists of responses to such objects, and that group life consists of the association of such reacting human organisms. In making his brilliant contributions along this line he did not map out a theoretical scheme of human society. However, such a scheme is implicit in his work. It has to be constructed by tracing the implications of the central matters which he analyzed. This is what I propose to do. The central matters I shall consider are (1) the self, (2) the act, (3) social interaction, (4) objects, and (5) joint action.

THE SELF

Mead's picture of the human being as an actor differs radically from the conception of man that dominates current psychological

*Reprinted by permission of *The American Journal of Sociology*, Vol. 71 (1965-6), pp. 535-544.

IMPLICATIONS OF THE THOUGHT OF MEAD

and social science. He saw the human being as an organism having a self. The possession of a self converts the human being into a special kind of actor, transforms his relation to the world, and gives his action a unique character. In asserting that the human being has a self, Mead simply meant that the human being is an object to himself. The human being may perceive himself, have conceptions of himself, communicate with himself, and act toward himself. As these types of behavior imply, the human being may become the object of his own action. This gives him the means of interacting with himself—addressing himself, responding to the address, and addressing himself anew. Such self-interaction takes the form of making indications to himself and meeting these indications by making further indications. The human being can designate things to himself—his wants, his pains, his goals, objects around him, the presence of others, their actions, their expected actions, or whatnot. Through further interaction with himself, he may judge, analyze, and evaluate the things he has designated to himself. And by continuing to interact with himself he may plan and organize his action with regard to what he has designated and evaluated. In short, the possession of a self provides the human being with a mechanism of self-interaction with which to meet the world—a mechanism that is used in forming and guiding his conduct.

I wish to stress that Mead saw the self as a process and not as a structure. Here Mead clearly parts company with the great bulk of students who seek to bring a self into the human being by identifying it with some kind of organization or structure. All of us are familiar with this practice because it is all around us in the literature. Thus, we see scholars who identify the self with the "ego," or who regard the self as an organized body of needs or motives, or who think of it as an organization of attitudes, or who treat it as a structure of internalized norms and values. Such schemes which seek to lodge the self in a structure make no sense since they miss the reflexive process which alone can yield and constitute a self. For any posited structure to be a self, it would have to act upon and respond to itself—otherwise, it is merely an organization awaiting activation and release without exercising any effect on itself or on its operation. This marks the crucial weakness or inadequacy of the many schemes such as referred to above, which misguidingly associate the self with some kind of psychological or personality structure. For example, the ego, as such, is not a self; it would be a self only by becoming reflexive, that is to say, acting toward or on itself. And the same thing is true of any other posited psychological structure. Yet, such reflexive action changes both the status and the character of the structure and elevates the process of self-interaction to the position of major importance.

We can see this in the case of the reflexive process that Mead has isolated in the human being. As mentioned, this reflexive process takes the form of the person making indications to himself, that is to say, noting things and determining their significance for his line of action. To indicate something is to stand over against it and to put oneself in the position of acting toward it instead of automatically responding to it. In the face of something which one indicates, one can withhold action toward it, inspect it, judge it, ascertain its meaning, determine its possibilities, and direct one's action with regard to it. With the mechanism of self-interaction the human being ceases to be a responding organism whose behavior is a product of what plays upon him from the outside, the inside, or both. Instead, he acts toward his world, interpreting what confronts him and organizing his action on the basis of the interpretation. To illustrate: a pain one identifies and interprets is very different from a mere organic feeling and lays the basis for doing something about it instead of merely responding organically to it; to note and interpret the activity of another person is very different from having a response released by that activity; to be aware that one is hungry is very different from merely being hungry; to perceive one's "ego" puts one in the position of doing something with regard to it instead of merely giving expression to the ego. As these illustrations show, the process of self-interaction puts the human being over against his world instead of merely in it, requires him to meet and handle his world through a defining process instead of merely responding to it, and forces him to construct his action instead of merely releasing it. This is the kind of acting organism that Mead sees man to be as a result of having a self.[1]

THE ACT

Human action acquires a radically different character as a re-

[1] The self, or indeed human being, is not brought into the picture merely by introducing psychological elements, such as motives and interests, along side of societal elements. Such additions merely compound the error of the omission. This is the flaw in George Homan's presidential address on "Bringing Man Back In" (*American Sociological Review*, XXIX, No. 6, 809–18).

IMPLICATIONS OF THE THOUGHT OF MEAD

sult of being formed through a process of self-interaction. Action is built up in coping with the world instead of merely being released from a pre-existing psychological structure by factors playing on that structure. By making indications to himself and by interpreting what he indicates, the human being has to forge or piece together a line of action. In order to act the individual has to identify what he wants, establish an objective or goal, map out a prospective line of behavior, note and interpret the actions of others, size up his situation, check himself at this or that point, figure out what to do at other points, and frequently spur himself on in the face of dragging dispositions or discouraging settings. The fact that the human act is self-directed or built up means in no sense that the actor necessarily exercises excellence in its construction. Indeed, he may do a very poor job in constructing his act. He may fail to note things of which he should be aware, he may misinterpret things that he notes, he may exercise poor judgment, he may be faulty in mapping out prospective lines of conduct, and he may be half-hearted in contending with recalcitrant dispositions. Such deficiencies in the construction of his acts do not belie the fact that his acts are still constructed by him out of what he takes into account. What he takes into account are the things that he indicates to himself. They cover such matters as his wants, his feelings, his goals, the actions of others, the expectations and demands of others, the rules of his group, his situation, his conceptions of himself, his recollections, and his images of prospective lines of conduct. He is not in the mere recipient position of responding to such matters; he stands over against them and has to handle them. He has to organize or cut out his lines of conduct on the basis of how he does handle them.

This way of viewing human action is directly opposite to that which dominates psychological and social sciences. In these sciences human action is seen as a product of factors that play upon or through the human actor. Depending on the preference of the scholar, such determining factors may be physiological stimulations, organic drives, needs, feelings, unconscious motives, conscious motives, sentiments, ideas, attitudes, norms, values, role requirements, status demands, cultural prescriptions, institutional pressures, or social-system requirements. Regardless of which factors are chosen, either singly or in combination, action is regarded as their product and hence is explained in their terms. The formula is simple: Given factors play on the human being to produce given types of behavior.

The formula is frequently amplified so as to read: Under specified conditions, given factors playing on a given organization of the human being will produce a given type of behavior. The formula, in either its simple or amplified form, represents the way in which human action is seen in theory and research. Under the formula the human being becomes a mere medium or forum for the operation of the factors that produce the behavior. Mead's scheme is fundamentally different from this formula. In place of being a mere medium for operation of determining factors that play upon him, the human being is seen as an active organism in his own right, facing, dealing with, and acting toward the objects he indicates. Action is seen as conduct which is constructed by the actor instead of response elicited from some kind of preformed organization in him. We can say that the traditional formula of human action fails to recognize that the human being is a self. Mead's scheme, in contrast, is based on this recognition.

SOCIAL INTERACTION

I can give here only a very brief sketch of Mead's highly illuminating analysis of social interaction. He identified two forms or levels—non-symbolic interaction and symbolic interaction. In non-symbolic interaction human beings respond directly to one another's gestures or actions; in symbolic interaction they interpret each other's gestures and act on the basis of the meaning yielded by the interpretation. An unwitting response to the tone of another's voice illustrates non-symbolic interaction. Interpreting the shaking of a fist as signifying that a person is preparing to attack illustrates symbolic interaction. Mead's concern was predominatly with symbolic interaction. Symbolic interaction involves *interpretation*, or ascertaining the meaning of the actions or remarks of the other person, and *definition*, or conveying indications to another person as to how he is to act. Human association consists of a process of such interpretation and definition. Through this process the participants fit their own acts to the ongoing acts of one another and guide others in doing so.

Several important matters need to be noted in the case of symbolic interaction. First, it is a formative process in its own right. The prevailing practice of psychology and sociology is to treat social interaction as a neutral medium, as a mere forum for the operation of outside factors. Thus psychologists are led to account for the behavior of people in interaction by resorting to elements of the psychological equipment of the participants—such elements as motives, feelings, attitudes, or personality organization. Sociologists do the same sort of thing by resorting to societal factors, such as cultural prescriptions, values, social roles, or structural pressures. Both miss the central point that human interaction is a positive shaping process in its own right. The participants in it have to build up their respective lines of conduct by constant interpretation of each other's ongoing lines of action. As participants take account of each other's ongoing acts, they have to arrest, reorganize, or adjust their own intentions, wishes, feelings, and attitudes; similarly, they have to judge the fitness of norms, values, and group prescriptions for the situation being formed by the acts of others. Factors of psychological equipment and social organization are not substitutes for the interpretative process. Symbolic interaction has to be seen and studied in its own right.

Symbolic interaction is noteworthy in a second way. Because of it human group life takes on the character of an ongoing process—a continuing matter of fitting developing lines of conduct to one another. The fitting together of the lines of conduct is done through the dual process of definition and interpretation. This dual process operates both to sustain established patterns of joint conduct and to open them to transformation. Established patterns of group life exist and persist only through the continued use of the same schemes of interpretation; and such schemes of interpretation are maintained only through their continued confirmation by the defining acts of others. It is highly important to recognize that the established patterns of group life just do not carry on by themselves but are dependent for their continuity on recurrent affirmative definition. Let the interpretations that sustain them be undermined or disrupted by changed definitions from others and the patterns can quickly collapse. This dependency of interpretations on the defining acts of others also explains why symbolic interaction conduces so markedly to the transformation of the forms of joint activity that make up group life. In the flow of group life there are innumerable points at which the participants are *re*defining each other's acts. Such redefinition is very common in adversary relations, it is frequent in group discussion, and it is essentially intrinsic to dealing with problems. (And I may remark here that no human group is free of problems.) Redefinition imparts a formative character to human interaction, giving rise at this or that point to new objects, new conceptions, new relations, and new types of behavior. In short, the reliance on symbolic interaction makes human group life a developing process instead of a mere issue or product of psychological or social structure.

There is a third aspect of symbolic interaction which is important to note. In making the process of interpretation and definition of one another's acts central in human interaction, symbolic interaction is able to cover the full range of the generic forms of human association. It embraces equally well such relationships as cooperation, conflict, domination, exploitation, consensus, disagreement, closely knit identification, and indifferent concern for one another. The participants in each of such relations have the same common task of constructing their acts by interpreting and defining the acts of each other. The significance of this simple observation becomes evident in contrasting symbolic interaction with the various schemes of human interaction that are to be found in the literature. Almost always such schemes construct a general model of human interaction or society on the basis of a particular type of human relationship. An outstanding contemporary instance is Talcott Parsons' scheme which presumes and asserts that the primordial and generic form of human interaction is the "complementarity of expectations." Other schemes depict the basic and generic model of human interaction as being "conflict," others assert it to be "identity through common sentiments," and still others that it is agreement in the form of "consensus." Such schemes are parochial. Their great danger lies in imposing on the breadth of human interaction an image derived from the study of only one form of interaction. Thus, in different hands, human society is said to be fundamentally a sharing of common values; or, conversely, a struggle for power; or, still differently, the exercise of consensus; and so on. The simple point implicit in Mead's analysis of symbolic interaction is that human beings, the interpreting and defining one another's acts, can and do meet each other in the full range of human relations. Proposed schemes of human society should respect this simple point.

OBJECTS

The concept of object is another fundamental pillar in Mead's scheme of analysis. Human beings live in a world or environment of objects, and their activities are formed around objects. This bland statement becomes very significant when it is realized that for Mead objects are human constructs and not self-existing entities with intrinsic natures. Their nature is dependent on the orientation and action of people toward them. Let me spell this out. For Mead, an object is anything that can be designated or referred to. It may be physical as a chair or imaginary as a ghost, natural as a cloud in the sky or man-made as an automobile, material as the Empire State Building or abstract as the concept of liberty, animate as an elephant or inanimate as a vein of coal, inclusive of a class of people as politicians or restricted to a specific person as President de Gaulle, definite as a multiplication table or vague as a philosophical doctrine. In short, objects consist of whatever people indicate or refer to.

There are several important points in this analysis of objects. First, the nature of an object is constituted by the meaning it has for the person or persons for whom it is an object. Second, this meaning is not intrinsic to the object but arises from how the person is initially prepared to act toward it. Readiness to use a chair as something in which to sit gives it the meaning of a chair; to one with no experience with the use of chairs the object would appear with a different meaning, such as a strange weapon. It follows that objects vary in their meaning. A tree is not the same object to a lumberman, a botanist, or a poet; a star is a different object to a modern astronomer than it was to a sheepherder of antiquity; communism is a different object to a Soviet patriot than it is to a Wall Street broker. Third, objects—all objects—are social products in that they are formed and transformed by the defining process that takes place in social interaction. The meaning of the objects—chairs, trees, stars, prostitutes, saints, communism, public education, or whatnot—is formed from the ways in which others refer to such objects or act toward them. Fourth, people are prepared or set to act toward objects on the basis of the meaning of the objects for them. In a genuine sense the organization of a human being consists of his objects, that is, his tendencies to act on the basis of their meanings. Fifth, just because an object is something that is designated, one can organize one's action toward it instead of responding immediately to it; one can inspect the object, think about it, work out a plan of action toward it, or decide whether or not to act toward it. In standing over against the object in both a logical and psychological sense, one is freed from coercive response to it. In this profound sense an object is different from a stimulus as ordinarily conceived.

This analysis of objects puts human group life into a new and interesting perspective. Human beings are seen as living in a world of meaningful objects—not in an environment of stimuli or self-constituted entities. This world is socially produced in that the meanings are fabricated through the process of social interaction. Thus, different groups come to develop different worlds—and these worlds change as the objects that compose them change in meaning. Since people are set to act in terms of the meanings of their objects, the world of objects of a group represents in a genuine sense its action organization. To identify and understand the life of a group it is necessary to identify its world of objects; this identification has to be in terms of the meanings objects have for the members of the group. Finally, people are not locked to their objects; they may check action toward objects and indeed work out new lines of conduct toward them. This condition introduces into human group life an indigenous source of transformation.

JOINT ACTION

I use the term "joint action" in place of Mead's term "social act." It refers to the larger collective form of action that is constituted by the fitting together of the lines of behavior of the separate participants. Illustrations of joint action are a trading transaction, a family dinner, a marriage ceremony, a shopping expedition, a game, a convivial party, a debate, a court trial, or a war. We note in each instance an identifiable and distinctive form of joint action, comprised by an articulation of the acts of the participants. Joint actions range from a simple collaboration of two individuals to a complex alignment of the acts of huge organizations or institutions. Everywhere we look in a human society we see people engaging in forms of joint action. Indeed, the totality of such instances—in all of their multitudinous variety, their variable connections, and their complex networks—constitutes the life of a society. It is easy to understand from these remarks why Mead saw joint action, or the social act, as the distinguishing characteristic of society. For him, the social act was the fundamental unit of society. Its analysis, accordingly, lays bare the generic nature of society.

To begin with, a joint action cannot be resolved into a common or same type of behavior on the part of the participants. Each participant necessarily occupies a different position, acts from that position, and engages in a separate and distinctive act. It is the fitting together of these acts and not their commonality that constitutes joint action. How do these separate acts come to fit together in the case of human society? Their alignment does not occur through sheer mechanical juggling, as in the shaking of walnuts in a jar or through unwitting adaptation, as in an ecological arrangement in a plant community. Instead, the participants fit their acts together, first, by identifying the social act in which they are about to engage and, second, by interpreting and defining each other's acts in forming the joint act. By identifying the social act or joint action the participant is able to orient himself; he has a key to interpreting the acts of others and a guide for directing his action with regard to them. Thus, to act appropriately, the participant has to identify a marriage ceremony as a marriage ceremony, a holdup as a holdup, a debate as a debate, a war as a war, and so forth. But, even though this identification be made, the participants in the joint action that is being formed still find it necessary to interpret and define one another's ongoing acts. They have to ascertain what the others are doing and plan to do and make indications to one another of what to do.

This brief analysis of joint action enables us to note several matters of distinct importance. It calls attention, first, to the fact that the essence of society lies in an ongoing process of action—not in a posited structure of relations. Without action, any structure of relations between people is meaningless. To be understood, a society must be seen and grasped in terms of the action that comprises it. Next, such action has to be seen and treated, not by tracing the separate lines of action of the participants—whether the participants be single individuals, collectivities, or organizations—but in terms of the joint action into which the separate lines of action fit and merge. Few students of human society have fully grasped this point or its implications. Third, just because it is built up over time by the fitting together of acts, each joint action must be seen as having a career or a history. In having a career, its course and fate are contingent on what happens during its formation. Fourth, this career is generally orderly, fixed and repetitious by virtue of a common identification or definition of the joint action that is made by its participants. The common definition supplies each participant with decisive guidance in directing his own act so as to fit into the acts of the others. Such common definitions serve, above everything else, to account for the regularity, stability, and repetitiveness of joint action in vast areas of group life; they are the source of the established and regulated social behavior that is envisioned in the concept of culture. Fifth, however, the career of joint actions also must be seen as open to many possibilities of uncertainty. Let me specify the more important of these possibilities. One, joint actions have to be initiated—and they may not be. Two, once started a joint action may be interrupted, abandoned, or transformed. Three, the participants may not make a common definition of the joint action into which they are thrown and hence may orient their acts on different premises. Four, a common definition of a joint action may still allow wide differences in the direction of the separate lines of action and hence in the course taken by the joint action; a war is a good example. Five, new situations may arise calling for hitherto unexisting types of joint action, leading to confused exploratory efforts to work out a fitting together of acts. And, six, even in the context of a commonly defined joint action, participants may be led to rely on other considerations in interpreting and defining each other's lines of action. Time does not allow me to spell out and illustrate the importance of these possibilities. To mention them should be sufficient, however, to show that uncertainty, contingency, and transformation are part and parcel of the process of joint action. To assume that the diversified joint actions which comprise a human society are set to follow fixed and established channels is a sheer gratuitous assumption.

From the foregoing discussion of the self, the act, social interaction, objects, and joint action we can sketch a picture of human society. The picture is composed in terms of action. A society is seen as people meeting the varieties of situations that are thrust on them by their conditions of life. These situations are met by working out joint actions in which participants have to align their acts to one another. Each participant does so by interpreting the acts of others and, in turn, by making indications to others as to how they should act. By virtue of this process of interpretation and definition joint actions are built up; they have careers. Usually, the course of a joint action is outlined in advance by the fact that the participants make a common identification of it; this makes for regularity, stability, and repetitiveness in the joint action. However, there are many joint actions that encounter obstructions, that have no pre-established pathways, and that have to be constructed along new lines. Mead saw human society in this way—as a diversified social process in which people were engaged in forming joint actions to deal with situations confronting them.

This picture of society stands in significant contrast to the dominant views of society in the social and psychological sciences—even to those that pretend to view society as action. To point out the major differences in the contrast is the best way of specifying the sociological implications of Mead's scheme of thought.

The chief difference is that the dominant views in sociology and psychology fail, alike, to see human beings as organisms having selves. Instead, they regard human beings as merely responding organisms and, accordingly, treat action as mere response to factors playing on human beings. This is exemplified in the efforts to account for human behavior by such factors as motives, ego demands, attitudes, role requirements, values, status expectations, and structural stresses. In such approaches the human being becomes a mere medium through which such initiating factors operate to produce given actions. From Mead's point of view such a conception grossly misrepresents the nature of human beings and human action. Mead's scheme interposes a process of self-interaction between initiating factors and the action that may follow in their wake. By virtue of self-interaction the human being becomes an acting organism coping with situations in place of being an organism merely responding to the play of factors. And his action becomes something he constructs and directs to meet the situations in place of an unrolling of reactions evoked from him. In introducing the self, Mead's position focuses on how human beings handle and fashion their world, not on disparate responses to imputed factors.

If human beings are, indeed, organisms with selves, and if their action is, indeed, an outcome of a process of self-interaction, schemes that purport to study and explain social action should respect and accommodate these features. To do so, current schemes in sociology and psychology would have to undergo radical revision. They would have to shift from a preoccupation with initiating factor and terminal result to a preoccupation with a process of formation. They would have to view action as something constructed by the actor instead of something evoked from him. They would have to depict the milieu of action in terms of how the milieu appears to the actor in place of how it appears to the outside student. They would have to incorporate the interpretive process which at present they scarcely deign to touch. They would have to recognize that any given act has a career in which it is constructed but in which it may be interrupted, held in abeyance, abandoned, or recast.

On the methodological or research side the study of action would have to be made from the position of the actor. Since action is forged by the actor out of what he perceives, interprets, and judges, one would have to see the operating situation as the actor sees it, perceive objects as the actor perceives them, ascertain their meaning in terms of the meaning they have for the actor, and follow the actor's line of conduct as the actor organizes it—in short, one would have to take the role of the actor and see his world from his standpoint. This methodological approach stands in contrast to the so-called objective approach so dominant today, namely, that of viewing the actor and his action from the perspective of an outside, detached observer. The "objective" approach holds the danger of the observer substituting his view of the field of action for the view held by the actor. It is unnecessary to add that the actor acts toward his world on the basis of how he sees it and not on the basis of how that world appears to the outside observer.

In continuing the discussion of this matter, I wish to consider especially what we might term the structural conception of human society. This conception views society as established organization, familiar to us in the use of such terms as social structure, social system, status position, social role, social stratification, institutional structure, cultural pattern, social codes, social norms, and social values. The conception presumes that a human society is structured with regard to (*a*) the social positions occupied by the people in it and with regard to (*b*) the patterns of behavior in which they engage. It is presumed further that this interlinked structure of social positions and behavior patterns is the over-all determinant of social action; this is evidenced, of course, in the practice of explaining conduct by such structural concepts as role requirements, status demands, strata differences, cultural prescriptions, values, and norms. Social action falls into two general categories: conformity, marked by adherence to the structure, and deviance, marked by departure from it. Because of the central and determinative position into which it is elevated, structure becomes necessarily the encompassing object of sociological study and analysis—epitomized by the well-nigh universal assertion that a human group or society is a "social system." It is perhaps unnecessary to observe that the conception of human society as structure or organization is ingrained in the very marrow of contemporary sociology.

Mead's scheme definitely challenges this conception. It sees human society not as an established structure but as people meeting their conditions of life; it sees social action not as an emanation of societal structure but as a formation made by human actors; it sees this formation of action not as societal factors coming to expression through the medium of human organisms but as constructions made by actors out of what they take into account; it sees group life not as a release or expression of established structure but as a process of building up joint actions; it sees social actions as having variable careers and not as confined to the alternatives of conformity to or deviation from the dictates of established structure; it sees the so-called interaction between parts of a society not as a direct exercising of influence by one part on another but as mediated throughout by interpretations made by people; accordingly, it sees society not as a system, whether in the form of a static, moving or whatever kind of equilibrium, but as a vast number of occurring joint actions, many closely linked, many not linked at all, many prefigured and repetitious, others being carved out in new directions, and all being pursued to serve the purposes of the participants and not the requirements of a system. I have said enough, I think, to point out the drastic differences between the Meadian conception of society and the widespread sociological conceptions of it as structure.

The differences do not mean, incidentally, that Mead's view rejects the existence of structure in human society. Such a position would be ridiculous. There are such matters as social roles, status positions, rank orders, bureaucratic organizations, relations between institutions, differential authority arrangements, social codes, norms, values, and the like. And they are very important. But their importance does not lie in an alleged determination of action nor in an alleged existence as parts of a self-operating societal system. Instead, they are important only as they enter into the process of interpretation and definition out of which joint actions are formed. The manner and extent to which they enter may vary greatly from situation to situation, depending on what people take into account and how they assess what they take account of. Let me give one brief illustration. It is ridiculous, for instance, to assert, as a number of eminent sociologists have done, that social interaction is an interaction between social roles. Social interaction is obviously an interaction between *people* and not between roles; the needs of the participants are to interpret and handle what confronts them—such as a topic of conversation or a problem—and not to give expression to their roles. It is only in highly ritualistic relations that the direction and content of conduct can be explained by roles. Usually, the direction and content are fashioned out of what people in interaction have to deal with. That roles affect in varying degree phases of the direction and content of action is true but is a matter of determination in given cases. This is a far cry from asserting action to be a product of roles. The observation I have made in this brief discussion of social roles applies with equal validity to all other structural matters.

Another significant implication of Mead's scheme of thought refers to the question of what holds a human society together. As we know, this question is converted by sociologists into a problem of unity, stability, and orderliness. And, as we know further, the typical answer given by sociologists is that unity, stability, and orderliness come from a sharing in common of certain basic matters, such as codes, sentiments, and, above all, values. Thus, the disposition is to regard common values as the glue that holds a society together, as the controlling regulator that brings and keeps the activities in a society in orderly relationship, and as the force that preserves stability in a society. Conversely, it is held that conflict between values or the disintegration of values creates disunity, disorder, and instability. This conception of human society becomes subject to great modification if we think of society as consisting of the fitting together of acts to form joint action. Such alignment may take place for any number of reasons, depending on the situations calling for joint action, and need not involve, or spring from, the sharing of common values. The participants may fit their acts to one another in orderly joint actions on the basis of compromise, out of duress, because they may use one another in achieving their respective ends, because it is the sensible thing to do, or out of sheer necessity. This is particularly likely to be true in our modern complex societies with their great diversity in composition, in lines of interest, and in their respective worlds of concern. In very large measure, society becomes the formation of workable relations. To seek to encompass, analyze, and understand the life of a society on the assumption that the existence of a society necessarily depends on the sharing of values can lead to strained treatment, gross misrepresentation, and faulty lines of interpretation. I believe that the Meadian perspective, in posing the question of how people are led to align their acts in different situations in place of presuming that this necessarily requires and stems from a sharing of common values, is a more salutary and realistic approach.

IMPLICATIONS OF THE THOUGHT OF MEAD 119

There are many other significant sociological implications in Mead's scheme of thought which, under the limit of space, I can do no more than mention. Socialization shifts its character from being an effective internalization of norms and values to a cultivated capacity to take the roles of others effectively. Social control becomes fundamentally and necessarily a matter of self-control. Social change becomes a continuous indigenous process in human group life instead of an episodic result of extraneous factors playing on established structure. Human group life is seen as always incomplete and undergoing development instead of jumping from one completed state to another. Social disorganization is seen not as a breakdown of existing structure but as an inability to mobilize action effectively in the face of a given situation. Social action, since it has a career, is recognized as having a historical dimension which has to be taken into account in order to be adequately understood.

In closing I wish to say that my presentation has necessarily skipped much in Mead's scheme that is of great significance. Further, I have not sought to demonstrate the validity of his analyses. However, I have tried to suggest the freshness, the fecundity, and the revolutionary implications of his point of view.

ALFRED SCHUTZ*

THE SOCIAL WORLD
AND THE THEORY OF
SOCIAL ACTION[†]

At first sight it is not easily understandable why the subjective point of view should be preferred in the social sciences. Why address ourselves always to this mysterious and not too interesting tyrant of the social sciences, called the subjectivity of the actor? Why not honestly describe in honestly objective terms what really happens, and that means speaking our own language, the language of qualified and scientifically trained observers of the social world? And if it be objected that these terms are but artificial conventions created by

*EDITORS' NOTE—The essay here published for the first time was found by Professor Arvid Brodersen of the New School's Graduate Faculty, in the course of preparing for publication a collection of papers by the late Alfred Schutz. It is presented in *Social Research* because the editors of the journal and the colleagues of Alfred Schutz believe it to be outstanding as a brief statement of his sociological thinking.

The essay was written in New York in the summer of 1940, the author's first work after his arrival in this country from his native Austria, then Nazi-occupied. It forms the final portion, about one-third, of a longer paper, the first two-thirds of which were devoted to a critical review of Talcott Parsons' *The Structure of Social Action* (1937). While he was still in Europe, Schutz had studied with the keenest interest that important American attempt to construct a general social theory on the foundations of the masters of modern sociology, mainly Weber, Durkheim, and Pareto. In his long paper he analyzed the book in detail, and concluded by briefly setting forth his own basic ideas of a theory of social action, conceived from his familiarity with those great scholars as well as with the modern philosophers whose work he considered most relevant to such a theory—Bergson and, above all, Husserl. It is this final part of the paper that is here presented.

The manuscript, with its footnotes, is published without change, except for slight bibliographical amplifications and the insertion of two minor passages and a single major one from the earlier pages (enclosed within brackets); the deletion of occasional brief references to matters relevant only to the preceding part of the paper; and occasional punctuation changes and paragraph divisions. The title under which the essay appears here was supplied by the editors.

[†]Reprinted by permission of *Social Research*, Vol. 27, No. 2 (Summer 1960), pp. 203–221.

our "will and pleasure," and that therefore we cannot utilize them for real insight into the meaning which social acts have for those who act, but only for our interpretation, we could answer that it is precisely this building up of a system of conventions and an honest description of the world which *is* and is alone the task of scientific thought; that we scientists are no less sovereign in our system of interpretation than the actor is free in setting up his system of goals and plans; that we social scientists in particular have but to follow the pattern of natural sciences, which have performed with the very methods we should abandon the most wonderful work of all time; and, finally, that it is the essence of science to be objective, valid not only for me, or for me and you and a few others, but for everyone, and that scientific propositions do not refer to my private world but to the one and unitary life-world common to us all.

The last part of this thesis is incontestably true; but doubtless even a fundamental point of view can be imagined, according to which social sciences have to follow the pattern of natural sciences and to adopt their methods. Pushed to its logical conclusion it leads to the method of behaviorism. To criticize this principle is not within the scope of the present study. We restrict ourselves to the remark that radical behaviorism stands and falls with the basic assumption that there is no possibility of proving the intelligence of "the fellow-man." It is highly probable that he is an intelligent human being, but that is a "weak fact" not capable of verification (Russell, similarly Carnap).

Yet, it is not then quite understandable why an intelligent individual should write books for others or even meet others in congresses where it is reciprocally proved that the intelligence of the other is a questionable fact. It is even less understandable that the same authors who are convinced that no verification is possible for the intelligence of other human beings have such confidence in the principle of verifiability itself, which can be realized only through cooperation with others by mutual control. Furthermore they feel no inhibition about starting all their deliberations with the dogma that language exists, that speech reactions and verbal reports are legitimate methods of behavioristic psychology, that propositions in a given language are able to make sense, without considering that language, speech, verbal report, proposition, and sense already presuppose intelligent alter egos, capable of understanding the language, of interpreting the proposition, and of verifying the sense.[1] But the phenomena of understanding and interpreting themselves cannot be explained as pure behavior, provided we do not recur to the subterfuge of a "covert behavior" which evades a description in behavioristic terms.[2]

These few critical remarks, however, do not hit the center of our problem. Behaviorism as well as every other objective scheme of reference in the social sciences has, of course, as its chief purpose, to explain with scientifically correct methods what really happens in the social world of our everyday life. It is, of course, neither the goal nor the meaning of any scientific theory to design and to describe a fictitious world having no reference whatsoever to our common sense experience and being therefore without any practical interest for us. The fathers of behaviorism had no other purpose than that of describing and explaining real human acts within a real human world. But the fallacy of this theory consists in the substitution of a fictional world for social reality by promulgating methodological principles as appropriate for the social sciences which, though proved true in other fields, prove a failure in the realm of intersubjectivity.

But behaviorism is only one form of objectivism in the social sciences, though the most radical one. The student of the social world does not find himself placed before the inexorable alternative either of accepting the strictest subjective point of view, and, therefore, of studying the motives and thoughts in the mind of the actor; or of restricting himself to the description of the overt behavior and of admitting the behavioristic tenet of the inacessibility of the other's mind and even of the unverifiability of the other's intelligence. There is rather a basic attitude conceivable—and, in fact, several of the most successful social scientists have adopted it—which accepts naively the social world with all the alter egos and institutions in it as a meaningful universe, meaningful namely for the observer whose only scientific task consists in describing and explaining his and his co-observers' experiences of it.

To be sure, those scientists admit that phenomena like nation,

---

[1] John B. Watson, *Psychology, from the Standpoint of a Behaviorist*, 3rd ed. (Philadelphia 1929) pp. 38 ff.

[2] The foregoing remarks are only partially true for the so-called behavioristic position of the great philosopher and sociologist G. H. Mead (*Mind, Self and Society*, for example, pp. 2 ff.).

government, market, price, religion, art, science refer to activities of other intelligent human beings for whom they constitute the world of their social life; they admit furthermore that alter egos have created this world by their activities and that they orient their further activities to its existence. Nevertheless, so they pretend, we are not obliged to go back to the subjective activities of those alter egos and to their correlates in their minds in order to give a description and explanation of the facts of this social world. Social scientists, they contend, may and should restrict themselves to telling what this world means to them, neglecting what it means to the actors within this social world. Let us collect the facts of this social world, as our scientific experience may present them in a reliable form, let us describe and analyze these facts, let us group them under pertinent categories and study the regularities in their shape and development which then will emerge, and we shall arrive at a system of the social sciences, discovering the basic principles and the analytical laws of the social world. Having once reached this point the social sciences may confidently leave the subjective analyses to psychologists, philosophers, metaphysicists, or however else you like to call idle people bothering with such problems. And, the defender of such a position may add, is it not this scientific ideal which the most advanced social sciences are about to realize? Look at modern economics! The great progress of this science dates exactly from the decision of some advanced spirits to study curves of demand and supply and to discuss equations of prices and costs instead of striving hard and in vain to penetrate the mystery of subjective wants and subjective values.

Doubtless such a position is not only possible but even accepted by the majority of social scientists. Doubtless on a certain level real scientific work may be performed and has been performed without entering into the problems of subjectivity. We can go far ahead in the study of social phenomena, like social institutions of all kinds, social relations, and even social groups, without leaving the basic frame of reference, which can be formulated as follows: what does all this mean for us, the scientific observer? We can develop and apply a refined system of abstraction for this purpose which intentionally eliminates the actor in the social world, with all his subjective points of view, and we can even do so without coming into conflict with the experiences derived from social reality. Masters in this technique—and there are many of them in all fields of social research—will always guard against leaving the consistent level within which this technique may be adopted and they will therefore confine their problems adequately.

All this does not alter the fact that this type of social science does not deal directly and immediately with the social life-world, common to us all, but with skillfully and expediently chosen idealizations and formalizations of the social world which are not repugnant to its facts. Nor does it make the less indispensable reference to the subjective point of view on other levels of abstraction if the original problem under consideration is modified. But then—and that is an important point—this reference to the subjective point of view always *can* be performed and should be performed. As the social world under any aspect whatsoever remains a very complicated cosmos of human activities, we can always go back to the "forgotten man" of the social sciences, to the actor in the social world whose doing and feeling lies at the bottom of the whole system. We, then, try to understand him in that doing and feeling and the state of mind which induced him to adopt specific attitudes towards his social environment.

In such a case the answer to the question "what does this social world mean for me the observer?" requires as a prerequisite the answering of the quite other questions "what does this social world mean for the observed actor within this world and what did he mean by his acting within it?" In putting our questions thus we no longer naively accept the social world and its current idealizations and formalizations as ready-made and meaningful beyond all question, but we undertake to study the process of idealizing and formalizing as such, the genesis of the meaning which social phenomena have for us as well as for the actors, the mechanism of the activity by which human beings understand one another and themselves. We are always free, and sometimes obliged, to do so.

This possibility of studying the social world under different points of view reveals the fundamental importance of the formula of Professor Znaniecki, [that all social phenomena can be described under one of the following four schemes of reference: social personality; social act; social group; social relations.] Each social phenomenon may be studied under the scheme of reference of social relationship or social groups (or may we be allowed to add social institutions) but with equal legitimacy under the scheme of social acts or social persons. The first group of schemes of reference is the objective one; such a scheme will do good service if applied exclusively to problems belonging to the sphere of objective phenomena for whose explanation its specific idealizations and formalizations have been designed, provided, however, that they do not contain any inconsistent element or elements incompatible with the other schemes (the subjective) and with our common-sense experience of the social world in general. Mutatis mutandis the same thesis is valid for the subjective schemes.[3]

In other words, the scientific observer's decision to study the social world under an objective or subjective frame of reference circumscribes from the beginning the section of the social world (or, at least, the aspect of such a section) which is capable of being studied under the scheme chosen once and for all. The basic postulate of the methodology of social science, therefore, must be the following: choose the scheme of reference adequate to the problem you are interested in, consider its limits and possibilities, make its terms compatible and consistent with one another, and having once accepted it, stick to it! If, on the other hand, the ramifications of your problem lead you in the progress of your work to the acceptance of other schemes of reference and interpretation, do not forget that with the change in the scheme all terms in the formerly used scheme necessarily undergo a shift of meaning. To preserve the consistency of your thought you have to see to it that the "subscript" of all the terms and concepts you use is the same!

This is the real meaning of the so often misunderstood postulate of "purity of method." It is harder than it seems to comply with it. Most of the fallacies in the social sciences can be reduced to a mergence of subjective and objective points of view which, unnoticed by the scientist, arose in the process of transgressing from one level to the other in the continuation of the scientific work. These are the dangers that the mixing up of subjective and objective points of view would involve in the concrete work of social scientists. But for a theory of action the subjective point of view must be retained in its fullest strength, in default of which such a theory loses its basic foundations, namely its reference to the social world of everyday

---

[3]To be as precise as possible: on the level of what we have just called objective schemes the dichotomy of subjective and objective points of view does not even become visible. It emerges at all within the basic assumption that the social world *may* be referred to activities of individual human beings and to the meaning those individuals bestow on their social life-world. But precisely this basic assumption which alone makes the problem of subjectivity in the social sciences accessible is that of modern sociology.

life and experience. The safeguarding of the subjective point of view is the only but sufficient guarantee that the world of social reality will not be replaced by a fictional non-existing world constructed by the scientific observer.

To make this matter clearer let us forget for a moment that we are social scientists observing the social world with a detached and disinterested mind. Let us see how each of us interprets the social world, common to us all, in which he lives and acts just as a man among fellowmen, a world which he conceives as a field of his possible action and orientation, organized around his person under the specific scheme of his plans and the relevances deriving from them, but mindful, too, that the same social world is the field of other people's possible action and from their point of view organized around them in an analogous manner.

This world is always given to me from the first as an organized one. I was, so to speak, born into this organized social world and I grew up in it. Through learning and education, through experiences and experiments of all kinds, I acquire a certain ill-defined knowledge of this world and its institutions. Above all I am interested in the objects of this world in so far as they determine my own orientation, as they further or hinder the realization of my own plans, as they constitute an element of my situation, which I have to accept or to modify, as they are the source of my happiness or uneasiness—in a word, in so far as they mean anything to me. This meaning to me implies that I am not satisfied with the pure knowledge of the existence of such objects; I have to understand them, and this means I have to be able to interpret them as possible relevant elements for possible acts or reactions I might perform within the scope of my life plans.

But from the beginning this orientation through understanding occur in cooperation with other human beings: this world has meaning not only for me but also for you and you and everyone. My experience of the world justifies and corrects itself by the experience of the others with whom I am interrelated by common knowledge, common work, and common suffering. The world, interpreted as the possible field of action for us all: that is the first and most primitive principle of organization to my knowledge of the exterior world in general. Afterwards I discriminate between natural things, which may be defined as things essentially given to me and you and everyone, such as they are, independent of any human interference, and on the other hand, social things, which are understandable only as products of human activity, my own or others' (the term "thing" used in both cases in its broadest sense, covering not only corporeal objects, but also "ideal"—mental—ones).

Concerning natural things my "understanding" is limited to the insight into their existence, variations, developments, in so far as all these elements are compatible with all my experiences and those of others within the natural world in general and with the basic assumptions about the structure of this world we all accept by common agreement. Within these limits prediction (though only of likelihood) is possible for us all. This thing here is, in my opinion and in the opinion of us all, a wild apple tree. This implies that it will bear blossoms in spring, leaves in summer, fruits in fall, and become bare in winter. If we want to have a better view, we may climb to its top; if we need relaxation in the summer, we may rest in its shade; if we are hungry in the fall, we may taste its fruits. All these possibilities are independent of any human agency; the cycle of natural events revolves without our interference.[4]

If I want to do so, there is no objection to calling this organized knowledge of natural facts an "understanding" of them. But used in this larger sense the term "understanding" means nothing else than the reducibility of known and tested facts to other known and tested facts. If I consult an expert in the physiology of plants in order to learn what is really behind the afore-named cycle in vegetative life, he will refer me to the chemistry of chlorophyl or to the morphological structure of cells; in short he will "explain" the facts by reducing them to others, which have a greater generality and which have been tested in a broader field.

Quite another "understanding" is peculiar to social things (this term embracing also human acts). In this case it is not sufficient to refer the fact under consideration to other facts or things. I cannot understand a social thing without reducing it to the human activity which has created it and, beyond it, without referring this human activity to the motives out of which it springs. I do not understand a tool without knowing the purpose for which it was designed, a sign or a symbol without knowing what it stands for, an institution if I am unfamiliar with its goals, a work of art if I neglect the intentions of the artist which it realizes.

[4]Of course the interpretation of natural things as products of the agency of another intelligence (though not a human one) is always an overt possibility. The life of the tree is then the result of the activities of a demon or of a dryad, etc.

[The present writer thinks that only a theory of motives can deepen an analysis of the act, provided that the subjective point of view is kept in its strictest and unmodified sense. He has tried elsewhere[5] to sketch the outline of such a theory and hopes to be allowed to repeat here some of its outstanding features.

His starting point was a distinction between action and behavior. The distinguishing characteristic of action is precisely that it is determined by a project which precedes it in time. Action then is behavior in accordance with a plan of projected behavior; and the project is neither more nor less than the action itself conceived and decided upon in the future perfect tense. Thus the project is the primary and fundamental meaning of the action. But this is an oversimplification, which can be used only as a first approach. The meaning attributed to an experience varies according to one's whole attitude at the moment of reflection. When an action is completed, its original meaning as given in the project will be modified in the light of what has been actually carried out, and it is then open to an indefinite number of reflections which can ascribe meaning to it in the past tense.

The simplest complex of meaning in terms of which an action is interpreted by the actor are its motives. But this term is equivocal and covers two different categories which have to be well distinguished: the in-order-to motive and the because motive.[6] The former refers to the future and is identical with the object or purpose for the realization of which the action itself is a means: it is a "terminus ad quem." The latter refers to the past and may be called its reason or cause: it is a "terminus a quo." Thus the action is determined by the project including the in-order-to motive. The project is the intended act imagined as already accomplished, the in-order-to motive is the future state of affairs to be realized by the projected action, and the project itself is determined by the because motive. The complexes of meaning which constitute the in-order-to motive and the because motive respectively differ from one another in that the first is an integral part of the action itself, whereas the latter requires a special act of reflection in the pluperfect tense, which will

---

[5] Alfred Schutz, *Der sinnhafte Aufbau der sozialen Welt* (Vienna 1932; 2nd ed. 1960) pp. 93–105.

[6] I borrow some English terms from the excellent study A. Stonier and Karl Bode published about my theory under the title "A New Approach to the Methodology of the Social Sciences," in *Economica* (November 1937) pp. 406–24.

be carried out by the actor only if there are sufficient pragmatic reasons for him to do so.

It must be added that neither the claims of in-order-to motives nor the claims of because motives are chosen at random by the actor performing a concrete act. On the contrary, they are organized in great subjective systems. The in-order-to motives are integrated into subjective systems of planning: life plan, plans for work and leisure, plans for the "next time," time table for today, necessity of the hour, and so on. The because motives are grouped into systems which are treated in American literature (W. James, G. H. Mead, Znaniecki, Allport, Parsons) correctly under the caption of (social) personality. The self's manifold experiences of its own basic attitudes in the past as they are condensed in the form of principles, maxims, habits, but also tastes, affects, and so on are the elements for building up the systems which can be personified. The latter is a very complicated problem requiring most earnest deliberation.]

Above all, I cannot understand other people's acts without knowing the in-order-to or the because motives of such acts. To be sure, there are manifold degrees of understanding. I must not (even more, I cannot) grasp the full ramifications of other people's motives, with their horizons of individual life plans, their background of individual experiences, their references to the unique situation by which they are determined. As we said before, such an ideal understanding would presuppose the full identity of my stream of thought with that of the alter ego, and that would mean an identity of both our selves. It suffices, therefore, that I can reduce the other's act to its typical motives, including their reference to typical situations, typical ends, typical means, etc.

On the other hand, there are also different degrees of my knowledge of the actor himself, degrees of intimacy and anonymity. I may reduce the product of human activity to the agency of an alter ego with whom I share present time and present space, and then it may occur that this other individual is an intimate friend of mine or a passenger I meet for the first time and will never meet again. It is not necessary even that I know the actor personally in order to have an approach to his motives. I can for instance understand the acts of a foreign statesman and discuss his motives without having ever met him or even without having seen a picture of him. The same is true for individuals who have lived long before my own time; I can understand the acts and motives of Caesar as well as of the caveman who left no other testimony of his existence than the firestone hatchet exhibited in the showcase of the museum. But it is not even necessary to reduce human acts to a more or less well known individual actor. To understand them it is sufficient to find typical motives of typical actors which explain the act as a typical one arising out of a typical situation. There is a certain conformity in the acts and motives of priests, soldiers, servants, farmers everywhere and at every time. Moreover, there are acts of such a general type that it is sufficient to reduce them to "somebody's" typical motives for making them understandable.

All this must be carefully investigated as an essential part of the theory of social action.[7] Summing up, we come to the conclusion that social things are only understandable if they can be reduced to human activities; and human activities are only made understandable by showing their in-order-to or because motives. The deeper reason for this fact is that as I naively live within the social world I am able to understand other people's acts only if I can imagine that I myself would perform analogous acts if I were in the same situation, directed by the same because motives, or oriented by the same in-order-to motives—all these terms understood in the restricted sense of the "typical" analogy, the "typical" sameness, as explained before.

That this assertion is true can be demonstrated by an analysis of the social action in the more precise sense of this term, namely of an action which involves the attitudes and actions of others and is oriented to them in its course.[8] As yet we have dealt in this study only with action as such without entering into the analysis of the modification which the general scheme undergoes with the introduction of social elements proper: mutual correlation and intersubjective adjustment. We have, therefore, observed the attitude of an isolated actor without making any distinction as to whether this actor is occupied with the handling of a tool or acting with others and for others, motivated by others and motivating them.

This topic is very complicated to analyze and we have to restrict ourselves to sketching its outlines. It can be proved that all social

---

[7] An attempt was made by the present writer in his book *Der sinnhafte Aufbau* . . . (cited above, note 5).

[8] Max Weber, *Wirtschaft und Gesellschaft* (Tübingen 1922; new ed. 1956). Parts of this important work are available in English translation in H. H. Gerth and C. Wright Mills, eds., *From Max Weber: Essays in Sociology* (New York 1946); other parts in the English translation by Talcott Parsons, under the title *The Theory of Social and Economic Organization* (New York 1947).

relations as they are understood by me, a human being living naively in the social world which is centered around myself, have their prototype in the social relation connecting myself with an individual alter ego with whom I am sharing space and time. My social act, then, is oriented not only to the physical existence of this alter ego but to the other's act which I expect to provoke by my own action. I can, therefore, say that the other's reaction is the in-order-to motive of my own act. The prototype of all social relationship is an intersubjective connection of motives. If I imagine, projecting my act, that you will understand my act and that this understanding will induce you to react, on your part, in a certain way, I anticipate that the in-order-to motives of my own acting will become because motives of your reaction, and vice-versa.

Let us take a very simple example. I ask you a question. The in-order-to motive of my act is not only the expectation that you will understand my question, but also to get your answer; or more precisely, I reckon *that* you will answer, leaving undecided what the content of your answer may be. *Modo futuri exacti* I anticipate in projecting my own act that you will have answered my question in some way or other, and this means I think there is a fair chance that the understanding of my question will become a because motive for your answer, which I expect. The question, so we can say, is the because motive of the answer, as the answer is the in-order-to motive of the question. This interrelationship between my own and your motives is a well tested experience of mine, though, perhaps, I have never had explicit knowledge of the complicated interior mechanism of it. But I myself had felt on innumerable occasions induced to react to another's act, which I had interpreted as a question addressed to me, with a kind of behavior of which the in-order-to motive was my expectation that the other, the questioner, might interpret my behavior as an answer. Over against this experience I know that I have succeeded frequently in provoking another person's answer by my own act called questioning and so on. Therefore I feel I have a fair chance of getting your answer when I shall have once realized my action of questioning.

This short and incomplete analysis of a rather trivial example shows the great complications inherent in the problem of the social act, but also gives an idea of the extension of the field to be explored by a theory of action worthy of its name. We do not intend to enter further into this topic here but we must draw some conclusions from our example concerning the role of the subjective point of view for the actor in the social world.

The social world in which I live as one connected with others through manifold relations is for me an object to be interpreted as meaningful. It makes sense to me, but by the same token I am sure it makes sense to others too. I suppose, furthermore, that my acts oriented to others will be understood by them in an analogous manner as I understand the acts of others oriented to me. More of less naively I presuppose the existence of a common scheme of reference for both my own acts and the acts of others. I am interested above all not in the overt behavior of others, not in their performance of gestures and bodily movements, but in their intentions, and that means in the in-order-to motives for the sake of which, and in the because motives based on which, they act as they do.

Convinced that they want to express something by their act or that their act has a specific position within the common frame of reference, I try to catch the meaning which the act in question has, particularly for my co-actors in the social world, and, until presented with counter-evidence, I presume that this meaning for them, the actors, corresponds to the meaning their act has for me. As I have to orient my own social acts to the because motives of the other's social acts oriented to me, I must always find out their in-order-to motives and disentangle the texture of social interrelationship by interpreting other people's acts from the subjective point of view of the actor. That is the great difference between the attitude of a man who lives amidst manifold social interrelations in which he is interested as a party and the pure observer who is disinterested in the outcome of a social situation in which he does not participate and which he studies with a detached mind.

There is another reason why man living naively among others in the social world tries above all to find out the motives of his co-actors. Motives are never isolated elements but grouped in great and consistent systems of hierarchical order. Having grasped a sufficient number of elements of such a system, I have a fair chance of completing the empty positions of the system by correct conjectures. Basing my assumption on the inner logical structure of such a motive system, I am able to make, with great likelihood of proving them right, inferences concerning those parts which remain hidden. But, of course, all this presupposes interpretation from the subjective point of view, i.e. answering the question "what does all this mean for the actor?"

This practical attitude is adopted by us all in so far as we not merely observe a social situation which does not touch us but are actors and reactors within the social world, and this is precisely the reason why the subjective point of view must be accepted by the social sciences too. Only this methodological principle gives us the necessary guarantee that we are dealing in fact with the real social life-world of us all, which, even as an object of theoretical research, remains a system of reciprocal social relations, all of them built up by mutual subjective interpretations of the actors within it.

But if the principle of safeguarding the subjective point of view in the social sciences were even admitted, how is it possible to deal scientifically—and that means in objective conceptual terms—with such subjective phenomena? The greatest difficulty lies, first of all, in the specific attitude the scientific observer has adopted towards the social world. As a scientist—not as a man among other men, which he is too—he is not a party in social interrelationship. He does not participate in the living stream of mutual testing of the in-order-to motives of his own acts by the reactions of others, and vice-versa. Strictly speaking, as a pure observer of the social world, the social scientist does not act. In so far as he "acts scientifically" (publishing papers, discussing problems with others, teaching) his activity is performed *within* the social world: he acts as man among other men, dealing with science, but he no longer has, then, the specific attitude of a scientific observer. This attitude is characterized by the fact that it is performed in complete aloofness. To become a social scientist the observer must make up his mind to step out of the social world, to drop any practical interest in it, and to restrict his in-order-to motives to the honest description and explanation of the social world which he observes.

But how should this job be performed? Not being able to communicate directly with the actors within the social world, he is unable to verify directly the data he has obtained about them from the different sources of information open to him within the social world. To be sure, he himself has, as a man among others, direct human experiences of the social world. In that capacity he can send out questionnaires, hear witnesses, establish test-cases. From these sources and others he gathers data which he will later use, once retired into the solitude of the theoretician. But his theoretical task as such begins with the building up of a conceptual scheme under which his information about the social world may be grouped.

It is one of the outstanding features of modern social science to have described the device the social scientists use in building up their conceptual scheme, and it is the great merit of [Durkheim, Pareto, Marshall, Veblen, and] above all of Max Weber, to have developed this technique in all its fullness and clarity. This technique consists in replacing the human beings which the social scientist observes as an actor on the social stage by puppets created by himself, in other words, in constructing ideal types of actors. This is done in the following way.

The scientist observes certain events within the social world as caused by human activity and he begins to establish a type of such events. Afterwards he coordinates with these typical acts typical because motives and in-order-to motives which he assumes as invariable in the mind of an imaginary actor. Thus he constructs a personal ideal type, which means the model of an actor whom he imagines as gifted with a consciousness. But it is a consciousness restricted in its content only to all those elements necessary for the performance of the typical acts under consideration. These elements it contains completely, but nothing beyond them. He imputes to it constant in-order-to motives corresponding to the goals which are realized within the social world by the acts under consideration; furthermore he ascribes to it constant because motives of such a structure that they may serve as a basis for the system of the presupposed constant in-order-to motives; finally he bestows on the ideal type such segments of life plans and such stocks of experiences as are necessary for the imaginary horizons and backgrounds of the puppet actor. The social scientist places these constructed types in a setting which contains all the elements of the situation in the social world relevant for the performance of the typical act under inquiry. Moreover, he associates with him other personal ideal types with motives apt to provoke typical reactions to the first ideal type's typical act.

So he arrives at a model of the social world, or better at a reconstruction of it. It contains all the relevant elements of the social event chosen as a typical one by the scientist for further examination. And it is a model which complies perfectly with the postulate of the subjective point of view. For from the first the puppet type is imagined as having the same specific knowledge of the situation—including means and conditions—which a real actor would have in the real social world; from the first the subjective motives of a real actor performing a typical act are implanted as constant elements of the specious consciousness of the personal ideal type; and it is the destiny of the personal ideal type to play the role the actor in the social world would have to adopt in order to perform the typical act. And as the type is constructed in such a way that it performs exclusively typical acts, the objective and subjective elements in the formation of unit-acts coincide.

On the other hand, the formation of the type, the choice of the typical event, and the elements considered as typical are conceptual terms which can be discussed objectively and which are open to criticism and verification. They are not formed by social scientists at random without check or restraint; the laws of their formation are very rigid and the scope of arbitrariness of the social scientist is much narrower than seems at first sight. We are unable to enter into this problem within this study. But briefly we will summarize what was brought out elsewhere.[9]

1. Postulate of relevance. The formation of ideal types must comply with the principle of relevance, which means that the problem once chosen by the social scientist creates a scheme of reference and constitutes the limits of the scope within which relevant ideal types might be formed.

2. Postulate of adequacy. It may be formulated as follows: each term used in a scientific system referring to human action must be so constructed that a human act performed within the life world by an individual actor in the way indicated by the typical construction would be reasonable and understandable for the actor himself as well as for his fellowman.

3. Postulate of logical consistency. The system of ideal types must remain in full compatibility with the principles of formal logic.

4. Postulate of compatibility. The system of ideal types must contain only scientifically verifiable assumptions, which have to be fully compatible with the whole of our scientific knowledge.

---

[9] I have sketched some of the principles ruling the formation of ideal types in a lecture delivered in the Faculty Club of Harvard University under the title "The Problem of Rationality in the Social World." (This lecture was published, under the same title, in *Economica*, May 1943—Eds.)

These postulates give the necessary guarantees that social sciences do in fact deal with the real social world, the one and unitary life-world of us all, and not with a strange fancy-world independent of and without connection to this everyday life-world. To go further into the details of the typifying method seems to me one of the most important tasks of a theory of action.

ROBERT REDFIELD

BOOK REVIEW*
OF SOCIAL RESEARCH[†]

This is a clear, readable, and, I think, a truly useful account of scientific method from the point of view, now so fashionable in the social sciences, that identifies "scientific method" with "quantitative method." For Lundberg science is "a technique of deriving knowledge about any type of phenomenon in the universe and then applying this derived knowledge for purposes of prediction and control." The functional aspect of modern social science is therefore the same as that of modern physics or chemistry. The historical-geographical method (Kroeber's "depiction") is recognized as a preliminary stage leading ultimately, through comparison, to the determination of uniform sequences. But such uniformities can chiefly, or perhaps only, be determined by quantification. "The statistical method is in any case the only method whereby types can be discovered and large numbers of cases classified" (p. 208). Therefore, in order for social science to become truly scientific, it must collect its data with a view to getting data that can be treated statistically. Data can be treated statistically only when they can be broken into equivalent units. The interest therefore lies in such devices, external to the observer, that make possible such objective categories: the schedule, the questionnaire, the "scale." On the other hand, the life history, the interview, the autobiographical document, may serve a purpose in suggesting hypotheses, but they cannot be treated "scientifically," i.e., "statistically." "The chief obstacle to the scientific utilization of case records and life history documents is the difficulty of .... generalizing them statistically" (p. 173).

The future historian of science, reflecting upon the scientific philosophy that Lundberg has here ably presented, will recognize that

*Reprinted by permission of *American Anthropologist*, Vol. 33, No. 1 (1931), pp. 106–107.

[†]George A. Lundberg. *Social Research. A Study in Methods of Gathering Data* (New York: Longmans, Green and Co., 1929).

in the early part of the twentieth century, the social sciences, not having had time to work out methods in accordance with their own materials and problems, set out to imitate the natural sciences, which by that time had achieved success and prestige. He will go on to tell our descendants that it was only an assumption that the goal of social science lay in prediction through generalization (although it may turn out that is indeed its goal). And in the second place, if he is any sort of historian of science at all, he will point out that statistical procedure is not the same as natural science. The term "statistics" must be very much enlarged if the procedure of the zoologist, distinguishing a genus or a family, is to be called statistical. Over and over again the natural scientist gets his types, arrives at his generalizations by studying cases, by getting intimate with them, by coming to know each in the light of the others, and then by a method that is quite informal, deriving a type from them. No mathematical handling of equivalent units is involved at all. If data are to be treated only by means of objective devices that permit statistical treatment, the cases can never be completely known, but only in fragments.

These objections receive support from the experience of ethnologists. Every general account of crisis rite or customary ceremonial involves an informal generalization of this sort, one made either by a native or by the ethnologist. At present ethnology is in that simple condition where the reputation of the ethnologist for accuracy and insight is the best guarantee of the validity of his account. But mere accuracy is not enough; he must be able to see sympathetically the meaning of the overt behavior in its full social context. We welcome the development of objective devices in ethnology; but it is hard to see how they can ever be more than auxiliaries, how cultural data can ever be reported so as to be treated only quantitatively. A culture is not a sum, it is a, yes, a "configuration"; the relation of the part to the whole and to the other parts is important. It is by no means obvious that observation and reporting would be more useful if it were done by filling out schedules. Intimate, thorough, and sympathetic scrutiny of the total situation is what is needed. At least it is too soon for the social sciences to confine themselves to data that can be treated quantitatively. The study of society, whether civilized or primitive, still has the opportunity of working out its methods, not by imitation, but in accordance with its own needs.

FRANCIS D. WORMUTH

MATCHED-DEPENDENT BEHAVIORALISM: THE CARGO CULT IN POLITICAL SCIENCE*

Neal E. Miller and John Dollard, in their study of imitation,[1] identify a type which they call "matched-dependent behavior." They illustrate it with a story. The father told Jim, aged six, and Bobby, aged three, that he had hidden a piece of candy for each of them in the living room. Jim looked in the fireplace: no candy. Bobby looked in the fireplace: no candy. Jim looked inside the piano bench: no candy. Bobby looked inside the piano bench: no candy. Jim looked under a cushion on the sofa, found a piece of candy, and ate it. Bobby looked under the cushion: no candy. "Bobby was now helpless"; he could think of no other place to look. Finally his father gave him the candy. "On a succeeding trial of the same game, exactly the same thing happened. The younger child would look only in the places already examined by his older brother. He would not respond to place cues by looking for himself."

More than twenty years ago Gordon W. Allport, in an address as Divisional President to the Division of Personality and Social Psychology of the American Psychological Association, complained that "many of us seem so stupefied by admiration of physical science that we believe psychology in order to succeed need only imitate the models, postulates, and methods of physical science."[2] The same stupefaction has gripped those political scientists who call themselves behavioralists. We may liken the physical scientist to Jim; the behavioralist, who emulates his models, postulates, and methods, is Bobby. Miller and Dollard called Bobby's behavior maladaptive, but

*Reprinted by permission of Western *Political Science Quarterly*, Vol. XX, No. 4 (December 1967), pp. 809–840.
[1]*Social Learning and Imitation* (New Haven: Yale U. Press, 1941), excerpted in Melvin H. Marx (ed.), *Psychological Theory: Contemporary Readings* (New York: Macmillan, 1951), pp. 543–49, at p. 545.
[2]"Scientific Models and Human Morals," in Marx, *op cit.*, pp. 156–70, at p. 157.

they were wrong, for he always got his candy. Similarly the behavioralists have never found a piece of candy; but they are given their candy by the Ford Foundation.

Gordon Allport was not complaining of the undertaking of psychology, but of the diversion of that undertaking into imitative and unrewarding channels. There is no intention here to complain of the undertaking in political science, as old as Aristotle, to deal dispassionately and systematically with the data. In particular there is no intention to condemn the use of psychology—or at any rate psychologies like Allport's—in the explanation of politics. But the use of psychology is not new; it goes back to Plato.

Harold D. Lasswell has said that the "behavioral upswing" dates from the work of Charles E. Merriam at the University of Chicago in the 1920's and early 1930's.[3] But in fact the method and the assumptions of Merriam were traditional. Behavioralism is novel; Robert A. Dahl has called it a successful revolution.[4]

Although the adjective "behavioral" was used occasionally in the 1930's, the term "behavioral science" appears to have been introduced by the Committee on Behavioral Sciences, an interdisciplinary group organized at the University of Chicago in 1951 under the leadership of a psychologist, James G. Miller, with the encouragement of Dean Ralph W. Tyler. Miller has recorded the "working assumptions" of the Chicago "theory group":

> First, we agreed to accept as confirmation of theorems only *objective* phenomena available to public inspection by more than one observer, excluding private experience. Second, we tried when possible to state hypotheses quantitatively, so that they might be precisely testable and could subsequently be corrected. Third, we attempted to make statements capable of being disproved as well as proved, by *crucial experiments.* Finally, as will be explained below, insofar as possible we employed dimensions of natural science related to the centimeter-gram-second system.[5]

The first assumption is negative rather than affirmative: it is the rejection, common to behavioralism and psychological behaviorism, of both subjective data and subjective method. The second and the fourth make a commitment to the mathematical method of natural

---
[3] *The Future of Political Science* (New York: Atherton Press, 1963), p. 37.
[4] "The Behavioral Approach in Political Science: Epitaph for a Monument to a Successful Protest," *American Political Science Review*, 55 (1965), 763–72, at p. 766.
[5] "Toward a General Theory for the Behavioral Sciences," *American Psychologist*, 10 (1955), 513–31, at p. 514.

science. The third appears to be a bow in the direction of Karl Popper.

But these were not in fact the controlling assumptions of the Chicago group. Miller says that "we have found most profit in *general behavior systems theory*," and he goes on to describe this. The term "system theory" was introduced in 1945 by Ludwig von Bertalanffy when he offered an alternative to the analytical method of natural science.

> In the world view called mechanistic, born of classical physics of the 19th century, the aimless play of the atoms, governed by the inexorable laws of mechanical causality, produced all phenomena in the world, inanimate, living, and mental. No room was left for any directiveness, order, or telos. The world of organisms appeared a mere product of chance, accumulated by a senseless play of mutation at random and selection; the mental world as a curious and rather inconsequential epiphenomenon of material events.[6]

This "scheme of isolable units acting in one-way causality has proved to be insufficient. Hence the appearance, in all fields of science, of notions like wholeness, holistic, organismic, *gestalt* and so forth, which all signify that in the last resort, we must think in terms of systems of elements in mutual interaction."[7] In short, Bertalanffy rejected "the inexorable laws of mechanical causality" in favor of an Aristotelian teleology. Lurking behind this teleology is a vitalism like that of Driesch. It is not an open-ended vitalism like Bergson's; it aims at a given "final state," an Aristotelian final cause.

Mathematical behavioralism, with its commitment to analytical method and to efficient cause, is at the opposite pole from general systems theory, built as it is on an Aristotelian or Thomistic foundation. Yet some behavioralists believe they can combine the two. David Easton, in a book entitled *A Systems Analysis of Political Life*,[8] says that his goal is "descriptive, empirically-oriented, behavioral, operational or causal theory."

In 1954 the Ford Foundation established the Center for Advanced Study in the Behavioral Sciences at Menlo Park, California, with Ralph Tyler from the University of Chicago as Director. The Center became the first training place for behavioral political sci-

---

[6]Ludwig von Bertalanffy, "General System Theory," in *General Systems*, 1 (1956), 1–10, at p. 6.
[7]*Loc. cit.*
[8]New York:Wiley, 1965, p. 5.

entists. It still functions, but now many graduate schools offer the same training. At Menlo Park, however, an atomistic and reductionist approach by way of mathematics very largely displaced the holistic approach of Miller's general systems theory, and the latter now has its strongholds at the University of Chicago and the Mental Health Research Institute at the University of Michigan, to which Miller migrated.

Behavioral projects, principally mathematical, are carried on by the RAND Corporation and the Pentagon; others are financed by various organs of the national government; the Ford Foundation has been generous with financial assistance. We may offer a behavioral hypothesis that the number of pages of behavioral literature published varies directly with the cube root of the number of dollars spent.

Harold Lasswell has said of the Center for Advanced Study:

> The chief intellectual stress was methodological. . . . The methodological concern was threefold—(1) to encourage mathematical thinking or comparably strict methods; (2) to stimulate thinking about social processes in human history by giving consideration to general biological theory; (3) to provide a setting appropriate to the planning of research on problems of importance that are neglected or pursued by inferior methods unless recognized and undertaken by interdisciplinary teams.[9]

The third topic can be dismissed. There have been collaborations of behavioral political scientists with economists, but this has not pooled methods familiar to the two disciplines. Rather, these teams have invariably had recourse to the tools of the mathematicians. Apparently Lasswell's second topic is an understatement of the ambition of general systems theory. Many persons call themselves systems theorists—in addition to Bertalanffy and Miller, Talcott Parsons, David Easton, Morton Kaplan, Coleman and Almond, Bertram Gross, and others. Although there are vague resemblances between the formulations of these authors, there are greater inconsistencies, and it is not feasible to review this literature here.

The chief impact of behavioralism has been Lasswell's first topic, the adoption of new mathematical tools. This is often unaccompanied by any degree of mathematical sophistication; and frequently it is entirely unaccompanied by political sophistication.

[9]*Loc. cit.*

Since Petty, at least, we have had political scientists who have used mathematics, but they have been, in the language of Karl W. Deutsch, " 'shorthaired' social scientists, the counters and verifiers, who are too often and too thoughtlessly identified with the behavioral approach in social science."[10] No one, not even the behavioralists, would deny the utility of such sources as the reports of the Census Bureau, or the value of the many empirical studies, such as voting studies, that have been drawn from these sources. But these are humble projects. The behavioralists have a more ambitious goal. They attribute the success of the physical scientists to the use of mathematics, and they believe that if they adopt this tool they will be able to achieve comparable results.

This issue is not a new one. A very long time ago Aristotle observed that a young man might become an expert mathematician, but he would lack practical wisdom, which is "concerned with things human and things about which it is possible to deliberate"—that is, not with invariables but with matters of choice. Mathematics deals with abstractions, whereas practical widsom comes from experience.[11]

In the latter part of the nineteenth century, Wilhelm Dilthey introduced the distinction between the *Naturwissenschaften*, which deal with the physical world, and the *Geisteswissenschaften* or the human sciences, which deal with meanings and motives.[12] The *Naturwissenschaften* employ laws of mechanical causality; the *Geisteswissenschaften* employ human understanding, *Verstehen*.

Through Rickert and Windelband the teaching of Dilthey passed to Max Weber, whose name is of course one of the most widely respected in the social sciences. For Weber, sociology dealt with interpersonal action to which the actor attached subjective meaning.[13] This meaning was comprehended by *Verstehen*.

> A correct causal interpretation of a concrete course of action is arrived at when the overt action and the motives have both been correctly apprehended and at the same time their relation has become meaningfully comprehensible. ... If adequacy in respect to

---

[10] "Toward an Inventory of Basic Trends and Patterns in Comparative and International Politics," *APSR*, 54 (1960), 34–57, at p. 38.

[11] *Ethica Nicomachea*, 1141b–1142a.

[12] See H. A. Hodges, *The Philosophy of Wilhelm Dilthey* (London: Routledge & Kegan Paul, 1952).

[13] *The Theory of Social and Economic Organization*, trans. A. M. Henderson and Talcott Parsons (New York: Free Press of Glencoe, n.d.), p. 88.

meaning is lacking, then no matter how high the degree of uniformity and how precisely its probability can be numerically determined, it is still an incomprehensible statistical probability, whether dealing with overt or subjective processes.[14]

In his very valuable examination of the methodology of social science,[15] Frederick A. Hayek contrasts the data of the natural sciences with those of the social sciences. Physical science breaks up sensory experience into elements which bear computable relations to each other. Mathematics is not merely an auxiliary tool, and quantification is not merely increased precision: "it is of the essence of this process of breaking up our immediate sense data and of substituting for a description in terms of sense qualitites one in terms of elements which possess no attributes but these relations with each other."[16] In contrast with this objectivist approach, social science must use a subjectivist approach; the data are the subjective meanings and purposes of human beings. We understand these meanings because we know our own subjective experience.[17]

Robert MacIver is a determinist, but he has said:

> There is no point in trying to apply to social systems the causal formula of classical mechanics, to the effect that if you know the state of a system at any instant you can calculate mathematically, in terms of a system of co-ordinates, the state of that system at any other time. We simply cannot use such a formula. It fits into another frame of reference. On the other hand we have the advantage that some of the factors operative in social causation are *understandable as causes*, are validated as causal by our own experience. This provides us a frame of reference that the physical sciences cannot use. We must therefore cultivate our own garden. We must use the advantages we possess and not merely regret the advantages we lack.[18]

Similarly Carl J. Friedrich has said:

> The physicist can merely note that every so often an atom deviates from the norm, but he is at present completely at a loss when it comes to accounting for it. Far be it from me to belittle the achievements of modern natural science; they are the more imposing precisely because the naturalist has to work without the

[14]*Ibid.*, p. 99.
[15]*The Counter-Revolution of Science* (Glencoe: Free Press, 1952).
[16]*Ibid.*, p. 23.
[17]*Ibid.*, chap. 3.
[18]*Social Causation* (Boston: Ginn, 1942), pp. 263-64.

guide of common human understanding. However, it is thoughtless, indeed, to deprive ourselves in the social sciences of the invaluable aid which such human understanding can give us, merely because the natural sciences have had to evolve techniques for getting along without it.[19]

Morton A. Kaplan, a behavioralist, identifies his approach with science and dismisses as "traditionalism" the view that "understanding, wisdom or tradition are required for areas where human purpose is involved."[20] It is certainly the case that subjective understanding has been the traditional reliance in the interpretation of politics. No one can read Merriam's *Political Power*, for example, without realizing that it relies throughout on the subjectivism of *Verstehen* and not the objectivism of behavioralism.

Of course a man might impose upon himself the obligation of walking on his hands, and might succeed in walking a hundred yards in this manner. It is conceivable that a student might take on the very considerable handicap of studying politics without the aid of understanding and might nevertheless arrive at one or more useful propositions about politics. There is a widespread opinion among political scientists that this has actually occurred.[21] Whether or not this is true can only be determined by reviewing the principal mathematical practices engaged in by political scientists and the major contributions of the mathematical behavioralists.

TRANSLATION

One of the most popular enterprises has been to translate vulgar speech into mathematics. Of course this could yield no scientific proposition that was not implicit in the English; nevertheless it is supposed that knowledge is advanced by converting statements into what Carnap called "physical language."

Herbert Simon has been the most active translator in the field of

[19]*Constitutional Government and Democracy* (rev. ed.; Boston: Ginn, 1946), p. 574.
[20]"The New Great Debate: Traditionalism vs. Science in International Relations," *World Politics*, 19 (1966), 1–20, at p. 1.
[21]When Frederick L. Schuman suggested that the *American Political Science Review* had published behavioral studies—including many of those reviewed below—in order to discredit the genre, the Editor denied this: "we publish what we publish because my referees and I think the articles make significant contributions." *APSR*, 61 (1967), 149.

political science. For Simon mathematics is "the most dulcet of languages,"[22] and he enjoys his task. So he has turned a set of propositions from Homans' *The Human Group* into mathematics; similarly he has translated a formulation of Leon Festinger's.[23] In addition, he has set up schemata of his own and has restated them symbolically.

Simon does not mistake a translation for a demonstration. He recognizes that it is merely a restatement whose form offers certain advantages:

> 1. Knowing more precisely what mechanisms or structural relations are being postulated, and sometimes calling attention to the need for further clarification of the operational meaning of definitions and statements;
> 2. Discovering whether certain postulates can be derived from others, and hence can be eliminated as independent assumptions; whether additional postulates need to be added to make the system complete and the deductions rigorous; and whether there are inconsistencies among the postulates;
> 3. Assisting in the discovery of inconsistencies between the empirical data and the theories used to explain them;
> 4. Laying the basis for further elaboration of theory, and to deductions from the postulates that suggest further empirical studies for verification;
> 5. Aiding in handling complicated, simultaneous interrelations among a relatively large number of variables, with some reduction of the obscuring circumlocutions entailed by nonmathematical language.[24]

This statement of advantages should be supplemented by a statement of disadvantages. Something is lost in the translation. The aureole of meaning that surrounds words is trimmed off when they become mathematical counters; or, conversely, it is possible that the central meaning is excised and a fragment of the aureole enters into the formula. On the other hand, the entire ambiguity of an English word may survive unimpaired in a symbol which gives it spurious precision: calling power P does not make this rich and untidy word suitable for definition in a single equivalence. Finally, mathematical formulation imports the assumptions of mathematics into the statement, and this may work an unobserved alteration in the meaning of the

---

[22] In Leonard D. White (ed.), *The State of the Social Sciences* (Chicago: U. of Chicago Press, 1956), p. 67.
[23] *Models of Man* (New York: Wiley, 1957), chaps. 6–8.
[24] *Ibid.*, p. 142.

verbal formulation. The assumption of game theory, for example, that utilities can be deprived of their subjective and variable character and can be rank-ordered and even represented as multiples of some common unit of measurement, is made possible by the device of mathematical formulation of verbal statements whose original meaning does not authorize such a claim.

An instructive example of simple translation is an essay by Otto A. Davis and Melvin Hinich, "A Mathematical Model of Policy Formulation in a Democratic Society."[25] They state their problem verbally:

> Given the precisely defined ... and unchangeable preferences of the voters in the population, candidates for public office compete for votes by announcing before an election their exact position on each of the relevant issues. Each voter compares the positions taken by the various candidates and casts his vote for that particular candidate whose position is "nearest" ... his own most preferred position. It is assumed that, once elected, a (former) candidate will adopt those policies which he announced during the campaign. Thus the questions to be answered are whether, and under what conditions, dominant strategies exist for the candidates.[26]

After elaborate manipulations of symbols, the results are translated back into English. "In other words, if the 1st candidate selects the policies in his platform to be exactly the same as the mean of the policies desired by the individuals in the voting population, and the other candidate does not make the same choice, then the 1st candidate is certain to win the election."[27] "Given that one of the mutually exclusive and exhaustive groups 'desires' one set of policies, that the other group 'desires' another set of policies, and that there is no conflict between the two sets of policies since each refers to a mutually exclusive set of issues, then the politician can enhance his chance of winning the election by giving each group what it desires."[28] Given a party system, the minority party will lose unless certain conditions are present. If there is a " 'smaller range' of taste and opinion about policy" in the minority party, and the position of the candidate of the party lies closer to the positions of a sufficient number of voters

---

[25] Joseph L. Bernd (ed.), *Mathematical Applications in Political Science, II* (Dallas: Southern Methodist U. 1966), pp. 175–208.
[26] *Ibid.*, p. 176
[27] *Ibid.*, p. 184.
[28] *Ibid.*, pp. 204–5.

of the majority party than that of the candidate of the majority party, the minority party will win.[29]

The authors confess that "simplifying assumptions" have been made. This is not necessarily a fault: the construction of models or ideal types may be useful, although it is certainly an error to assume that all are equally useful. The real infirmity of the argument lies in the very fact of mathematical expression; it is the assumption that people can be arrayed on a linear scale of preference on an issue, so that medians can be calculated and the diffuseness of positions determined. From this grows the related assumption that there exists a common unit of magnitude which can be used to reduce preferences on all issues to a common scale and ultimately to a single mean. It is not merely that as a Practical matter these measurements cannot be taken. The fault is more serious: the very conception is, to use the most damning words in the behavioral vocabulary, operationally meaningless.

Robert A. Dahl has translated the "intuitive idea of power" into a formula with four elements.[30] The power of A over a with respect to x is the probability that if A does w, a will do x, diminished by the probability that a would do x even though A did not do w. This can be rendered

$$M\left(\frac{A}{a} : w, x\right) = P(a, x \mid A, w) - P(a, x \mid A, \textit{not-w})$$

To translate the English into symbols does not advance science any more than a translation into Greek or Spanish would have done. But the translation is not faithful. One reads "probability" in the English as subjective probability, an expectation or guess on the part of the observer with regard to an individual event. The probability in the formula must be an objective probability, the ratio of the number of cases in which the outcome occurs to the total number of cases in the class of events. Dahl gives us no method of computing the elements in this ratio in any real case; and surely this is impossible. But then the formula is operationally meaningless.

The translation of a theory into mathematics requires a theory: "First catch your rabbit." Once one has a theory suitable for expres-

[29] *Ibid.*, p. 194. A similar formulation, but one which relies on graphic representation rather than explicit mathematical computation, is given in Gordon Tullock, *The Politics of Bureaucracy* (Washington: Public Affairs Press, 1965), chap. 7.

[30] "The Concept of Power," *Behavioral Science*, 2 (1957), 201–15.

sion in mathematical terms, translation may assist in exposing its meaning. The next step would be to test the theory by the use of empirical data.[31] Economists are accustomed to compare their theories with the actual behavior of prices. But the political world is more complex than the economic; and no one—neither Aristotle nor Machiavelli nor Hobbes nor Harrington nor Marx nor the inventors of Utopias—has ever succeeded in building into a political theory all the relevant variables. This means that the theory will not accord with actual behavior.

Of course physical theories do not state all the variables encountered in nature; but in physics it is very often possible to establish laboratory conditions which exclude the undesired variables and permit observation of the behavior of the variables expressed in the theory. When this cannot be done, the theory is unverifiable. If it is ever possible to set up laboratory tests for theories about politics, it will be for very trivial propositions about small groups.

This means that the term "political theory" is a misnomer. A theory must be susceptible to confirmation or disproof. Consequently the more modest term model is often used to describe such logical constructs as that of Hobbes and the formulations of mathematical behavioralists. Typically a model is unicausal; at most, it embraces only a few of the relevant variables. Therefore it is likely to have little predictive value for the real world. It does not follow that it is useless. One judges the merits of a model not by what comes out of it but by what is put into it; the famous models have rested on shrewd if partial insights into psychology or social relationships, on *Verstehen*. This means that individually they each report one of the multifarious causes that collectively shape events. In political science a model is not and cannot be a law; at most, it is a tendency statement. Because of the action of excluded variables, the tendency reported by a model may not emerge into the light in a given case. This does not necessarily invalidate the model; of course it does not validate it either.

Yet in debates about public policy tendency statements are continually offered as genuine cause-effect propositions which forecast practical results. In the case of economic proposals, these statements sometimes do indicate the direction, although not the magnitude, of change. So we can have some confidence as to the character of the re-

[31] The most impressive attempt is Lewis F. Richardson, *Arms and Insecurity* (1939; Pittsburgh: Boxwood Press, 1960).

sults of deficit spending or the relaxation of credit restrictions by the Federal Reserve Board.

Such forecasting is not confined to economics. Since the beginning of politics men have predicted the future on the basis of auguries or other formulae. Currently it is argued that prayer in the schools will reduce juvenile delinquency. The domino theory contends that the recognition of a military or diplomatic defeat by the United States entails the triumph of communism throughout the world. John Kenneth Galbraith has asserted that economic concentration produces "countervailing power."[32] All these propositions purport to be theories and not models. They could easily be formalized and tested against empirical fact. Probably the greatest service that mathematical translation could perform would be the evaluation of such theories.

NOMINAL DEFINITION

In a real definition, the right-hand term of the equation, the *definiens*, is an analysis of the meaning of the left-hand term, the *definiendum*. The analysis may be correct or incorrect; a real definition can be true or false. In a nominal definition, the entire meaning lies in the right-hand term, the *definiens*. The left-hand term is not a *definiendum*, for it has no meaning to be defined: it is merely a name arbitrarily attached by the speaker to the contents of the right-hand term. Consequently a nominal definition is neither true nor false: it exists by intention, "by definition."

Very frequently mathematical behavioralists pretend to solve a problem by taking a term which is ordinarily used to describe actual phenomena, emptying out its empirical content, and then equating the shell to a mathematical formulation on the right side of the equation. This yields no real definition of the term, but only a nominal definition of the mathematical formulation. This elementary logical error is often disguised by calling the definition "operational," and appealing to the authority of Percy Bridgman, who invented this term.[33] This is unwarranted. What Bridgman asserted was that "we must always demand that physical concepts be stated in terms of

---

[32] *American Capitalism: The Concept of Countervailing Power* (Boston: Houghton Mifflin, 1952).
[33] *The Nature of Physical Theory* (Princeton: Princeton U. Press, 1936), pp. 7–12.

physical operations."[34] He warned that mathematical operations "are mental operations, and have no necessary physical validity."[35] Moreover, he explicitly denied that any phenomenon could be successfully defined in terms of a single set of operations.

> "To define a phenomenon by the operations which produced it" involves unproved assumptions. It implies that the performance of the same operations will always be followed by the occurrence of the same phenomenon, and this statement is operationally meaningless unless there is some method of checking the truth of the statement. This again implies that it means something to say "same" phenomenon, which implies, unless we are dealing with a pure convention, that there is some other method of recognizing the phenomenon when it recurs than through the operation of the definition. Operational definitions, in spite of their precision, are in application without significance unless the situations to which they are applied are sufficiently developed so that at least two methods are known of getting to the terminus.[36]

That is to say, a "definition" of a phenomenon by a single operational method gives merely a conventional or nominal definition of the operation; it is not a definition of the phenomenon.

Behaviorist psychologists have also appropriated the word "operationism" from Bridgman. They have better reason than the behavioralists, for they do use it to describe external physical operations. Their purpose, indeed, is to reduce psychology to objective description of conduct, excluding mental states and consciousness. This elimination of all subjective phenomena has migrated into mathematical behavioralism. So both Dahl and March define power in terms of overt conduct: he who stimulates the response has power over the respondent.[37] It follows that the victim who incautiously displays a well-filled wallet has power over the thief who robs him. This does violence to the conception of power which one has by *Verstehen*, but here behavioralism meets behaviorism. And if one is

---

[34] *Ibid.*, p. 10. (Italics supplied.)

[35] *Ibid.*, p. 11. See *ibid.*, p. 24: "An essential difference between language and experience is that language separates out from the living matrix little bundles and freezes them; in doing this it produces something totally unlike experience, but nevertheless useful."

[36] Percy W. Bridgman, "Some General Principles of Operational Analysis," *Psychological Review*, 52 (1945), 246–49, at p. 248. This essay occurs in a symposium on operationism, *ibid.*, pp. 241–94.

[37] Dahl, *op cit.*; James G. March, "An Introduction to the Theory and Measurement of Influence," *APSR*, 49 (1955), 431–51.

satisfied with a merely nominal definition of power there is no objection to a definition that gives the victim power over the thief.

As we have seen, Robert Dahl has translated a verbal definition of power into a mathematical one, employing two probabilities which are operationally meaningless. When he came to make a study of power in a concrete case, therefore, he substituted certain events—votes—for the probabilities, and transformed his real definition into a nominal one.[38] He and his associates compiled the votes of 34 senators on roll calls on foreign policy and tax and economic policy during the years 1946–54. Each senator is paired with every other senator; the senator who more often votes with the majority is said to be the more powerful. The 34 senators are then rank-ordered.

A series of intellectual leaps is made. This table of data is treated as a probability table. Then the probability table is called a power index. But it cannot be that. According to Dahl's formula, Senator S has power over the Senate which is the probability that if Senator S does w—votes for a bill—the Senate will do x—pass the bill—or if he does $not\text{-}w$—votes against the bill—it will fail. This means that when Senator S votes in the majority he has demonstrated power over the Senate, including Senator T. But Senator T has also voted with the majority; thus he has demonstrated power over the Senate and over Senator S. Indeed, every member of the majority is simultaneously superior and inferior to every other member of the majority.

But the formula needs to be carried further. If we insist that the power of a senator really depends on the probability that his vote will determine the fate of the bill, all the senators are completely power-

---

[38]*Ibid.* Peter Bachrach and Morton S. Baratz, "Two Faces of Power," *APSR*, 56 (1962), 947–52, make the point that Dahl's approach considers only events as exercises of power, whereas nonevents, or "nondecision-making," as they put it, which gives effect to and maintains the existing bias in affairs, may be the best evidence of power. There are two significant classes of nonevents. Friedrich, *op cit.*, p. 589, has formulated the "rule of anticipated reactions:" often the exercise of power leaves no trace, for those influenced forestall a contest by compliance. It is also the case that authority may refrain from issuing commands that are likely to meet with noncompliance or resistance.

Duncan MacRae, Jr., and Hugh D. Price, "Scale Position and 'Power' in the Senate," *Behavioral Science*, 4 (1959), 212–18, offer a somewhat different nominal definition. Of course one nominal definition of power may be better than another in that it may be useful to have a name for one set of operations and of no use to have a name for another set of operations. But the utility of naming either set has not been shown. Certainly no useful purpose is served by calling any rank-ordering of senators by voting behavior a power index. MacRae and Price say: "We conclude that although the conceptualization of 'power' has been advanced [1], the operational definition of it has not yet been accompliehed." *Ibid.*, p. 218.

less on all roll calls except those yielding a majority of one or two. If there is a majority greater than two, it does not matter whether any Senator S does *w* or *not-w*; his vote cannot influence the outcome. Where there is a majority of one, every senator in the majority has complete power—what Dahl would call a probability of one—over the Senate, for the change of his vote would change the outcome. If the majority is two, every senator in the majority had the power to produce a tie—the power, that is, to give the Vice President complete power over the Senate.

To put the matter mathematically, let P_{im} equal the power of a member of the majority. Then

$$P_{im}\left(\frac{n}{2} + 3\right) = 0, \text{ and } P_{im}\left(\frac{n}{2} + 1\right) = 1$$

If power is equated to probability, is cannot exceed unity. But here we have multiple probabilities and multiplied power. Let $P([n/2] + 1)$ equal the power of all the members of a majority with a margin of 1. Then on a single vote $P([n/2] + 1) = (n/2) + 1$. Clearly we are not talking of probabilities. Nor are we talking of power.

Dahl recognizes certain imperfections in his scheme: a senator may achieve a high rating by correctly anticipating the vote of the majority; or he may do so by aping a genuinely powerful member. These are not the most important weaknesses in the scheme. Very often the vote of a senator demonstrates not his power but his powerlessness. When the President or the floor leader or a group of constituents does *w*, the senator does *x*. To define power in terms of votes is to invent a purely nominal definition of power.

In a study that has become famous, L. S. Shapley and Martin Shubik[39] offered a method for the a priori evaluation of the division of power among the various bodies and members of a legislature or

---

[39]"A Method for Evaluating the Distribution of Power in a Committee System," in John C. Wahlke and Heinz Enlau (eds.), *Legislative Behavior* (Glencoe: Free Press, 1959), pp. 358-61, at p. 358. In a study prompted by the Shapley and Shubik article, R. Duncan Luce and Arnold A. Rogow, "A Game Theoretic Analysis of Congressional Power Distributions for a Stable Two-Party System," *ibid.*, pp. 362-71, assume a bicameral Congress and a President, two parties, and the possibility of defection from both parties. They then tabulate eighteen situations and identify the locus or loci of power in each. The table supports familiar propositions— among others that the President is weak when his party is in the minority, but is strong when his party is in the majority and is committed to his program.

committee system. This is accomplished with simple fractions. Decisive power in a committee vote is attributed to the member whose vote completes the majority of one side or the other. If there are n members, each member has $1/n$th chance of being the pivotal member; therefore all members have equal power. The Vice President, with his power to break a tie, has as much power as any senator, unless it happens that an odd number of senators are present. The power indices of Senate, House, and President are 5:5:2, figures which reflect their tie-breaking power. "The indices for a *single* Congressman, a *single* Senator, and the President are in the proportion 2:9:350."[40] These computations, we are told, are not able to catch "all the subtle shades and nuances of custom and procedure that are to be found in most real decision-making bodies."[41] Nevertheless the a priori power index will serve as a standard the departure from which will constitute a measure of empirical factors.

Herbert Simon has said that this index consorts well with his intuitive notion of power,[42] and Richard C. Snyder regards it as a true report of "voting power."[43] This is odd. As we said above, a legislator's vote may be a response to power rather than the exercise of power. Moreover, it is rare that a measure carries by a single vote. Therefore it is seldom true that the member who first completes the majority is responsible for the passage of the measure; it would in any case be carried by one of the later affirmative votes on the roll call. Nor does it appear that the pivotal member actually contributes more to the passage of the bill than one of the earlier voters who has made his vote pivotal. But the most important shortcoming is the psychology of the scheme. Do legislators actually value the occupancy of a mathematically defined position in a series? Did any Southern senator ever vote in favor of a civil rights bill because he discovered that his position in the roll call would enable him to carry the measure if he voted in the affirmative? What Shapley and Shubik offer us is a permutation index, called a power index by an act of nominal definition.

William H. Riker undertook "A Test of the Adequacy of the

[40]*Ibid.*, p. 359.
[41]*Ibid.*, p. 360.
[42]*Op cit.*, p. 7.
[43]"Game Theory and the Analysis of Political Behavior," in *Research Frontiers in Politics and Government* (Washington: Brookings Institution, 1955), pp. 70–103, at p. 93.

Power Index."[44] His purpose was to test the assumption that men seek power, "the kind of power that the index measures"—the status, that is, of "the last added member of a minimal winning coalition."[45] He calls his investigation an empirical test of the assumption; since the question is psychological, one would expect him to use opinions as data. Instead he uses changes of party affiiliation. He adopts the a priori method of Shapley and Shubik and complicates it by introducing political parties. The power of a party—the frequency, that is, with which a party occupies a pivotal position in a scheme of random voting—varies with the size of the party; but a weighted index for all the parties can be computed from the theory of games. The power of an individual member in a party of m members will be $1/m$ of the party's power, since he will occupy the pivotal position once out of m times in a scheme of random voting. The test itself is to measure the power of members who migrated from party to party in the French National Assembly before and after their change of parties. If the assumption is sound, such migrations should show an improvement in the power of the migrants. But the study shows an average power loss of 5.9 per cent for each migrant. (By assuming that the party benefited by the migrant makes a payoff to the migrant of its "total gain" from the migration, Riker reduces the loss to 1.7 per cent. In what currency the party makes the payoff we are not told. The only units of value in the system are the values of the position of pivot man in the party and the position of pivot party in the legislature. The party cannot alter either of these figures, which means that the values are not transferable.) These results seem to discredit the formula, but Riker finds fault with his empirical test. He rejects the suggestion that more than 40 of the 600-odd members of the National Assembly were moved by ideology; and for him the sole remaining motive is playing the role of pivot man. One objection to the test might be the fact that parties have different capacities for entering into coalitions, and the power indices are therefore inaccurate. Riker rejects this explanation. More plausible to him is the suggestion that the power computations were so complicated that the migrants made errors in their calculations. Both these obstacles seem so formidable that, aside from the frivolous character of the thesis, one wonders why Riker undertook the

[44] *Behavioral Science,* 4 (1959), 120–31.
[45] *Ibid.,* p. 121.

study, and why he published it when it failed. Or did it fail? Perhaps it demonstrated that the behavior of legislators is not controlled by the ambition to be the $(n/2) + 1$ man on one side—no matter which—on a roll call.

Riker is also the author of "A Method for Determining the Significance of Roll Calls in Voting Bodies."[46] What is needed is a "quasi-objective scale of significance." A single observer, and a panel of observers, will suffer from bias. "But it is both impossible and foolish to attempt to eliminate bias from judgments of significance. Significance involves meaning; and meaning must have reference to some persons. The problem is not to eliminate subjective judgment, but to select the persons whose subjective judgment will be used to weight roll calls. It seems intuitively justifiable that the persons whose judgments are so used ought to be those who, by their actions, make the significance, that is, the members of the legislature themselves."[47]

> Therefore I suggest the following definitions: the *most significant* roll call possible is one in which (1) all members vote, and (2) the difference between the majority and the minority is the minimum possible under the voting rules. Conversely, the *least significant* roll call is one in which (1) a bare quorum votes, and (2) the outcome is unanimous.[48]

Riker then contrives a formula for significance in which the total number of members, the number voting on each side, and the quorum requirements are all represented.

A mathematical measure of significance is of course absurd. Mathematics measures magnitudes and not significance. The formula yields only a number, nothing more.

But it is worthwhile to examine the assumptions Riker put into the formula. Clearly he has equated significance with intensity of feeling. He thinks that a large vote indicates such intensity, although a large turnout is not inconsistent with indifference. It is of course also true that there may be a small turnout and yet every member may vote at white heat. He considers that a closely divided vote indicates high feeling on both sides. But this is not necessarily true; and it is possible that when there is a huge majority, as for a declaration of war, all the members are experiencing very intense emo-

---

[46] Wahlke and Eulau, *op cit.*, pp. 377–84.
[47] *Ibid.*, p. 378.
[48] *Loc. cit.*

tions. In short, Riker's formula is a very unsatisfactory attempt at a real definition of the psychological state of agitation of the legislators. Specialists in this field have a more direct method; they measure the perspiration rate. But when a false definition of agitation is converted into a nominal definition of significance, it becomes impossible to complain.

A real definition of significance would have to take account of the fact that a judgment of significance is not merely an emotional experience. It involves an intellectual appraisal of the consequences of an action for one or another value. Judgments of significance—forecasts of the future—may therefore be in error. In the case of legislators, it is of course notorious that they often vote on bills without reading them and without making any forecast except of the consequences of their votes for their own personal fortunes. It would not be difficult to show that when they do make forecasts of the general consequences of their votes they are usually in error. Congressmen are poor judges of significance.

James G. March has given another mathematical treatment of the problem of power or, as he calls it, influence.[49] He sets up matrices concerning the probability of given outcomes when the incumbents of certain positions—say, the President and the Speaker—support or oppose a bill. This elaborate exercise involves two solecisms: it is impossible to supply empirical values for the symbolically designated values, which would be necessary if the formulations were to be meaningful; and the mathematical concept of probability is inapplicable to unique events, which the outcomes would be if they were given an empirical content. But the argument is mathematically unexceptionable. If the President's influence in favor of a bill is α, and in opposition $-\alpha$, if the Speaker's influence in favor is β and in opposition $-\beta$, then when they both favor the bill the sum is $\alpha + \beta$; when the President favors the bill and the Speaker opposes it the sum is $\alpha - \beta$, and so on. We are given no reason why the influence of a President or a Speaker in favor of a bill should be of the same absolute magnitude as his influence against it; but since the formulations are operationally meaningless there is no need to quarrel with them. In fact, of course, what we have here is an exercise in arithmetic and not a scientific formulation about influence. As children we learned that if John has three apples and James has one apple,

[49]"Measurement Concepts in the Theory of Influence," *Journal of Politics,* 19 (1957), 202–26.

together they have four apples. This problem bears the same relation to the science of promology that March's formulations bear to political science.

Charles D. Farris has given us a nominal definition of ideology.[50] There are, he says, three ways of dealing with this phenomenon: "verbalism about the meaning of the word"; postponement of research "until most members of the profession agree on what the word means"; and behavioral research by "operational criteria." Being, apparently, an impatient man, he adopted the last course.

Farris examined roll-call votes on five issues in the House of Representatives in 1946. There were "32 logically possible groupings of pro and con positions on five issues." Each of these he calls a distinct ideology. Another roll call would produce 64 ideologies; by the end of the session the number of ideologies would be astronomical. And the ideology of a legislator would change every time he cast another vote. But most of these ideologies were empty houses. Only 12 of Farris' 32 possible ideologies were represented in the House. What we have here, of course, is a report of voting clusters in the House, the smallest 0.9 per cent and the largest 23.3 per cent. These clusters become tenants of 12 of the 32 possible ideologies by an act of nominal definition. Certainly the *definiens* is operational—it is an exercise in the mathematics of combinations—but the *definiendum* is meaningless. One does not supply empirical content to the *definiendum* by putting an empirical content in 12 of the 32 empty boxes in the *definiens*.

These are some of the better known nominal definitions. The reader can recall others; or, if he likes, he can invent new ones *ad libitum*.

GAME THEORY

In 1944 John von Neumann and Oskar Morgenstern introduced "decision-making" into economics under the name of game theory.[51] They were able to show that if two or more players competed with each other under agreed rules for an agreed good, or utility, and if adequate knowledge and data were available, there

---

[50] "A Scale Analysis of Ideological Factors in Congressional Voting," in Wahlke and Eulau, *op cit.*, pp. 339–413.
[51] *Theory of Games and Economic Behavior* (Princeton: Princeton U. Press, 1944).

was, or might be, a preferred strategy or range of strategies for each. This could be computed in terms of probabilities of outcome.

Game theory has evoked more enthusiasm among political scientists than any other technique. But is has three fatal disabilities: it assumes the objectivity, measurability, and commensurability of values; it makes indefensible psychological assumptions; and, on the practical level, it assumes that it is possible to obtain the empirical data necessary to compute the probabilities.

In the application of game theory in economics, values are allowed to collapse into dollars, which have the convertibility and measurability which the theory demands, and which present the necessary appearance of objectivity. Of course utility always has a subjective foundation; and for logical positivists like game theorists it is exclusively subjective. Insofar as they rest on subjective states of mind, utilities are not stable but variable. Northrop has shown that economics cannot be a science in the sense of the physical sciences because the central concept is value and values wax, wane, and change in time; science, however, requires invariability.[52]

Some political scientists attempt to use dollars as the values of a political system. So Buchanan and Tullock reduce politics to the bids and side-payments of three farmers jockeying to obtain the most favorable location of a road, a location which has a precise dollar value for each.[53] But most political contests—including this one—cannot be expressed in dollars.

William H. Riker has constructed a *Theory of Political Coalitions*[54] by means of game theory. The purpose of a coalition is to despoil others. Rational calculation keeps the winning coalition as small as possible; this maximizes the share of each partner. Riker treats of costs in the building of a coalition, and recognizes that the cost may exceed the prospective gain from the coalition. Costs may be in money or charisma or love; payments may be in threats of reprisal or money or policy or promises or emotional satisfaction. Unfortunately these things cannot be computed: "utiles are just a convention for theorizing, not an actual measure which real persons can use."[55] A formula in terms of such utiles is clearly not operational.

---

[52]F. S. C. Northrop, *The Logic of the Sciences and the Humanities* (New York: Macmillan, 1947), chap. 13.

[53]James M. Buchanan and Gordon Tullock, *The Calculus of Consent* (Ann Arbor: U. of Michigan Press, 1962).

[54]New Haven: Yale U. Press, 1962.

[55]*Ibid.*, p. 118.

In discussing the conflicts for which coalitions are built—markets and elections and war—Riker ignores cost. The conflict is treated as a zero-sum game, one in which the whole loss of the loser is imputed to the victor, and the victor retains his original utilities, as in poker. The "payoff" is in money or power or success.[56] "Often, and especially now when there is threat of nuclear war, the game has seemed non-zero-sum, that is the common benefits of peace and civilization have seemed greater than any possible gain from conflict."[57] Nevertheless "total war," which apparently means nuclear war, can be treated as a zero-sum game because "the loss of the losers, i.e., their destruction, is the announced object of the winners. The gain is the exact reverse of the loss."[58]

No other author has been more successful in establishing standardized utiles for a political game. The theory is also weak on the psychological side. It is not only necessary that there be measurable objective utiles at stake in the conflict; the decision-maker must attach exclusive value to these utiles. Riker solves this problem by pointing out that government is conducted by trustees, and attributing a special character to a trustee: "the one duty of the fiduciary agent is to guard the position of the beneficiary of the trust."[59] He has "one overriding moral standard: promote the interests of the beneficiary."[60] It is curious that in other mathematical discussions of the actions of fiduciary agents, Riker attributes to them the sole motive of promoting their own interests, which are described as maximizing personal power. In fact, of course, the whole vocabulary of value and emotion is needed to describe the conduct of any man, whether he is a trustee or not.

It is perplexing that anyone with the slightest acquaintance with history could suppose that decisions are reached on the motives and by the calculations postulated by game theory. "At the sight of the actions of man displayed on the great stage of the world," said Emmanuel Kant, "it is impossible to escape a certain degree of disgust":

> With all the occasional indications of wisdom scattered here and there, we cannot but perceive the whole sum of these actions to be a web of folly, childish vanity, and often even of the idlest wickedness and spirit of destruction. Hence, at last, one is puzzled to

[56]*Ibid.*, p. 23.
[57]*Ibid.*, p. 67.
[58]*Loc. cit.*
[59]*Ibid.*, p. 24.
[60]*Ibid.*, p. 25.

know what judgment to form of our species so conceited of its high advantages.[61]

If the psychology of game theory were applicable anywhere, it would be in games, where the utiles are defined and definite, the player has no motive except to acquire utiles, and the probabilities are calculable. Yet the psychological studies of gambling show that players regularly behave with less than the complete rationality imputed to them by game theory.[62]

Even more impressive a defect of game theory in politics, perhaps, is the flat impossibility of computing the probabilities which are supposed to govern rational decision. At a time when such matters were infinitely more simple than now, Clausewitz wrote:

> In order to ascertain the real scale of the means which we must put forth for war, we must think over the political object both on our side and on the enemy's side; we must consider the power and position of the enemy's State as well as our own, the character of his Government and of his people, and the capacities of both, and all that again on our own side, and the political connections of other States, and the effect which the War will produce on those States. That the determination of these diverse circumstances and their diverse connections with each other is an immense problem, that it is the true flash of genius which discovers here in a moment what is right, and that it would be quite out of the question to become master of the complexity merely by a methodical study, it is easy to conceive. In this sense Buonaparte was quite right when he said that it would be a problem in algebra before which a Newton might stand aghast.[63]

---

[61]"Idea of a Universal History on a Cosmo-Political Plan," trans. Thomas DeQuincey, in DeQuincey, *Works* (Edinburgh: Adam and Charles Black, 1863), Vol. 12, pp. 133–52, at p. 134.

[62]See for example the series of articles in the *American Journal of Psychology*: four articles by Ward Edwards, "Probability Preferences in Gambling," 66 (1953), 349–64; "Probability Preferences among Bets With Differing Expected Values," 67 (1954), 56–67; "The Reliability of Probability Preferences," 67 (1954), 68–95; "Variance Preferences in Gambling," 67 (1954), 441–52; C. H. Combs and S. S. Komorita, "Measuring Utility of Money through Decisions," 71 (1958), 383–89; Robert F. Munson, "Decision-Making in an Actual Gambling Situation," 75 (1962), 640–43.

There is not agreement among game theorists themselves as to the prescriptions of rationality. See R. D. Luce and H. Raiffa, *Games and Decisions* (New York: Wiley, 1957), chap. 13; William J. Baumol, *Economic Theory and Operations Analysis* (New York: Wiley, 1961), chap. 19.

[63]Joseph I. Greene (ed.), *Clausewitz on the Art of Warfare* (Philadelphia: McKay, 1943), p. 138.

Whence, then, come the empirical data that game theorists sometimes build into their studies? The answer is simple: they are invented. Philip Green has shown that the computations of Herman Kahn for thermonuclear war lack both evidence and plausibility.[64]

Game theory is a branch of economics; its utiles derive from the hedonistic calculus of Utilitarianism. One is tempted to say, as Macaulay said of the Utilitarians, that game theorists do not particular harm: they might as well be game theorists as jockeys or dandies; "it certainly hurts the health less than hard drinking, and the fortune less than high play."[65] But in fact they are dangerous. The incredibly superficial outlook of game theory is mistaken for a foreign policy.[66] Officials of the RAND Corporation complain that Secretary McNamara has drafted so many of their experts to the Pentagon that they have not enough left to man the computers.

Richard Snyder considered that John Foster Dulles was an intuitive game theorist. In 1955 he wrote:

> It is interesting to consider the present problem confronting Secretary of State Dulles over the defense of Formosa. If the United States is considered to be in a two-person, non-zero-sum game with Communist China, the theory suggests that the optimum strategy for the United States is to move first and commit itself to a defense of Formosa by some sort of device that would make it impossible to reverse the decision. This is so because often in a non-zero-sum game both players can lose, especially if one of the payoffs is war. If the Formosa situation were a zero-sum game, the early commitment of the United States to a strategy might not be desirable. Although in such a game it does not matter whether one

---

[64] *Deadly Logic: The Theory of Nuclear Deterrence* (Columbus: Ohio State U. Press, 1966), chap. 2. One wishes that Secretary McNamara could read this admirable book.

[65] Thomas Babington Macaulay, "Mill on Government," in G. M. Young (ed.), *Macaulay: Prose and Poetry* (Cambridge: Harvard U. Press, 1952), pp. 579–609, at p. 609.

[66] Roger Fisher, "Constructing Rules That Affect Governments," in Donald G. Brennan (ed.), *Arms Control, Disarmament, and National Security* (New York: Braziller, 1961), pp. 56–67, at p. 61, says that "the science of game theory has shown that an understanding of international relations may be acquired by comparing the rules of governmental conduct to those of a game." In an intelligent book on foreign policy one of the authors of game theory, Oskar Morgenstern, found no occasion to make use of this tool. He commented: "terms are frequently employed that have the appearance of authority while behind them there is exactly nothing. 'Sound military decision' and 'calculated risk' are some of these phrases. The first expression is entirely empty and the second never indicates what the risk is, how it is measured and what the alleged calculation actually consists of." *The Question of National Defense* (2nd ed.; New York: Random House, 1961), p. 4.

is predictable or not, bluff may offer one's opponent an opportunity for error that can be turned into a gain.

On the contrary, bluff in a non-zero-sum game may tempt your opponent into the use of a strategy that results in a negative pay-off for both players. From the standpoint of the safest course of action in Formosa, an automatic defense of Formosa—perhaps triggered by some automatic mechanism—would be most desirable because the opponent (in this case Communist China) must know that the strategy cannot be altered. . . . If the Secretary's diagnosis happens to coincide with the diagnosis of the theory, it is probable that it coincided because his reasoning followed the pattern indicated by the theory.[67]

Thus game theory leads directly to Herman Kahn's Doomsday Machine. The United States, said Kahn, might deliver ultimata to the Soviet Union, and make them plausible by irrevocably activating nuclear devices capable of blowing up the earth which would be triggered automatically by a violation of any ultimatum.[68] If the earth were destroyed, the fault would lie with the irrationality of the adversary. This proposal, which according to Kahn is technologically quite feasible, evoked little enthusiasm even in the Pentagon. It could appeal only to intellectual and moral cretins. But, as Snyder has pointed out, it is the logical culmination of game theory.

At least since the advent of nuclear weapons, it has been inappropriate for states to behave as Rome and Cathage behaved. Such a conception of national interest is operationally meaningless. No state any longer has an interest distinguishable from the interest of the whole world. As John H. Herz has said: "Under the standards of a new humanism which places the preservation of the human race above any and all partial interests, the same behavior pattern now emerges as indispensable to national policy if the entire race is not to perish." He warns that if we continue the pursuit of "national interest narrowly conceived, . . . a catastrophic blowup will become an almost mathematical certainty."[69]

---

[67] *Op cit.*, pp. 99.

[68] *On Thermonuclear War* (Princeton: Princeton U. Press, 1960), pp. 145–49. Kahn proposed only to control the conduct of the Soviet Union, but today he would undoubtedly add China. And why not include France, Cuba, and Vietnam, and indeed all the other nations that might adopt policies inconsistent with those of Washington—that is, all the nations in the world? And why not apply the device in domestic politics, and thus eliminate riots in the ghettos, tax evasion, and Sabbath-breaking?

[69] "International Politics and the Nuclear Dilemma," in John C. Bennett (ed.), *Nuclear Weapons and the Conflict of Conscience* (New York: Scribner's, 1962), pp. 13–38, at pp. 31–32.

The certainty is indeed almost mathematical, but the computations lie outside the mathematics of game theorists. In the course of a torrent of prescriptions for American foreign policy, Morton A. Kaplan, on the basis, no doubt, of his confidence in game theory, asks for evidence that arms races lead to war, and opines:

> If one thing is clear about the present, it is that some aspects of the arms race have improved the stability of peace in the world we live in, have diminished the probability that a nuclear accident or a provocative situation will produce war, and have made it possible to control nuclear war, if it occurs. Perhaps much of the "detente" which we perceive can be attributed to this greater military stability. Whether a continued arms race would have similar felicitous consequences or whether these would be overbalanced by unfavorable aspects of the arms race is a matter for sober and cautious analysis.[70]

Kaplan does not have the usual hospitable attitude of the behavioralist toward the other social sciences: "Practitioners would do well to avoid the half-digested contributions of psychologists, anthropologists, and sociologists to the problems of foreign policy."[71] But game theory rests on a psychology, one that has been obsolete for nearly a hundred years. To be sure, one cannot tell how far Kaplan accepts the psychology on which his system is founded. He finds the United States deficient in the qualities of the game theorist: "We lack the will to act, the coldness to engage in counterterror, and the skill to discriminate among the contenders for favor."[72] And he considers that the Communist leaders do not pursue the utiles of the game and do not behave rationally; they are "paranoids."[73] Under these circumstances, what is left of game theory? Game theory assumes the rationality of both parties. Responses intended to counter the moves of a rational adversary will be inappropriate against an irrational adversary. Whatever may be the proper strategy against paranoids, it is not game theory.

But of course game theory is not a discipline and cannot solve any political problem. Its real function is to restate the problem that faces the world. Certainly Utilitarian psychology and economics had a broader purpose, but they were used in the nineteenth century to

---

[70]"Old Realities and New Myths," *World Politics,* 17 (1965), 334–65, at p. 355.
[71]*Ibid.,* p. 361.
[72]*Ibid.,* p. 363.
[73]*Ibid.,* p. 357.

justify the world view of Dickens' Gradgrind and thus foreclose attempts at the solution of social problems. Game theory employs the same psychology to argue for the inevitability of the cold war. The one real consequence of the adoption of game theory is to bottom the discussion of international affairs on the assumption of reciprocal intransigent hostility. Game theory is academically more respectable than the philosophy of the John Birch Society; but it performs the same social function. And it performs no other function.

JURIMETRICS[74]

In 1941, C. Herman Pritchett introduced the "box-score" method of displaying the agreement and disagreement of the several Supreme Court justices in the 1939 and 1940 terms.[75] In 1951 the psychologist Louis L. Thurstone, after Spearman the author of factor analysis, applied this technique to divided voted in the 1943 and 1944 terms as "an exploration in scientific method on the problem of identifying the blocs or sub-groups within a larger group as in a legislature, council, or court, in terms of the voting records of the members"; but he refrained from drawing any psychological conclusions.[76]

In the past decade several political scientists have used mathematical techniques to compare divided votes and pairs of justices; even more frequently they have exhibited the voting records of justices on a Guttman scale. When the data can be so scaled, they display a quite regular descending order of concurrence like a stairway.

A summary of data, mathematically or graphically presented, is authentic fact, and can be used for whatever this fact is useful for. The behavioralists believe that from past votes of justices it is possible to

---

[74]This term was introduced by Lee Loevinger in 1949 in an essay, "Jurimetrics," which is reprinted in Glendon Schubert (ed.), *Judicial Behavior* (Chicago: Rand McNally, 1964), pp. 72–76, to describe "the scientific investigation of legal problems." He did not confine it to any particular techniques, but the word has been appropriated by the behvaioralists, even though Loevinger's interest was in facilitating purposive change in the law and their is merely in prediction.

[75]"Divisions of Opinion among Justices of the United States Supreme Court," *APSR*, 35 (1941), pp. 890–98. See also Pritchett, *The Roosevelt Court: A Study in Judicial Politics and Values* (New York: Macmillan, 1948), and *Civil Liberties and the Vinson Court* (Chicago: U. of Chicago Press, 1954).

[76]Louis L. Thurstone and J. W. Degan, "A Factorial Study of the Supreme Court," reprinted in Schubert, *op cit.*, pp. 335–40.

predict future votes. Prediction has not merely practical but scientific value; it is the "verification of theory."[77]

The most popular school of thought believes that it is also possible to establish the significant features of the personality structures of the participating justices by techniques of comparison. In this case, personality is the mediating factor between the past votes and the predicted judicial behavior.

The comparative method of the behavioralists is applicable only to divided votes. Nevertheless Glendon Schubert, the chief of those who distill psychological attitudes from votes, has offered a psychological explanation for unanimity. He points out that more than 90 per cent of the decisions of the Supreme Court are unanimous,[78] and attributes this fact to "the homogeneity of values common to the justices as a group"[79] and "high communality in perception of the issues deemed relevant."[80] No doubt this is true of those decisions that follow the rule of *stare decisis*, but decisions that make new law must be explained in other terms. When the Court unanimously overthrew "separate but equal" in *Brown* v. *Board of Education*,[81] it was not applying settled legal values. Clearly a majority of the justices were determined to introduce a new value, but it seems unlikely that all of them really desired this. Probably some concurred for political reasons—most important, perhaps, the desirability of presenting a united front in the battle that was sure to follow.

Schubert has enumerated some of the occasional and personal factors that may influence a judge.

> Out of the entire situation (including the record, briefs, oral argument, conversation with colleagues, newspaper and television commentary, law review articles, the competence of his clerk, the current state of mental and physical health of himself and his family, perhaps the war news from Viet Nam, et cetera, ad infinitum, plus the remembered and the sublimated historical antecedents of all of these events) a judge defines the issue to which he will react in his decision. Much of his training as a lawyer, and of his socialization as a judge, combine with the customs and institutional proce-

---

[77]Schubert, "Prediction from a Psychometric Model," in Schubert, *op cit.*, pp. 548–87, at p. 554.
[78]*Judicial Decision-Making* (New York: Free Press of Glencoe, 1963), p. 61.
[79]*Loc. cit.*
[80]"Ideologies and Attitudes, Academic and Judicial," *Journal of Politics*, 29 (1967), 3–40, at p. 14.
[81]347 U.S. 483 (1954).

dures for judicial decision-making to provide maximal (within the range of possible variation for human beings) assurance that his cognition of the situation will be highly structured, especially when he defines the question for decision.[82]

In addition to the influences listed by Schubert, we might point to the diversity of the ideological factors that affect judges. Justice Holmes charged the majority of the Court with coining Herbert Spencer's *Social Statics* into law.[83] Holmes himself coined Darwinism into law.[84] Justice Field's conception of due process was derived from the Christian idea of vocation.[85] Justice Burton dissented from a decision up-holding the dismissal of public employees for past membership in the Communist party because the law contravened the Christian doctrine of repentance.[86] And it is familiar that a great variety of ethical and social ideas have supplied the content of due process on such subjects as procedure, economic regulation, speech, picketing, obscenity, and freedom of religion.

The number and the diversity of these influences might make one despair; it might lead to the pessimism of the rule-skeptics among the legal realists. But Schubert is confident that the data can be ordered: "the number of basic attitudinal dimensions that are relevant to the decision-making of the United States Supreme Court is very small."[87]

The explicit reliance of such authors is on attitude psychology. But they do not undertake to establish the judge's personality structure by psychological evidence, and then relate his personality to his votes.[88] Like orthodox lawyers, they confine themselves to the decisions. They define the problem, sometimes in terms of the legal issue before the court, sometimes in terms of the legal or social roles of the litigants, and then they compare the votes of the judges. If the vote is unanimous, nothing can be concluded. A single divided vote

[82] *Op. cit.*, pp. 13–14.
[83] *Lochner* v. *New York*, 198 U.S. 45 (1905).
[84] See Martin B. Hickman, "Mrs. Justice Holmes: A Reappraisal," *Western Political Quarterly*, 5 (1952), 66–83.
[85] Clay P. Malick, "Justice Field and the Concept of the Calling," *Western Political Quarterly*, 13 Supp. (September 1960), 52–53.
[86] *Garner* v. *Los Angeles*, 341 U.S. 716 (1951).
[87] Schubert, "Prediction from a Psychometric Model," p. 552.
[88] However, Stuart S. Nagel, "Off-the-Bench Judicial Attitudes," in Schubert (ed.), *Judicial Decision-Making*, pp. 29–53, has attempted to characterize judges by their responses to a questionnaire and to show that votes correspond to character thus established.

tells nothing. But if a substantial series of cases involving the same problem, whether defined in terms of issues or of litigants, can be discovered, and if the votes of each judge are consistent, or fairly consistent, in relation to the votes of his brother judges, this is taken to demonstrate two things. The problem is a real problem, in the sense that the factual determinant of judicial votes has been isolated. And the psychological determinant has also been isolated. The responses of the judges to the facts attest to the presence or absence of a psychological attitude. Sometimes the cases simply display a permanent division of the court into blocs, like the "liberal" and "conservative" blocs identified by Pritchett. Sometimes the cases in the series present not a single issue but a succession of graded issues, progressing from one extreme to another. In this case each judge has a "break point" which represents the extremity of his attitude; his vote changes when this point is passed. The several judges will have different break points, so that their differential adhesion to the value in question can be exhibited on a Guttman scale.

No attitude psychologist has undertaken to explain reasoned decisions in terms of attitudes. Attitudes or dispositions or biases are raw materials that go into decisions; but there are involved also rational calculation of the relation of means to ends and a rational evaluation of the end itself—a weighing of alternatives, costs, and consequences. It is in this sense that a choice among values can be said to be correct or incorrect: the decision inevitably involves reasoning, and this may be in error.[89] The obvious explanation of the consistency of the votes of a judge on an issue is that he has arrived at a settled opinion on the merits. An attitude or attitudes contributed to this conclusion; but rational appraisal of the problem and the outcome entered in as well. More than one variable is involved. Attitude a, coupled with propositions m and n, may lead to vote v; attitude b, compled with propositions x and y, may lead to vote v. This is clearly demonstrated in some concurring opinions. Judicial behavioralists, however, believe that votes have a one-to-one correspondence to appropriate attitudes.

So behavioralism puts on attitude psychology a burden beyond its powers. There are two other difficulties. The attitudes employed by behavioralists are not established by any psychological test but are

---

[89] On the process of decision see Ralph Barton Perry, *General Theory of Value* (Cambridge: Harvard U. Press, 1950).

borrowed from political polemics; they are versions of the political formula of "liberal-conservative" applied to judges in the controversial literature of the 1920's and 1930's. Moreover, the method of judicial behavioralism requires that attitudes come in pairs—"liberal" and "conservative"—and constitute polar opposites between which judges can be arrayed on a scale. But in psychology the opposite of an attitude is the absence of the attitude; it is not another attitude. Richard S. Cruchfield has summarized the literature:

> We have tended to call someone liberal if he rejected the values of conservatism.... All persons who reject conservatism may not be liberals, for as in the case of the "authoritarian-democratic" dimension, liberalism-conservatism may not be variables, paired in such a way that a high score on one necessarily signifies a low score on the other.[90]

Schubert's first venture in scaling arrayed the justices on the question: "How sympathetic are you to claims of the right to counsel under the Fourteenth Amendment?"[91] Such a sympathy is not one of the attitudes one encounters in psychological literature. Nor is a subjective experience like sympathy very accurately measured by a vote on the real question before the Court: "Shall this defendant have a new trial?" The ordering of the judges by their votes is not an ordering by greater and lesser quantities of sympathy; it merely discloses how judges have voted on the question of right to counsel in the immediate case. It is a report of outcomes and not of causes.

Right to counsel involves a highly specialized attitude. Subsequently Schubert generalized his scale to a liberalism-conservatism scale; but then he began to break it down topically, and now he recognizes at least seven attitudinal dimensions: liberalism and conservatism on civil liberties; economic liberalism and economic conservatism;[92] social liberalism and social conservatism; a fiscal scale, for cases between government and taxpayers; a judicial activism-restraint scale; a federalism scale; and a scale on the authority of the Supreme Court over the inferior courts.[93] Harold J. Spaeth has divided the economic scale into two, one measuring attitude toward

---

[90]"Comformity and Character," *American Psychologist,* 10 (1955), 191–98, at p. 194.
[91]"The Study of Judicial Decision-Making as an Aspect of Political Behavior," *APSR,* 52 (1958), 1007–25, at p. 1015.
[92]*Judicial Policy-Making* (Chicago: Scott, Foresman, 1965), p. 120.
[93]Schubert, "Prediction from a Psychometric Model," p. 569.

labor unions and one measuring attitude toward government regulation of business.[94]

Certainly this is moving in the right direction. If the business regulation scale were further divided topically, to distinguish, for example, between cases involving antitrust laws and cases involving fair-trade acts, even greater consistency would be achieved. But this process of analysis is not an increasingly accurate exploration of the personality structures of judges: it is a topical analysis of holdings in terms of legal categories. If the analysis is carried far enough we will have, not a psychology, but a legal text which reports the holdings on concrete problems and the dissenting votes.

In fact, the behavioral method of interpreting decisions comes down in the end precisely to the common law method. At common law, as for the behavioralists, the opinion is not the law, but only the holding on the facts of the case. In an early study, Fred Kort analyzed the right-to-counsel cases in terms of the presence or absence of certain sets of facts.[95] There was no mention of attitudes or of psychology. Instead, Kort undertook to establish empirical constants for each relevant fact. If the facts, thus weighted, added to a critical sum, the Court would require that counsel be afforded. Subsequently Kort has argued that both simultaneous equations and Boolean algebra can be used "to obtain a *precise and exhaustive* distinction between combinations of facts that lead to decisions in favor of one party and combinations of facts that lead to decisions in favor of the opposing party."[96] These methods however, cannot predict "doctrinal changes and the adoption of new rules of law."[97] Similarly Stuart S. Nagel has recommended that the weights of sets of facts in right-to-counsel cases be determined by obtaining coefficients of correlation; when the sum of these weights in a particular case passes an empirically deter-

---

[94]"Warren Court Attitudes toward Business," in Schubert (ed.), *Judicial Decision-Making*, pp. 79–108.

[95]"Predicting Supreme Court Decisions Mathematically: A Quantitative Analysis of the 'Right to Counsel' Cases," *APSR*, 51 (1957), 1–12. Franklin M. Fisher has argued that there was logical error in identifying the relevant facts, and that the assignment of weights was not justified. "The Mathematical Analysis of Supreme Court Decisions: The Use and Abuse of Quantitative Methods," *ibid.*, 52 (1958), 321–38.

[96]"Simultaneous Equations and Boolean Algebra in the Analysis of Judicial Decisions," in Schubert (ed.), *Judicial Behavior*, pp. 477–91, at p. 477.

[97]*Ibid.*, p. 490.

mined number, one expects the defendant to win.[98] Reed C. Lawlor has proposed the use of symbolic logic to relate facts to decisions.[99] Lawlor has quite correctly identified his method and Kort's and Nagel's as the practice of *stare decisis*, and has recognized that it is necessary to take account of "personal *stare decisis*"—the positions adopted on previous factual situations by individual justices.

This is a very reminiscent scheme; it is what Jerome Frank[100] called "legal fundamentalism." Like James C. Carter,[101] these authors believe that anyone who examines the facts and applies himself to the precedents is bound to arrive at the right conclusion. A legal problem is merely a problem of cognition. But if it is necessary to employ a computer to work the sums, may not a judge make an error? Joseph H. Beale, whom Frank made his principal target, was more realistic. He recognized that a judge might err in applying the precedents to the facts, in which case his decision simply was not law.

[98]"Using Simple Calculations to Predict Judicial Decisions," *American Behavioral Scientist*, 4 (December 1960), 24–28.

[99]"Stare Decisis and Electronic Computers," in Schubert (ed.), *Judicial Behavior*, pp. 492–505. See also Lawlor, "Foundations of Logical Legal Decision Making," *Modern Uses of Logic in Law*, June 1963, pp. 98–110.

[100]*Law and the Modern Mind* (New York: Brentano, 1930), chap. 6. It is an extraordinary thing that the judicial behavioralists should represent themselves as continuing the tradition of Jerome Frank. Frank was interested in "(1) what courts actually do, (2) what they are supposed to do, (3) whether they do what they are supposed to do, and (4) whether they should do what they are supposed to do." Jerome Frank, "A Conflict with Oblivion: Some Observations on the Founders of Legal Pragmatism," *Rutgers Law Review*, 9 (1954), 425–63, at p. 451 n. The behavioralists address themselves only to the first question, which had no independent significance for Frank: it was preliminary to the later questions. And they do so on assumptions that were explicitly rejected by Frank. "Lawyers and judges purport to make large use of precedents; that is, they purport to rely on the conduct of judges in past cases as a means of procuring analogies for action in new cases. But since what was actually decided in the earlier cases is seldom revealed, it is impossible, in a real sense, to rely on these precedents. They could approximate a system of real precedents only if the judges, in rendering those former decisions, had reported with fidelity the precise steps by which they arrived at their decisions." "The facts of all but the simplest controversies are complicated and unlike those of any other controversy; in the absence of a highly detailed account by the judge of how he reacted to the evidence, no other person is capable of reproducing his exact reactions." "The uniqueness of the facts and of the judge's reaction thereto is often concealed because the judge so states the facts that they appear to call for the application of a settled rule. But the concealment does not mean that the judge's personal bent has been inoperative or that his emotive experience is simple and reproducible." Frank, *Law and the Modern Mind*, pp. 148–49, 150–51.

[101]*Law: Its Origin, Growth and Function* (New York: Putnam, 1907).

Schubert very properly rebukes these authors for ignoring psychological considerations, and for the artificial division between law and fact which is one aspect of the failure to consider psychology.[102] Lawlor asserts that it is unnecessary to make the personal factors explicit: "Even if the judge's personal inclinations are unknown, they are implicit in the equations."[103] Psychological factors, then can be ignored: fact and law are linked in an invariable manner.

But in fact Schubert adds to Kort only an unwarranted assumption. He identifies the significant facts in the same way as Kort, and regards the vote of the judge as a direct response to this stimulus.[104] In addition, he assures us that what mediates between stimulus and response is a psychological attitude. But he confesses that his attitudes are not empirical; they are "logical inferences from sets of decisional responses."[105] At no point does Schubert offer evidence on the question of the personality structure of a judge. Operationally, he merely adduces data of two sorts. Like Kort, he shows that in many cases a given stimulus is followed by a given response; but no more than Kort does he supply the causal link between the two. And he shows that in many cases the responses of judges on an issue can be ranked; but he does not demonstrate that this ranking is in terms of differential quantities of a given psychological attitude.

If one could measure psychological attitudes (A's) independently, and then relate them to a fixed stimulus and varying responses, so that the scale reads $S\text{-}A_1\text{-}R_1$, $S\text{-}A_2\text{-}R_2$, ... $S\text{-}A_n\text{-}R_n$, we could conclude, as Schubert does, that "the votes of judges are attitudinal responses to the public policy issues raised for decision by cases."[106] But Schubert offers us $A_1 = S\text{-}R_1$, $A_2 = S\text{-}R_2$, ... $A_n = S\text{-}R_n$. The A's are not otherwise identified or measured. This is merely a series of nominal definitions of attitudes which begs the question as to whether decisions are in fact simply functions of psychological attitudes.

Still other behavioral explanations of judicial conduct have been offered. In a study of the 1936 term of the Supreme Court, Schubert identified a three-man bloc moved by a liberal attitude, a four-man

---

[102] Schubert, "Introductory Note," in Schubert (ed.), *Judicial Behavior*, pp. 443-60, at pp. 451-53.

[103] "Stare Decisis and Electronic Computers," p. 496.

[104] *Op cit.*, p. 15.

[105] "Ideologies and Attitudes, Academic and Judicial," pp. 27-28.

[106] "A Psychometric Model of the Supreme Court, *American Behavioral Scientist*, 4 (November 1961), 14-18, at p. 18.

bloc moved by a conservative attitude, and a two-man bloc consisting of Chief Justice Hughes and his supporter Justice Roberts—Schubert calls the bloc Hughberts.[107] Inexplicably, it is asserted that Hughberts is neigher liberal nor conservative. Nevertheless, on all the occasions on which this was possible except two, Hughberts joined with the three-man liberal bloc to form a majority rather than with the four-man conservative bloc. Schubert offers two explanations. The first is in terms of the Shapley-Shubik power index. If the members are rotated, a member of a five-man bloc is the swing-man making up a majority once of every five times; in a six-man bloc, he occupies the prized position which carries power only once of six times. Hughberts has maximized his power by voting with the three-man bloc. The second explanation is not supported by mathematics, but one can accept it by *Verstehen*; by giving decisions favorable to the New Deal, Hughberts hoped to ward off legislation directed against the Court.

If one employed Schubert's usual method, he would explain the votes of Hughes and Roberts by attributing liberal attitudes to them. There is no more reason to ascribe an appetite for Shapley-Shubik power, which after all brings only mathematical satisfactions, to the two-man Hughberts bloc that joined the three-man bloc than to the three-man bloc that joined the two-man Hughberts bloc. And it appears that Hughberts was not moved by a lust for Shapley-Shubik power in the 1931–35 terms, for then he regularly formed majorities with the four-man bloc;[108] but perhaps he had not yet learned to calculate permutations.

In the Hughberts game only two justices sought Shapley-Shubik power by practicing game theory, but S. Sidney Ulmer has ranked all the justices on a Shapley-Shubik index.[109] And both Samuel Krislov[110] and Schubert[111] have offered abstract discussions of coalition-formation on the Supreme Court in Shapley-Shubik terms. This is less plausible than Riker's theory of coalitions: in Riker's scheme, the majority coalition can exclude and expél members, whereas on the Supreme Court any justice can leave the minority

---

[107]*Constitutional Politics* (New York: Holt, Rinehart and Winston, 1960), pp. 161–71.

[108]*Ibid.*, p. 161.

[109]"The Analysis of Behavior Patterns on the United States Supreme Court," *Journal of Politics*, 22 (1960), 629–53.

[110]"Power and Coalition in a Nine-Man Body," in Schubert (ed.), *Judicial Behavior*, pp. 461–64.

[111]"The Power of Organized Minorities in a Small Group," *ibid.*, pp. 465–76.

position of powerlessness and achieve a fractional share of majority power simply by changing his vote. Schubert makes no effort to reconcile the Shapley-Shubik psychology with his attitude psychology.

Schubert recognizes three contemporary schools in the study of public law: the traditional, the conventional or political, and the behavioral.[112] Traditionalists explain a judge's decisions in part in terms of an authoritative structure of norms, in part in terms of his legal philosophy. For the conventionalists, the judge is "a transmission belt for the articulation of group (social) interests."[113] "Behavioralists assign a predominant weight to judicial personality as a source of substantive decisional norms."[114]

All three schools have a common purpose: it is to establish a causal explanation for judicial decisions. This would be a useful and gratifying accomplishment. But most students of public law belong to a fourth school; in the new literature they would bear the flattering name of "policy scientists."[115] They regard law not merely as a phenomenon but as an instrument. They are not primarily interested in the explanation of past events, or even in forecasting the future in terms of the past. They are interested in controlling the future. They study opinions rather than votes because the outcomes they are concerned with are not votes but the social consequences of decisions.

Law is the making of choices; to a degree, it is the shaping of society and of the future. Like ethics, law is concerned with goals, with objectives. A judicial opinion is a statement of values and a forecast of the consequences for one or another value of the policy adopted by the court. But constitutional decisions are problems; they are not always solutions. Often the judges are mistaken. What the social scientist has to contribute is an understanding of inherited values, or history; an account of the shaping of new values, through psychology and sociology; and a projection of the consequences of choice, by ideal types, developmental constructs, analogy, or *Verstehen*. Almost certainly this is not enough. But it is an enterprise of

---

[112]"Ideologies and Attitudes, Academic and Judicial," pp. 6–10; *Judicial Policy-Making,* ch. 7.
[113]"Ideologies and Attitudes, Academic and Judicial," p. 12.
[114]*Loc. cit.*
[115]"The policy science approach not only puts the emphasis upon basic problems and complex models but also calls forth considerable clarification of the value goals involved in policy." Harold D. Lasswell, "The Policy Orientation," in Daniel Lerner and Harold Lasswell (eds.), *The Policy Sciences* (Stanford: Stanford U. Press, 1951), pp. 3–15, at p. 9.

enormously greater importance than the exhibition of past events on a Guttman scale, or the calculation of the tactics by which judges can most frequently attain the position of swingman on a vote.

THE GREAT LEAP UPWARD

Unlike the other schools described above, the jurimetricians concern themselves with empirical data. They report and correlate certain facts. Such an ordering of data is not a scientific achievement, but it may be immediately useful to one who is interested in these facts; and it may suggest an hypothesis and lead to further inquiry.

The compilation of mathematical summaries of empirical data is as old as taxation. The comparison of two series of events goes back at least to the seventeenth century; sophisticated techniques of correlation are more recent. Since many propositions in politics assert the existence of a correlation of one sort or another, devices for testing such propositions can be very useful.

Some branches of physics have found it convenient to describe their findings as statistical probabilities rather than deterministic laws. Behavioral political scientists sometimes talk as though social science were in an analogous position, and they too by the use of statistics of correlation could obtain something equivalent to a theoretically elaborated law.

But the analogy fails. Physics deals with the behavior of entities which have been reduced to identities. One hydrogen atom is indistinguishable from another hydrogen atom. No such reduction has been achieved in social science. Personality factors, cultural factors, differences in the immediate environment, and historical factors— the past, the present, and the anticipated future—make it impossible to treat the members of a voting population as interchangeable units. Considerations of the same order make it impossible to assume that the structure of one voting population will resemble the structure of another voting population. Until we know better, we shall assume that one population of hydrogen atoms will behave in the same way as another population of hydrogen atoms. Since we know that the members of one human population are identical with the members of another human population only in a few biological respects, we do not expect these populations to behave alike.[116]

---

[116] Any viable society must satisfy the conditions of viability, and systems theory undertakes to specify those conditions. See Talcott Parsons, *The Social System* (Glencoe: Free Press, 1951); Marion J. Levy, Jr., *The Structure of Society* (Princeton: Princeton U. Press, 1952).

A. A. Tschuprow emphasizes "the difference between statistical correlation and natural law."

> The regression equation of Y on X expresses the functional relationship between the conditional mathematical expectation of Y and X....
>
> Yet the law of nature is always reversible. If Y is an explicit function of X one can express X as an explicit function of Y by means of formal-mathematical operations and suitable symbols: if $Y = X^2$, then X equals the square root of Y.... On the contrary, the regression equation of Y on X and the regression equation of X on Y are not deducible from each other.... By no ingenuity of mathematical reasoning can one equation be deduced from the other: each must be obtained independently by the consideration of the joint frequency distribution. This is itself by no means surprising, since the regression equations do not connect the same magnitudes: the one connects the conditional mathematical expectation of Y with X, the other, the conditional mathematical expectation of X with Y; they have just as little in common as an equation which connects X and Y with another equation which connects two variables, U and V.[117]

To put it another way, a nomothetic formula is a logical proposition; a regression equation is a factual description—a report of the values an empirical Y can have, and their frequencies, when an empirical X assumes a given value.

Sometimes, when a table of empirical data reports varying outcomes, the fraction of the total which an outcome constitutes is called a probability. The Jury Verdict Research Company began in 1960 a two-volume loose-leaf service, *Verdict Expectancies* and a *Valuation Handbook*. Reviewing the data, Stuart S. Nagel[118] says that a pedestrian hit by an automobile at a point other than a crosswalk has a 34 per cent chance of winning a lawsuit; a plaintiff bitten by dog has a 46 per cent chance of winning. The data, of course, show nothing about the chances of any litigant: they show that 34 and 46 per cent of the persons who brought the specified actions within the specified period of time won. But some pedestrians and some victims of dog bites who might conceivably have won never contemplated suit; an unknown number who presumably would have lost were dissuaded

---

[117] *Principles of the Mathematical Theory of Correlation* (London: William Hodge & Co., 1939), pp. 45–46.

[118] "Statistical Prediction of Verdicts and Awards," *Modern Uses of Logic in Law*, September 1963, pp. 135–39.

by their attorneys from suing. Aside from this, all the conditions for assessing probability in an individual case are lacking. The only meaning of probability when a lawsuit is contemplated is the subjective estimate of an attorney concerning what he and the defense attorney can persuade an as yet unknown jury to believe and to feel.

William H. Riker and Ronald Schaps have undertaken to establish an "index of disharmony" in federal government and to validate it by correlation.[119] Using the Shapley-Shubik power index described above, they computed the power of the two political parties in the national government and in the states for the years 1937–56. When party A has a power index of more than 0.5 in the national government, an index of disharmony can be computed. This is arrived at by subtracting the power index of the same party for all the states from 1.0. If the remainder, the index of disharmony, exceeds 0.5, this means that rival parties dominate the national government and the states. The higher the index, the greater the power of party B in the states and, according to the hypothesis, the greater the disharmony between the national government, controlled by party A, and the states.

Riker and Schaps offered an empirical test for their thesis that parties are the source of harmony and disharmony in federal government. For the period embraced by their study, they counted the lawsuits which reached the Supreme Court, at least to the point of denial of certiorari, in which the United States was a litigant against a state or submitted a brief *amicus curiae* against a state as a litigant, and those in which the United States was a litigant and a state or states submitted a brief *amicus curiae* against the United States. Then these episodes of disharmony were reduced by subtracting from them cases in which the United States and a state were on the same side of one of them submitted a brief *amicus curiae* in support of the other. No reason for introducing these evidences of harmony is given, but it considerably improves the result.

> Assuming that federal cases in the Supreme Court reveal the existence of actual federal disharmony, we counted the number of such events and correlated this number, by bienniums, with the index of disharmony. This calculation resulted in a coefficient of correlation of about + .79. Testing this coefficient against the hypothesis that it might have occurred by chance, it appears that the

[119]"Disharmony in Federal Government," *Behavioral Science,* 2 (1957), 276–90.

coefficient is just within the 2 per cent level of confidence, which is to say that a correlation this high would occur by chance only in 2/100 of the possible correlations.[120]

In fact, the authors assure us, "the correlation is more impressive than it appears."

Of course lawsuits very frequently array national policies or interests against state policies or interests, and this is disharmony of a kind. Much more often than not these collisions occur in suits between private persons, or suits in which the national government or a state is involved, but not both. Riker and Schaps have rejected this body of data; they have limited their survey to cases in which both governments appear, if only as *amici curiae*. This must be because there have been two governmental decisions to participate in the immediate lawsuit. The next appropriate step would be to show that in suits between the national government and states one party controlled the one and the other party the other, and that in suits in which they were on the same side the same party controlled both governments. This would be a more meaningful correlation between political parties and lawsuits than that of Riker and Schaps—a correlation between lawsuits and gross electoral results. But the considerations that array the national government and the states against each other in court, or on the same side, very seldom have anything to do with Republicans and Democrats.

We have here no real definition of disharmony, but two different nominal definitions. On the one hand, disharmony is equated with the situation in which the national government and a majority of the states are controlled by different political parties. On the other, it is equated with the occurrence of lawsuits between the national government and the states, whether or not these are controlled by different political parties. These nominal definitions are inconsistent with each other, since they name two different sets of data. But the authors believe that the two nominal definitions amalgamate and form a real definition because for a twenty-year period they found a high correlation between the two sets of data. The proper way to express their findings is to omit the word disharmony and to report the data: For a twenty-year period, when one party controlled the national government and the other controlled the states, the number of lawsuits in which the national government and the states appeared on opposite

---

[120] *Ibid.*, p. 284.

sides increased. But, in the absence of a showing that the lawsuits arrayed political parties as well as governments against each other, this can be nothing more than an accidental correlation.

In like fashion, unwarranted conclusions have been drawn from studies of the votes of legislators. George M. Belknap has shown that in their votes on amendments to the Taft-Hartley bill the senators can be roughly ordered on a one-dimensional scale.[121] Belknap avoids the assumption of personality types of liberal and conservative and falls back on more specialized attitudes: there are pro- and anti-labor attitudes. To the extent that the votes of senators express their attitudes, it is proper to infer the attitude from the votes, for the attitude is nothing more than a propensity to cast such votes. But of course a senator's attitude on the issue is only one influence on his vote; and it is often on the weaker side. Self-preservation may be a stronger motive. The general character of the senator's constituency affects his voting on labor questions. The voting behavior of Representative Keating from a conservative rural upstate district in New York differed markedly from that of Senator Keating from the urban state of New York; yet one doubts that his personality was restructured when he changed his constituency.

Dean R. Brimhall and Arthur S. Otis have introduced a variant on this method. They took the opinion of the editors of the *New Republic* as to whether a vote on one of eighteen issues was "progressive" or "conservative," and ranked senators and representatives in seven groups for each of four sessions.[122] They found that "there are 46 chances in 100 that a congressman's scale value will not change at all from any given year to the next; there are 83 chances in 100 that his scale value will not change more than one unit; and there are 95 chances in 100 that his scale value will not change more than 2 units."[123] This is supposed to support the inference that there is consistency in voting behavior. It is true that in the case of congressmen whose averages placed them in the "progressive" classes 1 or 2 during the four sessions, one has a voting pattern—which does not necessarily yield an inference as to psychological type—which approaches the *New Republic's* estimate of the merits of bills. In the

---

[121] "Scaling Legislative Behavior," in John C. Wahlke and Heinz Eulau (eds.), *Legislative Behavior* (Glencoe: Free Press, 1959), pp. 388–98.

[122] "A Study of Consistency in Congressional Voting," in Wahlke and Eulau, *op cit.,* pp. 384–87.

[123] *Ibid.,* p. 387.

case of those whose averages placed them in the "conservative" classes 6 and 7 for four years, one has a significant negative correlation with the judgment of the *New Republic*. These two groups account for 26 of the 96 senators. For the 70 senators in the intermediate classes 3, 4, and 5, there is no significant correlation with the judgment of the editors of the *New Republic*. The only "consistency in Congressional voting" shown by the study is the fact that the opinions of the *New Republic* do not relate in a significant way to Congressional voting. This, of course, does not mean that consistency in voting is necessarily lacking. It does mean that the authors have chosen the wrong yardstick.

Considerably more ambitious is the attempt to establish a causal chain of several factors whose relations to each other and to the outcome are purportedly demonstrated by correlation. Hayward R. Alker, Jr., has offered alternative causal chains involving political participation, Communist vote, per capita gross national product, urbanization, literacy, polyarchy, and other topics.[124] Likewise he has identified voting clusters on roll calls in the United Nations, and has attributed these to causal factors.[125]

Arthur S. Goldberg took five characteristics of 645 voters in the 1956 presidential election and examined the correlation of these factors with each other and with the votes of the respondents.[126] The candidates and the issues, or the voters' opinions on these, were not included; campaign strategy was not considered; the contemporary state of affairs—economic conditions affecting the respondents, domestic and foreign political and social problems—and the respondents' perceptions of these, and their hopes and apprehensions about the future, were all omitted. It is not surprising that Goldberg found it impossible to establish satisfactory correlations between his variables and the votes cast. He concluded that the contemporary scene must be included by building into the model an indeterminate number of perceptions of political events "as they arise in the political

---

[124]"Casual Inference and Political Analysis," in Bernd, *op cit.*, pp. 7–43.
[125]"The Long Road to International Relations Theory: Problems of Statistical Nonadditivity," *World Politics*, 18 (1966), 623–55. See also Bruce M. Russett, "The Analysis of Bloc Voting in the General Assembly: A Critique and a Proposal," *APSR*, 57 (1963), 902–17, and the criticism by John E. Mueller, "Some Comments on Russett's 'Discovering Voting Groups in the United Nations,'" *ibid.*, 61 (1967), 146–48.
[126]"Discerning a Causal Pattern among Data on Voting Behavior," *APSR*, 60 (1966), 913–22.

arena, probing in each case for evaluation of the party's handling of the events." Obviously an indefinite number of variable perceptions could not be built into a formula. We cannot expect regression equations to displace polling techniques.

Empirical correlations, like those of Alker and Goldberg, are mathematical descriptions of unique sets of facts. A description is not an explanation. Alker has said: *"Surely one can hypothesize that the coefficients in any statistical investigation of international behavior making additivity assumptions have 'realistic' or 'causal' significance. Until and unless some attempt has been made to verify the pattern of the causal interdependence among the variables involved, however, these hypotheses must remain largely conjectural."*[127] Where are these hypotheses? The coefficients of correlation within a limited population of events are a set of statements about those events; they are not hypotheses about other events. Alker's hypotheses are not conjectural; they are unformulated.

Surely the most ambitious attempt to soar into the empyrean on wings composed of nothing more than mathematical reports of empirical data is an essay by William N. McPhee,[128] who is well known for voting studies. Given only the number of television programs surviving from year to year—given no standards for the classification of television programs into A, B, and C ratings, and the identification of no single program in terms of quality—he purported to establish what percentages of A, B, and C programs survived in the second half of the 1950's.[129] It was 81 per cent for both A and B programs,

---

[127] *Op. cit.*, p. 652.

[128] "Survival Theory in Culture," in *Formal Theories of Mass Behavior* (New York: Free Press of Glencoe, 1963), pp. 26–73. McPhee acknowledges the assistance of Bernard Berelson, James S. Coleman, Lee M. Wiggins, Jack Ferguson, Robert B. Smith, Harry Milholland, the Ford Foundation, the National Science Foundation, and the Center for Advanced Study in the Behavioral Sciences.

[129] Obviously this is mathematically impossible. McPhee obtains his formula by using the same symbol C for an unknown constant and for a variable. The C of equations 19–21 on page 68 is not the C of equation 22.

McPhee begins with the formula $S = A + B + C$, where S is "total culture," and A, B, and C are the unknown percentages made up of A, B and C offerings in the first year. He designates the percentage of A programs that survives the first year by a, of B programs by b, of C programs by c. For the second year he offers us the formula $S = A + B + C + aA + bB + cC$. For the nth year, assuming that the percentage values of A, B, C, a, b, and c are uniform from year to year, he gives us

$$S = \frac{A}{1-a} + \frac{B}{1-b} + \frac{C}{1-c}.$$

24 per cent for C or inferior programs. If we redefine the symbols, the formulae will equally well support the conclusion that 24 per cent of the best programs survived, and 81 per cent of the intermediate and poor programs. One can do a number of things with an algebraic formula, but one cannot get milk from it, as McPhee has tried to do.

What is wrong with these studies, of course, is not that they use statistics. We shall never be able to dispense with counters and verifiers. But it is wrong to suppose that merely by compiling figures we can arrive at science. There is something wistful about the practice. During the last war the natives of New Guinea became accustomed to receiving goods from airplanes of which they knew nothing except that they came from the sky. After the war the planes came no more. Then there developed a new form of the "cargo cult": the natives built landing strips and facsimiles of airplanes on the ground, in the hope that they would attract planes loaded with cargo from the sky.[130] Mathematical behavioralists admire the natural sciences. They have built their facsimiles on the ground. But they have not drawn down bounty from the sky.

But the first equation should read $S = AS + BS + CS$; A, B, and C are percentages of S, which McPhee equates to unity. In the second year, because of the surviving programs aA, bB, cC, the input of A, B, and C programs will be less than unity, and the formula should read $S = A(S - aA - bB - cC) + B(S - aA - bB - cC) + C(S - aA - bB - cC) + aA + bB + cC$, or, substituting one for S on the right, $S = (A + B + C)(1 - aA - bB - cC) + aA + bB + cC$. A, B, and C are constant percentages of the new input, but the new input, and the magnitudes of A, B, and C, will steadily diminish each yeas as the number of surviving programs increases. But McPhee's formula for the nth year treats the input of A, B and C programs in the $(n - 1)$th year, and every preceding year, as equal in magnitude to those in the first year.

[130] This was a revision of the nineteenth-century "steamship cult." Robert E. Dowse, "A Functionalist's Logic," *World Politics,* 18 (1966), 607–22, at p. 611n., has likened systems theory to the cargo cult.

BIBLIOGRAPHY

Becker, Howard S. "Problems of Inference and Proof in Participant Observation," *American Sociological Review*, XXIII, No. 6 (December 1958), pp. 653–660.

Blumber, Herbert. "Psychological Import of the Human Group," in Muzafer Sherif and M. O. Wilson, eds., *Group Relations at the Crossroads*. New York: Harper, 1953, pp. 185–202.

_____. "Society as Symbolic Interaction," in Arnold M. Rose, ed., *Human Behavior and Social Processes*. Boston: Houghton, Mifflin, 1962, pp. 179–92.

Bolton, Charles D. "Behavior, Experience, Relationships," *American Journal of Sociology*, LXIV, No. 1 (July 1958), pp. 45–58.

_____. "Mate Selection as the Development of a Relationship," *Marriage and Family Living*, XXIII, No. 3 (August 1961), pp. 234–240.

Bowman, Claude C. "Imagination in Social Science," *American Sociological Review*, I, No. 4 (August 1936), pp. 632–40.

Duncan, Hugh D. *Communication and Social Order*. New York: Oxford University Press, 1968.

Foote, Nelson. "Concept and Method in the Study of Human Development," in Muzafer Sherif and M. O. Wilson, eds., *Emerging Problems in Social Psychology*. Norman, Oklahoma: University Book Exchange Duplicating Service, 1957, pp. 29–53.

Goffman, Erving. *The Presentation of the Self in Everyday Life*. Garden City, New York: Doubleday Anchor, 1959.

Gold, Raymond L. "Roles in Sociological Field Observations," *Social Forces*, XXXVI, No. 3 (March 1958), pp. 217–223.

Gottschalk, Louis, Kluckohn, Clyde, and Angell, Robert C. *The Use of Personal Documents in History, Anthropology and Sociology*. New York: Social Science Research Council, 1945.

Junker, Buford H. *Field Work: An Introduction to the Social Sciences.* Chicago: University of Chicago Press, 1960.

Manis, Jerome G., and Meltzer, Bernard, eds. *Symbolic Interaction.* Boston: Allyn & Bacon, 1967.

Mead, George H. *Mind, Self and Society.* Chicago: University of Chicago Press, 1934.

Mills, C. Wright, and Gerth, Hans. *Character and Social Structure.* New York: Harcourt, Brace, 1953, (new edition in preparation).

Park, Robert E. *Race and Culture.* Glencoe, Ill.: The Free Press, 1950.

———. *Society.* Glencoe, Ill.: The Free Press 1955.

Rose, Arnold M. ed. *Human Behavior and Social Processes.* Boston: Houghton, Mifflin, 1962.

Strauss, Anselm. *Mirrors and Masks: The Search for Identity.* Glencoe, Ill.: The Free Press, 1959.

———, and Glaser, Barney. *The Discovery of Grounded Theory: Strategies for Qualitative Research.* Chicago: Aldine Publishing Co., 1967.

Turner, Ralph H. "Role-Taking, Role Standpoint and Reference Group Behavior," *American Journal of Sociology*, LXI, No. 1 (January 1956), pp. 316–328.

Waller, Willard. "Insight and Scientific Method," *American Journal of Sociology*, XL, No. 3 (November 1934), pp. 285–297.

Webb, Eugene L. *et al. Unobtrusive Measures: Nonreactive Research in the Social Sciences.* Chicago: Rand McNally Co., 1966.

Winch, Peter. *The Idea of a Social Science.* London: Routledge & Kegan Paul, 1958.

PART **III**

REORIENTATION OF
SOCIAL SCIENCE TEACHING
AND RESEARCH

INTRODUCTION

What are we to do? This pragmatic question is the subject of the final selection of readings in this volume. The purpose of this collection has been not simply to make some abstract and academic (in the invidious sense) points about the limitations of positivism in social science, but rather to suggest a practical reorientation of the sociological disciplines. The critical state of Western civilization has become a commonplace, and the need for better knowledge of human behavior an unassailable necessity. In order that the social sciences might contribute insight and understanding to the grave difficulties which confront man, we must utilize to the fullest extent the resources at our command. This cannot be done if the very subject matter is disregarded in the pursuit of a seeming methodological purity.

As the readings in the previous section demonstrate, the most important fact which must be understood about human behavior is that it includes an element which makes social knowledge different from other varieties of knowing. This is the subjective dimension or indeterminate equation. Many attempts, none successful in all respects, have been made to isolate the specific factors which make human behavior different qualitatively from the behavior of other living organisms. Probably the symbolic process holds the key to the difference, but most important for our purposes is simply to emphasize that the *fact* of qualitative difference must be taken for granted. Whatever the label applied— "purposeful," "motivated," "free"— the fact of the distinctive qualitative difference of human behavior sets the starting point for the reorientation of social science.

The reorientation of contemporary social science must proceed in full recognition of the ineluctable subjectivity of human experience and hence of the knowing enterprise as it involves social objects. We do not assume, to repeat, that a shift in method will solve all the empirical problems of the social sciences, but we reiterate that present intellectual fashions retard the progress of social research by discouraging reflection on exactly those aspects of the subject matter which most need attention. All the man-hours spent on irrelevant quantification, operational definition, and the like are hours not spent in reflection and research on the pressing problems set by the group nature of human living. The methodological foundations of social science are as yet mainly unformulated. Reflections on the implications of group life are still far from having accurately mapped the territory of human experience. Social inquiry has far to go before anything approaching a full understanding may be said to have been achieved.

But group nature and the subjective dimension of experience have set all manner of obstacles in the path of the social scientist. These are challenges, hard and stubborn ones, which must be met. But the purpose of this book is to remove an unnecessary obstacle—an inhibiting methodology—which has slowed the progress of the social sciences. The present social science orientation is positivistic in inclination, and this final section offers a critique of and an alternative to it. The definition of science posited by popular positivism identifies the aims of science as prediction and control. We may begin with some critical remarks on this definition.

The identification of the aims of science as prediction and control is erroneous as the following examples make clear. A sailor tossed about on a life raft may have a perfect knowledge of meteorology and thus be able to explain the typhoon without, as a drowning man, being able to do much to better his empirical situation. Political examples are also relevant on this point. A political scientist's informed critique of American policy in Vietnam, for instance, may be based upon a deep and penetrating knowledge of the situation in that unfortunate country and yet be devoid of policy suggestions. There is no reason to criticize the political scientist for not offering suggestions for control. The infinite number of variables involved in a complex social situation, the vested interests at stake, the limited power often available to advisers—these factors and others make any identification of science (which aims at understanding and control, involving a link of logical necessity) unwarranted.

The element of chance, unpredictability, or indeterminacy in human behavior has already been noted. This is due to the human ability to make self-indications, to mark out things and hence to manipulate them. The human ability to exercise choice does not rule out prediction and is not incompatible with determinism (choices are in a sense "caused"), but it is incompatible with predeterminism and with any attempt to forge a necessary link between science and prediction.

INTRODUCTION

Prediction is useful, and the limited prediction involved in testing hypotheses is certainly indispensable, but prediction *per se* is not a necessary part of the scientific enterprise. The aim of science is explanation, and while prediction and control are features of some research, the overriding purpose is understanding.

We may now sketch briefly our alternative conception of the philosophy of social science. As Dewey once remarked, at one time it was thought that reconstruction *in* philosophy would be enough, but later it was seen that reconstruction *of* philosophy was needed. That is, the traits which were undermining the enterprise were ingrained deeply enough to make their removal no easy task. Such a change in the orientation of a going concern would necessitate a major reworking of assumptions, practices, skills, and training. Yet nothing less than this is often demanded by the exigencies of many situations. In the case here under consideration, if the social sciences are to realize their promise as purveyors of knowledge about man and society, nothing less than such a major reconstruction seems to be called for by the present state of affairs.

Specification of the exact changes which are desirable in the focus, orientation, and practical arrangements of the social disciplines is a task clearly requiring a major treatise, or perhaps a series of them. Yet a brief enumeration of some of the general premises or working assumptions of reconstructed social sciences is possible. These principles admittedly are tentative and offer few precise suggestions as to how the needed revisions of theory and practice may be made, yet they may serve to indicate the main drift of reconstructionist thought. The philosophical foundations of the social sciences are mainly as yet unformulated, though beginnings of a systematic view can be found in the writings of such scholars as Robert Redfield, Alfred Schuetz, C. Wright Mills, and Kurt Riezler.

1. The first need of a reconstructed philosophy of social inquiry is a more flexible and open philosophical empiricism which will guide research in human behavior. Empiricism in the past has often evinced a healthy hostility to mysticism, obfuscation, supernaturalism, and non-experimental sources of evidence and authority, but it has committed sins of its own in constant attempts to force experience into prior categories drawn from a mechanistic or mechanical model. The positivist brand of empiricist metaphysics has especially been concerned with the reduction of all phenomena to mechanical or physical processes. Such an empiricism fails to do justice to the

richness of the empirical world and the qualities of human experience.

The failure of much of empirical philosophy to do justice to human experience has led to the revival of professedly trans-empirical philosophies and to the rise of subjectivist philosophies such as existentialism and phenomenology. As John Dewey once noted,

> Men who are balked of a legitimate realization of their subjectivity, men who are forced to confine innovating need and projection of ideas to technical modes . . . , and to specialized or 'scientific' fields of intellectual activity, will compensate by finding release within their inner consciousness. There will be one philosophy, a realistic one, for mathematics, physical science and the established social order; another, and opposed, philosophy for the affairs of personal life.[1]

Such a state of affairs has in effect come to pass, with empirical philosophy dominating the philosophy of science and mathematics, while its rivals can claim more genuine concern with the problems of man and hence can claim greater popular appeal. It would be too much to suggest that a reworking of empirical philosophy would of necessity heal the so-called division between "two cultures,"—the sciences and the humanities—but a revitalized empiricism could contribute powerfully to such an event.

A more flexible formulation would enable us to do justice to experience. As Walter Kaufman suggests in his stimulating book, *The Critique of Religion and Philosophy,* a sensible empiricism would avoid the pitfalls of an idealism which transcends evidence and of a positivism which empties experience of content. The empirical philosophy of the sort suggested could deal with the logic of inquiry in a more penetrating manner because of the firm grounding in an appraisal of the subject matter with which inquiry is concerned. The reason behind the failure of men previously attempting formalization of a philosophy of social science may be found in their avoidance of the distinctive traits of the "social."

2. The second needed component of a realistic logic of social inquiry would be a truly experimental and flexible attitude toward experience. The social sciences in their zeal for exactness and precision have often so over-formulated their requirements for research that many important problems could not really be dealt with at all

---

[1]John Dewey, *Experience and Nature* (New York: Dover, 1958), p. 241.

INTRODUCTION

within their methodological approach. A good example of this phenomenon may be found in the literature which has accumulated around C. Wright Mills' suggestion in his book *The Power Elite* that America is governed by a military-political industrial elite.

Charles H. Cooley, to make the point clearer, developed many of his stimulating ideas on the genesis of the self through observing his own children. The present overly formal approach to experimentation, which rules out much of experience in favor of utilizing only controlled situations that can easily be manipulated, must be eradicated. Any data, any situation, which might yield important information or theory for social science should be utilized to the utmost. To condemn any research which does not meet antecedent categories of methodological purity as "simply impressionistic" is to deprive social science of both meaningful data and the possibility of progress in theory. All this is not to suggest that the highest degree of precision possible should not be a goal, but simply to point out that there are other values which must be taken into account.

Experimentalism must be rescued from connotations of the laboratory, the white jacket, and the test-tube. John Dewey, to cite a pertinent example, did not have in mind such an uncritical emulation of the natural sciences when he indicated that the social sciences would progress only through becoming truly experimental. What he did mean was that social scientists should eschew armchair speculation in favor of action research. Participant observation, it might be suggested, is a good example of the less constrained notion of experimentation we have in mind. Experience must be met on its own terms. Refined models and simulated situations are in most cases not good enough, as the slow progress of the discipline of economics, which has been addicted to model-building, perhaps makes clear.

3. The third aspect of a reconstructed philosophy of social science would be a sensible and realistic approach to values. In the social sciences what *is* is inextricably bound up with what *should be.* It is possible to avoid rational consideration of values in social research, but it is not possible to banish the values themselves. Not only are values an integral part of the subject matter, but the process of evaluation is a necessary component of the logic of social inquiry. It is evaluation which determines the problems investigated in social research, in the sense that standards and values determine the understanding of our definition of situations. Judgments of value also determine which hypotheses or antecedent assumptions set the exact

framework of inquiry. And in the last analysis, values, together with the data which research accumulates, determine the conclusions to which we come.[2]

A philosophy of social science which ignores values on the surface as does contemporary positivism leaves those values imbedded in the foundations all the more secure and undisturbed. As a matter of fact, those who most ignore value considerations usually simply unreflectively repeat current evaluations. Presuppositions which are unrecognized and hence never reflectively analyzed, as Charles Beard once put it, are usually likely to be poor ones. The much vaunted value neutrality of contemporary positivist social science has nothing to do with any real quality of being *wertfrei*. Rather, so closely do positivist value assumptions mirror the "common sense" values of American society that, except to someone sensitive to the preconceptions of inquiry, they are often almost imperceptible. But the value premises are there and exercise close determination of the course of research.

Thus, the starting point of any fruitful reassessment of social philosophy, as Charles Beard pointed out in a striking series of essays as early as 1941,[3] must be a thorough-going reconsideration of values. That suggestion completes the triad of our position on the problem of reconstructing the philosophy of social science. A nonpositivist yet empirical social philosophy would be able to do justice to the subject matter. It would liberate experiment from self-imposed methodological inhibitions and make possible a sensible and realistic approach to the question of the place of values in the study of society. Such a logic of social inquiry would allow us to get down to the business at hand: the development of warranted knowledge about man in society.

[2] See Beck and Barak, "The Place of Values in the Study of Society," *op. cit.*
[3] See Charles A. Beard, *Public Policy and General Welfare* (New York: Farrar and Rinehart, 1941), chaps. 1–3.

HERBERT BLUMER*

WHAT IS WRONG WITH SOCIAL THEORY?[†]

My concern is limited to that form of social theory which stands or presumes to stand as a part of empirical science.[1]

The aim of theory in empirical science is to develop analytical schemes of the empirical world with which the given science is concerned. This is done by conceiving the world abstractly, that is in terms of classes of objects and of relations between such classes. Theoretical schemes are essentially proposals as to the nature of such classes and of their relations where this nature is problematic or unknown. Such proposals become guides to investigation to see

*Paper read at the annual meeting of the American Sociological Society, August, 1953.

†Reprinted by permission of *American Sociological Review*, Vol. 19, No. 1 (February 1954), pp. 3–10.

[1] There are two other legitimate and important kinds of social theory which I do not propose to assess. One of them seeks to develop a meaningful interpretation of the social world or of some significant part of it. Its aim is not to form scientific propositions but to outline and define life situations so that people may have a clearer understanding of their world, its possibilities of development, and the directions along which it may move. In every society, particularly in a changing society, there is a need for meaningful clarification of basic social values, social institutions, modes of living and social relations. This need cannot be met by empirical science, even though some help may be gained from analysis made by empirical science. Its effective fulfillment requires a sensitivity to new dispositions and an appreciation of new lines along which social life may take shape. Most social theory of the past and a great deal in the present is wittingly or unwittingly of this interpretative type. This type of social theory is important and stands in its own right.

A second type of theory might be termed "policy" theory. It is concerned with analyzing a given social situation, or social structure, or social action as a basis for policy or action. It might be an analysis of communist strategy and tactics, or of the conditions that sustain racial segregation in an American city, or of the power play in labor relations in mass production industry, or of the morale potential of an enemy country. Such theoretical analysis is not made in the interests of empirical science. Nor is it a mere application of scientific knowledge. Nor is it research inquiry in accordance with the canons of empirical science. The elements of its analysis and their relations have a nature given by the concrete situation and not by the methods or abstractions of empirical science. This form of social theorizing is of obvious importance.

whether they or their implications are true. Thus, theory exercises compelling influence on research—setting problems, staking out objects and leading inquiry into asserted relations. In turn, findings of fact test theories, and in suggesting new problems invite the formulation of new proposals. Theory, inquiry and empirical fact are interwoven in a texture of operation with theory guiding inquiry, inquiry seeking and isolating facts, and facts affecting theory. The fruitfulness of their interplay is the means by which an empirical science develops.

Compared with this brief sketch of theory in empirical science, social theory in general shows grave shortcomings. Its divorcement from the empirical world is glaring. To a preponderant extent it is compartmentalized into a world of its own, inside of which it feeds on itself. We usually localize it in separate courses and separate fields. For the most part it has its own literature. Its lifeline is primarily exegesis—a critical examination of prior theoretical schemes, the compounding of portions of them into new arrangements, the translation of old ideas into a new vocabulary, and the occasional addition of a new notion as a result of reflection on other theories. It is remarkably susceptible to the importation of schemes from outside its own empirical field, as in the case of the organic analogy, the evolutionary doctrine, physicalism, the instinct doctrine, behaviorism, psychoanalysis, and the doctrine of the conditioned reflex. Further, when applied to the empirical world social theory is primarily an interpretation which orders the world into its mold, not a studious cultivation of empirical facts to see if the theory fits. In terms of both origin and use social theory seems in general not to be geared into its empirical world.

Next, social theory is conspicuously defective in its guidance of research inquiry. It is rarely couched in such form as to facilitate or allow directed investigation to see whether it or its implications are true. Thus, it is gravely restricted in setting research problems, in suggesting kinds of empirical data to be sought, and in connecting these data to one another. Its divorcement from research is as great as its divorcement from its empirical world.

Finally, it benefits little from the vast and ever growing accumulation of "facts" that come from empirical observation and research inquiry. While this may be due to an intrinsic uselessness of such facts for theoretic purposes, it also may be due to deficiency in theory.

These three lines of deficiency in social theory suggest that all that is needed is to correct improper preoccupations and bad working practices in theorizing. We hear repeatedly recommendations and injunctions to this effect. Get social theorists to reduce drastically their preoccupation with the literature of social theory and instead get in touch with the empirical social world. Let them renounce their practice of taking in each other's washing and instead work with empirical data. Let them develop their own conceptual capital through the cultivation of their own empirical field instead of importing spurious currency from alien realms. Get them to abandon the practice of merely interpreting things to fit their theories and instead test their theories. Above all, get them to cast their theory into forms which are testable. Have them orient their theory to the vast bodies of accumulated research findings and develop theory in the light of such findings.

These are nice injunctions to which all of us would subscribe. They do have a limited order of merit. But they neither isolate the problem of what is basically wrong with social theory nor do they provide means of correcting the difficulties. The problem continues to remain in the wake of studies made with due respect to the injunctions. There have been and there are many able and conscientious people in our field, alone, who have sought and are seeking to develop social theory through careful, sometimes meticulous preoccupation with empirical data—Robert E. Park, W. I. Thomas, Florian Znaniecki, Edwin Sutherland, Stuart Dodd, E. W. Burgess, Samuel Stouffer, Paul Lazarsfeld, Robert Merton, Louis Wirth, Robin Williams, Robert Bales and dozens of others who equally merit mention. All of these people are empirically minded. All have sought in their respective ways to guide research by theory and to assess their theoretical propositions in the light of empirical data. Practically all of them are familiar with the textbook canons of empirical research. We cannot correctly accuse such people of indifference to the empirical world, or of procedural naivete, or of professional incompetence. Yet their theories and their work are held suspect and found wanting, some theories by some, other theories by others. Indeed, the criticisms and counter-criticisms directed to their respective work are severe and box the compass. It is obvious that we have to probe deeper than the level of the above injunctions.

In my judgment the appropriate line of probing is with regard to the concept. Theory is of value in empirical science only to the extent to which it connects fruitfully with the empirical world. Concepts are the means, and the only means of establishing such connection, for it is the concept that points to the empirical instances about which a theoretical proposal is made. If the concept is clear as to what it refers, then sure identification of the empirical instances may be made. With their identification, they can be studied carefully, used to test theoretical proposals and exploited for suggestions as to new proposals. Thus, with clear concepts theoretical statements can be brought into close and self-correcting relations with the empirical world. Contrariwise, vague concepts deter the identification of appropriate empirical instances, and obscure the detection of what is relevant in the empirical instances that are chosen. Thus, they block connection between theory and its empirical world and prevent their effective interplay.

A recognition of the crucial position of concepts in theory in empirical science does not mean that other matters are of no importance. Obviously, the significance of intellectual abilities in theorizing, such as originality and disciplined imagination, requires no highlighting. Similarly, techniques of study are of clear importance. Also, profound and brilliant thought, an arsenal of the most precise and ingenious instruments, and an extensive array of facts are meaningless in empirical science without the empirical relevance, guidance and analytical order that can come only through concepts. Since in empirical science everything depends on how fruitfully and faithfully thinking intertwines with the empirical world of study, and since concepts are the gateway to that world, the effective functioning of concepts is a matter of decisive importance.

Now, it should be evident that concepts in social theory are distressingly vague. Representative terms like mores, social institutions, attitudes, social class, value, cultural norm, personality, reference group, social structure, primary group, social process, social system, urbanization, assommodation, differential discrimination and social control do not discriminate cleanly their empirical instances. At best they allow only rough identification, and in what is so roughly identified they do not permit a determination of what is covered by the concept and what is not. Definitions which are provided to such terms are usually no clearer than the concepts which they seek to define. Careful scrutinizing of our concepts forces one to recognize that they rest on vague sense and not on precise specification of attributes. We see this in our common experience in explaining concepts to our students or outsiders. Formal definitions are of little use.

WHAT IS WRONG WITH SOCIAL THEORY? 197

Instead, if we are good teachers we seek to give the sense of the concept by the use of a few apt illustrations. This initial sense, in time, becomes entrenched through the sheer experience of sharing in a common universe of discourse. Our concepts come to be taken for granted on the basis of such a sense. It is such a sense and not precise specifications that guides us in our discipline in transactions with our empirical world.

This ambiguous nature of concepts is the basic deficiency in social theory. It hinders us in coming to close grips with our empirical world, for we are not sure what to grip. Our uncertainty as to what we are referring obstructs us from asking pertinent questions and setting relevant problems for research. The vague sense dulls our perception and thus vitiates directed empirical observation. It subjects our reflection on possible relations between concepts to wide bands of error. It encourages our theorizing to revolve in a separate world of its own with only a tenuous connection with the empirical world. It limits severely the clarification and growth that concepts may derive from the findings of research. It leads to the undisciplined theorizing that is bad theorizing.

If the crucial deficiency of social theory, and for that matter of our discipline, is the ambiguous nature of our concepts, why not proceed to make our concepts clear and definite? This is the nub of the problem. The question is how to do this. The possible lines of answer can be reduced a lot by recognizing that a great deal of endeavor, otherwise conscientious and zealous, does not touch the problem. The clarification of concepts is not achieved by introducing a new vocabulary of terms or substituting new terms—the task is not one of lexicography. It is not achieved by extensive reflection on theories to show their logical weaknesses and pitfalls. It is not accomplished by forming or importing new theories. It is not achieved by inventing new technical instruments or by improving the reliability of old techniques—such instruments and techniques are neutral to the concepts on behalf of which they may be used. The clarification of concepts does not come from piling up mountains of research findings. As just one illustration I would point to the hundreds of studies of attitudes and the thousands of items they have yielded; these thousands of items of finding have not contributed one iota of clarification to the concept of attitudes. By the same token, the mere extension of research in scope and direction does not offer in itself assurance of leading to clarification of concepts. These various lines of endeavor, as the results themselves seem abundantly to testify, do not meet the problem of the ambiguous concept.

The most serious attempts to grapple with this problem in our field take the form of developing fixed and specific procedures designed to isolate a stable and definitive empirical content, with this content constituting the definition or the reference of the concept. The better known of these attempts are the formation of operational definitions, the experimental construction of concepts, factorial analysis, the formation of deductive mathematical systems and, although slightly different, the construction of reliable quantitative indexes. Although these attempts vary as to the kind of specific procedure that is used, they are alike in that the procedure is designed to yield through repeated performances a stable and definitive finding. A definition of intelligence as being the intelligence quotient is a convenient illustration of what is common to these approaches. The intelligence quotient is a stable and discriminating finding that can be checked through a repetition of clearly specified procedures. Ignoring questions as to the differential merit and the differential level of penetration between these approaches, it would seem that in yielding a specific and discriminating content they are the answer to the problem of the ambiguous concept in social theory. Many hold that resolute employment of one or the other of these methods will yield definitive concepts with the consequence that theory can be applied decisively to the empirical world and tested effectively in research inquiry.

So far, the suitability of these precision endeavors to solving the problem of the ambiguous concept remains in the realm of claim and promise. They encounter three pronounced difficulties in striving to produce genuine concepts related to our empirical world.

First, insofar as the definitive empirical content that is isolated is regarded as constituting by itself the concept (as in the statement that, "X is the intelligence quotient") it is lacking in theoretic possibilities and cannot be regarded as yielding a genuine concept. It does not have the abstract character of a class with specifiable attributes. What is "intelligence quotient" as a class and what are its properties? While one can say that "intelligence quotient" is a class made up of a series of specific intelligence quotients, can one or does one point out common features of this series—features which, of course, would characterize the class? Until the specific instances of empirical content isolated by a given procedure are brought together in a class with common distinguishing features of content, no concept with theoretic character is formed. One cannot make proposals about the class or abstraction or relate it to other abstractions.

Second, insofar as the definitive empirical content that is isolated is regarded as qualifying something beyond itself (as in the statement that, "Intelligence is the intelligence quotient" wherein intelligence would now be conceived as including a variety of common sense references such as ability to solve business problems, plan campaigns, invent, exercise diplomatic ingenuity, etc.), the concept is constituted by this something which is beyond the definitive empirical content. But since this "something beyond" is not dealt with by the procedure yielding the definitive empirical content, the concept remains in the ambiguous position that originally set the problem. In other words, the concept continues to be constituted by general sense or understanding and not by specification.

Third, a pertinent question has to be faced as to the relation of the definitive empirical content that is isolated, to the empirical world that is the concern of the discipline. One has to have the possibilities of establishing the place and role of the specific content, in the empirical world in order for the empirical content to enter into theory about the world. A specific procedure may yield a stable finding, sometimes necessarily so by the internal mechanics of the procedure. Unless this finding is shown to have a relevant place in the empirical world under study, it has no value for theory. The showing of such relevancy is a critical difficulty confronting efforts to establish definitive concepts by isolating stable empirical contents through precise procedures. Incidentally, the establishment of such relevancy is not accomplished by making correlations. While classes of objects or items covered by concepts may be correlated, the mere establishment of correlations between items does not form concepts or, in other words, does not give an item as an instance of a class, a place or a function. Further, the relevance of an isolated empirical content to the empirical world is not established merely by using the concept to label given occurrences in that empirical world. This is a semantic pit into which scores of workers fall, particularly those working with operational definitions of concepts or with experimental construction of concepts. For example, a careful study of "morale" made in a restricted experiment may yield a stable finding; however, the mere fact that we customarily label many instances in our empirical world with the term, "morale," gives no assurance, whatsoever, that such an experimental construct of "morale" fits them. Such a relation has to be established and not presumed.

Perhaps these three difficulties I have mentioned may be successfully solved so that genuine definitive concepts of theoretic use can be formed out of the type of efforts I have been considering. There still remains what I am forced to recognize as the most important question of all, namely whether definitive concepts are suited to the study of our empirical social world. To pose such a question at this point seems to move in a reverse direction, to contradict all that I have said above about the logical need for definitive concepts to overcome the basic source of deficiency in social theory. Even though the question be heretical I do not see how it can be avoided. I wish to explain why the question is very much in order.

I think that thoughtful study shows conclusively that the concepts of our discipline are fundamentally sensitizing instruments. Hence, I call them "sensitizing concepts" and put them in contrast with definitive concepts such as I have been referring to in the foregoind discussion. A definitive concept refers precisely to what is common to a class of objects, by the aid of a clear definition in terms of attributes or fixed bench marks. This definition, or the bench marks, serve as a means of clearly identifying the individual instance of the class and the make-up of that instance that is covered by the concept. A sensitizing concept lacks such specification of attributes or bench marks and consequently it does not enable the user to move directly to the instance and its relevant content. Instead, it gives the user a general sense of reference and guidance in approaching empirical instances. Whereas definitive concepts provide prescriptions of what to see, sensitizing concepts merely suggest directions along which to look. The hundreds of our concepts—like culture, institutions, social structure, mores, and personality—are not definitive concepts but are sensitizing in nature. They lack precise reference and have no bench marks which allow a clean-cut identification of a specific instance and of its content. Instead, they rest on a general sense of what is relevant. There can scarcely be any dispute over this characterization.

Now, we should not assume too readily that our concepts are sensitizing and not definitive merely because of immaturity and lack of scientific sophistication. We should consider whether there are other reasons for this condition and ask particularly whether it is due to the nature of the empirical world which we are seeking to study and analyze.

I take it that the empirical world of our discipline is the natural social world of every-day experience. In this natural world every object of our consideration—whether a person, group, institution, practice or what not—has a distinctive, particular or unique character and lies in a context of a similar distinctive character. I think that it is this distinctive character of the empriical instance and of its setting which explains why our concepts are sensitizing and not definitive. In handling an empirical instance of a concept for purposes of study or analysis we do not, and apparently cannot meaningfully, confine our consideration of it strictly to what is covered by the abstract reference of the concept. We do not cleave aside what gives each instance its peculiar character and restrict ourselves to what it has in common with the other instances in the class covered by the concept. To the contrary, we seem forced to reach what is common by accepting and using what is distinctive to the given empirical instance. In other words, what is common (i.e. what the concept refers to) is expressed in a distinctive manner in each empirical instance and can be got at only by accepting and working through the distinctive expression. All of us recognize this when we commonly ask, for instance, what form does social structure take in a Chinese peasant community or in an American labor union, or how does assimilation take place in a Jewish rabbi from Poland or a peasant from Mexico. I believe that you will find that this is true in applying any of our concepts to our natural empirical world, whether it be social structure, assimilation, custom, institution, anomie, value, role, stratification or any of the other hundreds of our concepts. We recognize that what we are referring to by any given concept shapes up in a different way in each empirical instance. We have to accept, develop and use the distinctive expression in order to detect and study the common.

This apparent need of having to make one's study of what the concept refers to, by working with and through the distinctive or unique nature of the empirical instance, instead of casting this unique nature aside calls, seemingly by necessity, for a sensitizing concept. concept. Since the immediate data of observation in the form of the distinctive expression in the separate instances of study are different, in approaching the empirical instances one cannot rely on bench marks or fixed, objective traits of expression. Instead, the concept must guide one in developing a picture of the distinctive expression, as in studying the assimilation of the Jewish rabbi. One moves out from the concept to the concrete distinctiveness of the instance instead of embracing the instance in the abstract framework of the concept. This is a matter of filling out a new situation or of picking one's way in an unknown terrain. The concept sensitizes one to this task, providing clues and suggestions. If our empirical world presents itself in the form of distinctive and unique happenings or situations and if we seek through the direct study of this world to establish classes, we are, I think, forced to work with sensitizing concepts.

The point that I am considering may be put in another way, by stating that seemingly we have to *infer* that any given instance in our natural empirical world and its content are covered by one of our concepts. We have to make the inference from the concrete expression of the instance. Because of the varying nature of the concrete expression from instance to instance we have to rely, apparently, on general guides and not on fixed objective traits or modes of expression. To invert the matter, since what we infer does not express itself in the same fixed way, we are not able to rely on fixed objective expressions to make the inference.

Given current fashions of thought, a conclusion that concepts of social theory are intrinsically sensitizing and not definitive will be summarily dismissed as sheer nonsense by most people in our field. Others who are led to pause and give consideration to such a conclusion may be appropriately disquieted by what it implies. Does it mean that our field is to remain forever in its present state of vagueness and to forego the possibilities of improving its concepts, its propositions, its theory and its knowledge? This is not implied. Sensitizing concepts can be tested, improved and refined. Their validity can be assayed through careful study of empirical instances which they are presumed to cover. Relevant features of such instances, which one finds not be to covered adequately by what the concept asserts and implies, become the means of revising the concept. To be true, this is more difficult with sensitizing concepts than with definitive concepts precisely because one must work with variable instead of fixed forms of expression. Such greater difficulty does not preclude progressive refinement of sensitizing concepts through careful and imaginative study of the stubborn world to which such concepts are addressed. The concepts of assimilation and social disorganization, for instance, have gained more fitting abstraction and keener discrimination through insightful and realistic studies, such as those of W. I. Thomas and Robert E. Park. Actually, all that I am saying here is that careful and probing study of occurrences in our natural social world provide the means of bringing sensitizing concepts more and more in line with what such study reveals. In short, there is nothing esoteric or basically unusual in correcting and refining sensitizing concepts in the light of stubborn empirical findings.

It should be pointed out, also, that sensitizing concepts, even though they are grounded on sense instead of on explicit objective traits, can be formulated and communicated. This is done little by formal definition and certainly not by setting bench marks. It is accomplished instead by exposition which yields a meaningful picture, abetted by apt illustrations which enable one to grasp the reference in terms of one's own experience. This is how we come to see meaning and sense in our concepts. Such exposition, it should be added, may be good or poor—and by the same token it may be improved.

Deficiency in sensitizing concepts, then, is not inevitable nor irremediable. Indeed, the admitted deficiency in our concepts, which certainly are used these days as sensitizing concepts, is to be ascribed to inadequacy of study of the empirical instances to which they refer, and to inadequacy of their exposition. Inadequate study and poor exposition usually go together. The great vice, and the enormously widespread vice, in the use of sensitizing concepts is to take them for granted—to rest content with whatever element of plausibility they possess. Under such circumstances, the concept takes the form of a vague stereotype and it becomes only a device for ordering or arranging empirical instances. As such it is not tested and assayed against the empirical instances and thus forfeits the only means of its improvement as an analytical tool. But this merely indicates inadequate, slovenly or lazy work and need not be. If varied empirical instances are chosen for study, and if that study is careful, probing and imaginative, with an ever alert eye on whether, or how far, the concept fits, full means are provided for the progressive refinement of sensitizing concepts.

Enough has been said to set the problem of what is wrong with social theory. I have ignored a host of minor deficiencies or touched them only lightly. I have sought to pin-point the basic source of deficiency. This consists in the difficulty of bringing social theory into a close and self-correcting relation with its empirical world so that its proposals about that world can be tested, refined and enriched by the data of that world. This difficulty, in turn, centers in the concepts of theory, since the concept is the pivot of reference, or the gateway, to that world. Ambiguity in concepts blocks or frustrates contact with the empirical world and keeps theory apart in a corresponding unrealistic realm. Such a condition of ambiguity seems in general to be true of concepts of social theory.

How to correct this condition is the most important problem of our discipline insofar as we seek to develop it into an empirical science. A great part, if not most, of what we do these days does not touch the problem. Reflective cogitation on existing theory, the formulation of new theory, the execution of research without conceptual guidance or of research in which concepts are accepted uncritically, the amassing of quantities of disparate findings, and the devising and use of new technical instruments—all these detour around the problem.

It seems clear that there are two fundamental lines of attack on the problem. The first seeks to develop precise and fixed procedures that will yield a stable and definitive empirical content. It relies on neat and standardized techniques, on experimental arrangements, on mathematical categories. Its immediate world of data is not the natural social world of our experience but specialized abstractions out of it or substitutes for it. The aim is to return to the natural social world with definitive concepts based on precisely specified procedures. While such procedures may be useful and valuable in many ways, their ability to establish genuine concepts related to the natural world is confronted by three serious difficulties which so far have not been met successfully.

The other line of attack accepts our concepts as being intrinsically sensitizing and not definitive. It is spared the logical difficulties confronting the first line of attack but at the expense of forfeiting the achievement of definitive concepts with specific, objective bench marks. It seeks to improve concepts by naturalistic research,[2] that is by direct study of our natural social world wherein empirical instances are accepted in their concrete and distinctive form. It depends on faithful reportorial depiction of the instances and on analytical probing into their character. As such its procedure is markedly different from that employed in the effort to develop definitive concepts. Its success depends on patient, careful and imaginative life study, not on quick short-cuts or technical instruments. While its progress may

---

[2] I have not sought in this paper to deal with the logic of naturalistic research.

be slow and tedious, it has the virtue of remaining in close and continuing relations with the natural social world.

The opposition which I have sketched between these two modes of attack sets, I believe, the problem of how the basic deficiency of social theory is to be addressed. It also poses, I suspect, the primary line of issue in our discipline with regard to becoming an empirical science of our natural social world.

C. WRIGHT MILLS

TWO STYLES OF RESEARCH IN CURRENT SOCIAL STUDIES*

When in the course of our work we are uncertain, we sometimes become more concerned with our methods than with the content of our problems. We then try to clarify our conceptions and tighten our procedures. And as we re-examine studies that we feel have turned out well, we create conscious models of inquiry with which we try to guide our own work-in-progress.

It is in terms of these models that we sometimes gain that sense of craftsmanship that is one subjective yield of work well done.

Modern men have generally been happier in their sense of craftsmanship when they have felt that they were at least approximating the generalized model of the laboratory. "Every step in science," Charles Peirce wrote, "has been a lesson in logic." In our search for a general model of inquiry, we have usually seized upon the supposed Method of Physical Science, and we have often fetichized it.

In the sociological disciplines, this grateful acceptance of "Science" is often more formal than operative and always more ambiguous than clear-cut. As a going concern, in the social studies, scientific empiricism means many things, and there is no one accepted version, much less any systematic sue of any one model of science. The same work, admired by some as "great," is disparaged by others as "journalism." Professional expectations about method are quite confused, and our sense of craftsmanship may be realized in terms of quite different modes of inquiry.

There are, in fact, at least two working models of inquiry now available in current social studies, and accordingly two senses of craftsmanship in terms of which work is judged, and on the basis of which controversies over method occur.

*Reprinted by Permission of *Philosophy of Science*, Vol. 20, No. 4 (October 1953), pp. 266–275.

I

The first of these two research-ways might be called for macroscopic. It has a venerable history, reaching notable heights, for example, in the work of Weber and Ostrogorski, Marx and Bryce, Michels, Simmel and Mannheim. These men like to deal with total social structures in a comparative way; their scope is that of the world historian; they attempt to generalize types of historical phenomena, and in a systematic way, to connect the various institutional spheres of a society, and then relate them to prevailing types of men and women. How did the Crusades come about? Are Protestantism and the rise of capitalism related? If so, how? Why is there no socialist movement in the U. S.?

The other way of sociological research might be called the molecular. It is, at first glance, characterized by its usually small-scale problems and by its generally statistical models of verification. Why are 40 per cent more of the women who give marketing advice to their neighbors during a given week on a lower income level than those who gave it during another week? Molecular work has no illustrious antecedents, but, by virtue of historical accident and the unfortunate facts of research finance, has been developed a great deal from studies of marketing and problems connected with media of mass communication. Shying away from social philosophy, it often appears as technique and little else.

Everyone involved in the social studies will recognize these two styles, and by now, a good many will readily agree that "we ought to get the two together." Sometimes this program is put in terms of the statement that the sociologist's ideal task during the next decades is to unite the larger problems and theoretical work of the 19th century, especially that of the Germans, with the research techniques predominant in the 20th century, especially that of the Americans. Within this great dialectic, it is felt, signal and continuous advances in masterful conception and rigorous procedure will be made.

If we inquire more closely into just how the two research-ways differ, we find that there is sometimes a confusion of differences that are non-logical with those that are logical in character. This is revealed, for example, in statements of the difference between the two styles as a political and intellectual dilemma: the more socially or politically significant our problems and work (the more macroscopic), the less rigorous is our solution and the less certain our knowledge (the less molecular).

There is much social truth in such statements; as they have so far been used these two styles of thought do differ in their characteristic value-relevance and political orientation. But this does not mean that any political orientation is inherent in the logic of either style of thought. The evaluative choice of problems characteristic of each of the two methods has not been *necessarily* due to logical capabilities or limitations of either. Molecular work of great political relevance is logically possible; and macroscopic work is not necessarily of broad significance, as a glance at many "political science" monographs proves all too well. No, many of the differences between the two styles are not logical, but social.

From the standpoint of the individual researcher, the choice of problems in either sytle of work may be due to academic timidity, political disinterest, or even cowardice; but above all it is due to the institutional facts of the financial life of molecular research. Molecular work requires an organization of technicians and administrators, of equipment and money, and, as yet, of promoters. It can not proceed until agencies of research are sufficiently developed to provide detailed materials. It has arisen in definite institutional centers: in business, since the twenties among marketing agencies, and since the thirties, in the polling agencies; in academic life at two or three research bureaux; and in research branches of government. Since World War Two the pattern has spread, but these are still the centers.

This institutionalization of the molecular style has involved the applied focus, which has typically been upon specific problems, presented so as to make clear alternatives of practical—which is to say, pecuniary and administrative—action. It is *not* true that only as general principles are discovered can social science offer "sound practical guidance"; often the administrator needs to know certain detailed facts and relations, and that is all he needs to know.

The sociologist in the applied focus no longer addresses "the public"; more usually he has specific clients with particular interests and perplexities. This shift, from public to client, clearly destroys the idea of objectivity as aloofness, which perhaps meant responsiveness to vague, unfocused pressures, and thus rested more on the individual interests of the researcher. In applied research of the molecular style, the client's social operations and economic interests have often supplied the sometimes tacit but always present moral meaning and use to the problem and to its solution. This has meant that most molecular work of any scale has been socially guided by the concerns and worries set by practical government and business interests and has been responsible to them. Accordingly, there is little doubt that the applied focus has tended to lower the intellectucal initiative and to heighten the opportunism of the researcher. However technically free he may be, his initiative and interest are in fact usually subordinate to those of the client, whether it be the selling of pulp magazines or the administration of army's morale.

Very little except his own individual limitations has stood between the individual worker and macroscopic work of the highest order. But the rise of the molecular style means that the unattached man cannot pursue such research on any scale, for such work is dependent upon organization and money. If we would "solve" the problem raised by the coexistence of these two styles we must pay attention to the design of work that is possible for the unattached men who still comprise the bulk of those claiming membership in the sociological community.

The rise of applied molecular work, as it is now being organized, makes questions of moral and political policy of the social studies all the more urgent. As a bureaucratization of reflection, the molecular style is quite in line with dominant trends of modern social structure and its characteristic types of thought. I do not wish to consider these problems here except to say that they should not be confused with any differences of a logical character between the two styles of inquiry.

II

There are at least three relative differences of a logical sort between the macroscopic and the molecular styles of work as they are now practiced: the molecular is more objective; it is more open to cumulative development; and it is more open to statistical quantification.

Objectivity means that the work is so done and so presented that any other qualified person can repeat it, thus coming to the same results or showing that the results were mistaken. Subjectivity means the reverse, and thus that there is usually a persistent individual variation of procedure—and of solution. Under this difference lies the fact that when work is objective the procedures used are systematized or even codified and hence are available to any qualified operator; whereas in subjective work the procedures are often not systematized, much less standardized or codified.

This in turn means that in objective work there is a more distinct possibility of cumulation—or at least replication!—both in terms of empirical solutions and in terms of the procedures used. In the more subjective macroscopic work the sensitivity and talent of the individual worker weigh more heavily and although there may be those who "take up where he left off," this is usually a continuity of subject-matter, general ideas, and approach rather than an accumulation of procedure. It is possible within a few years to train competent persons to repeat a Sandusky job,[1] it is not so possible to train them to repeat a Middletown study. Another sample of soldiers in another war can be located on a morale scale and comparisons built up; Max Weber's analytic and historical essay on bureaucracy has not been repeated or checked in the same way, however much it has been criticized and "used." Macroscopic work has not experienced the sort of cumulative development that molecular work during the current generation of sociologists has.

It is descriptively true that the molecular style has been heavily statistical, whereas the macroscopic has not. This, again, is an aspect of the greater codification and the lower level of abstraction that molecular work entails. And it can be confidently supposed that as macroscopic work is made more systematic it will become more quantitative—at least as a general form of thought. For example, Darwin's *Origin* as well as many of Freud's theories are quantitative models of reflection.

Each of these three points is underpinned by the fact that molecular procedures can be, and have been, more explicitly codified than those of the macroscopic style; and by the fact that molecular terms are typically on a lower level of abstraction than most macroscopic conceptions.

Insofar as the logical differences between the two styles concern *procedures*, they are differences in the degree of systematic codification. Insofar as they involve *conceptions*, they are differences in level of abstraction.

III

When we say that molecular terms are on *lower* levels of abstraction we mean that they isolate from larger contexts a few precisely observed elements; in this sense they are of course quite abstract.

[1] Paul F. Lazarsfeld, et al., *The People's Choice* (New York: Duell, Sloan and Pearce, 1944).

When we say that macroscopic concepts are on *higher* levels of abstraction, we mean they they are more generalized, that the number of single variables which they cover are more numerous. The molecular term is narrow in scope, and specific in reference: it deals with a few discrete variables; the macroscopic researcher gains his broader scope by using concepts that cover, usually less specifically, a much larger number of variables.

There is no one clear-cut variable, the presence or absence of which allows application of the concept, "capitalism": under such concepts are not only high-level but their index structure is an elaborately compounded affair. Put technically, most big macroscopic concepts already have under them rather elaborate, and often unsystematic, cross-tabulations of several variables; most molecular terms stand for single variables useful for the stubs of such tables.

We can consider a term in its relation to some empirical item(s) —that is, its semantic dimension; and we can consider a term in its relation to other terms—that is, its syntactical dimension, or if you like, its conceptual implications.[2] It is characteristic of molecular terms that their semantic dimensions are pronounced, although syntactical relations may also be there. It is characteristic of macroscopic terms that their syntactical dimensions are pronounced, although semantical relations may also be available.

The higher macroscopic levels are more syntactically elaborate; semantically they involve a hierarchy of compounded indices pointing to whole gestalts of attributes. Macroscopic concepts are often sponge-like and unclarified in their semantic dimensions. Sometimes, in fact, they do not have any index structure that enables us to touch empirically observable facts or relations.[3] They have under them

---

[2] We can also consider it in relation to its users—the pragmatic dimension—which I am not here considering. These are the three dimensions of meaning which Charles M. Morris has systematized in his "Foundations of the Theory of Signs," International Encyclopedia of Unified Science, Volume I: Number 2. University of Chicago Press, 1938.

[3] To sort out the dimensions of a macroscopic concept requires us to elaborate it syntactically, while keeping our eyes open for semantic indices for each implication so elaborated. To translate each of these points into molecular terms requires us to trace the hierarchy of inference down to single, clear-cut variables. In assertions using macroscopic concepts, we must watch for whether or not the assertion (1) states a proposition, or (2) unlocks an implication. The guide-rule is whether the statement involves only one factor, then it simply "spells out" or specifies one of the conceptual implications of that one factor; its meaning is syntactical. If the assertion involves two factors, it may be a proposition, as statement of a relation which can be true or false; its meaning is semantical.

only a vague kind of many-dimensional indicator rather than an index. Yet, with all this, it may be that whether a statement is macroscopic or molecular is a matter of degree—a question of at what level we introduce our syntactical elaboration.

IV

Our choice of level of abstraction occurs, if I may simplify the matter, in at least two distinct junctions of our research act: The character and scope of the unit that we take as problematic, the what-is-to-be-explained;[4] and the model of explanation—the concepts we use in the solution of the problem.[5]

The grand tradition in social studies has been to state both problem and explanation in more or less macroscopic terms. In contrast, the *pure* molecular student goes through the whole research act on the molecular level. In the simplest scheme of observation and explanation are four possibilities:

Explanations	Observations To Be Explained:	
	Macroscopic	Molecular
Macroscopic	I	II
Molecular	III	IV

I. Both what is to be explained and its explanation can be on the macroscopic level. E.g.: Why do many people follow Hitler? Answer: Because in the bureaucratization of modern society, life-plans are taken over by centralized bureaucracies in such a way that when crises occur, people are disoriented and feel that they need guidance. Bu-

---

[4]In either style, one may of course start with a simple declaration of descriptive intent, finding more precisely-put problems as one goes along. In either style, too, the assembly of stray facts without any general significance or interconnection may be found; the new (molecular) ideography is no different in this respect from the older macroscopic kind. Both are composed of details not connected with any problem and entailing no evident syntactical implications.

[5]The difference here is not a difference in the general logic of explanation: in both styles of work a third factor (or fourth or fifth factor) is appealed to in the explanation of some relation observed.

The explanatory intent of the macroscopic style is to *locate* the behavior to be explained within a structural totality or a cultural milieu; it finds its explanation in this "meaningful location"—which means that it seeks to interpret in the terms of a highly intricate, inter-related complex of variables.

The explanatory intent of the molecular student is to break down the behavior of the individuals involved into component parts and to find the explanation in the association of further simplified attributes of these individuals.

reaucracy has thus resulted in a trained incapacity of people to steer themselves. In crises the bureaucratic routine that trained them is gone: they therefore follow Hitler. Etc.

II. When the problematic observations are molecular, but the explanation macroscopic, the question is thought to be too general and figures on the vote, pro-Hitler sentiment, and urban residence, for example, are taken as what is to be explained. Then they are explained macroscopically, although usually in a more modest way because of the molecular problem-setting. E.g.: The urban people were more disoriented and this in need of the image of a Father who would promise to plan their lives and take care of them. They therefore voted pro-Hitler. Etc.

III. The problematic observations may be macroscopic and the explanation molecular. Why do some people follow Hitler? Answer: We know that only 5 per cent of the population went to college: this is a fact pointing to social ignorance, which is further confirmed by the correlation of education and political information, revealed in all our polls. Ignorance, thus established, goes far to explain why some people follow Hitler. Etc.

IV. In this type of procedure, both phases are held to the molecular level. E.g.: The question is too general to be appropriately answered, it must be rephrased: 30 percent of the adult population voted for Hitler in a given election. Why? Answer: When we take into account the rural-urban distribution, the religious, and the income level of the population, we find that 80 per cent of the rural, Protestant, high income level voted pro-Hitler, only 15 per cent of the urban, Catholic, low income. These three factors in the combination indicated seem to explain something about why certain people voted pro-Hitler and others did not. Etc.[6]

Notice the following characteristics of these four models of thought:

The inadequacies of the purely macroscopic and the purely molecular (I and IV) are tied in with the fact that in both cases there is no shuttle between levels of abstraction. Since rigorous proof only exists empirically on the molecular levels, in the pure macroscopic there is no proved connection between problematic observation and explanation; when you are persuaded by such work, it is only because "it makes so much sense," it is syntactically convincing. On the

---

[6]All illustrative facts and figures in this paper are products of the imagination.

purely molecular level there is a connection proved between problematic observation and explanatory observation, yet here the larger implications and meaning of that association are neither explored nor explained. When you are unsatisfied with such work it is because, although it is "neat" and "ingenious," you feel "there is more to it all."

In procedures II and III there is a shuttle between the macroscopic and molecular levels but it does *not* occur in the same phase of the total research act: we do not move from macroscopic to molecular inside the problematic phase, and we do not do so inside the explanatory phase. This means that the problematic observation and the explanation are not logically connected.

When the problem is molecular and the explanation macroscopic (II), there is an error of *falsely concretizing a concept*: in explaining some molecular observation by appealing, *ad hoc*, to a macroscopic concept, that concept tends to be handled in discussion as if it were a definite variable statistically related to the molecular observation.

When the problem is macroscopic and the solution molecular (III), the error might be called *unduly stretching an index*: in explaining some macroscopic observation by appealing to a molecular variable, that variable is unduly generalized and handled in discussion as if it were a carefully built index. The molecular explanation is *imputed* to explain the macroscopic observation, not connected.[7]

What all this (II and III) amounts to is the use of statistics to illustrate general points, and the use of general points to illustrate statistics. The general points are not tested, nor necessarily enlarged; they are conveniently adapted to the figures, as the arrangement of figures are cleverly adapted to them. The general points and explanations can be used with other figures too; so can the figures be used with other points.

Perhaps there is nothing expecially wrong in all this; it is almost respectable procedure in some circles. But it does fall short of what is coming to be our vision of what social inquiry might be.

---

[7]In some research shops, the term "bright" is frequently applied when molecular facts or relations are cogently explained by macroscopic suppositions (II).

When further molecular variables, whose meaning is generalized very far—i.e., stretched—are brought in to explain, and they work, the result may be referred to as a "cute" table (III).

I mention this only to indicate that there is slowly emerging a shop language to cover the procedures I am trying to assert.

V

I have discussed these research-ways at length in order to be able to set forth an "ideal" procedure, which we can use as a sort of lordly measuring rod for any piece of work in current social studies. The inadequacies indicated above may be summarized in one positive statement: If our work is to be clarified, we must be able to shuttle between levels of abstraction *inside each phase* of our simplified two-step act of research. This, of course, is simply another way of referring to the problem of indices and their place in the research process. Examine this simplified chart:

	Problematic	Explanatory
Macroscopic	I	II
Molecular	III	IV

Only by moving grandly on the macroscopic level can we satisfy our intellectual and human curiosities. But only by moving minutely on the molecular level can our observations and explanations be adequately connected. So, if we would have our cake and eat it too, we must shuttle between macroscopic and molecular levels in instituting the problem *and* in explaining it—developing the molecular index structure of general concepts and the general conceptual implications of molecular variables. We move from macroscopic to molecular in both problem and in solution phase (I to III and II to IV); then we relate the two on the molecular level (III and IV); then we go back to the macroscopic (III to I and IV to II). After that we can speak cautiously (i.e., bearing in mind the shuttles made), of relations on the macroscopic level (I and II).

To illustrate these shuttles, we may now design one ideal way of asking and answering a general question: Why *do* some people follow Hitler?

First, we accept the question macroscopically, and without losing any of its intended meaning, break it into more manageable (molecular) parts: "following Hitler" means: Expressing pro-Hitler sentiments to an interviewer, consistently voting for him, going out on the street to demonstrate when he or his agents request it, urging others to follow Hitler. Etc.

Each individual in a cross-section of the population may be classified in terms of a table composed of such items, and the tables reduced to a scale of types. Thus we build an index for "following Hitler;" our observation of what-is-to-be-explained is molecularly translated: transparent and specific indices are available.

We also accept, as a rather complicated hypothesis, the macroscopic statements (A) that people follow Hitler because of an inability to plan their own life-ways, (B) that this inability has been trained into them by work and life in bureaucratic structures, (C) that it was the crises and collapse of these bureaucracies that precipitated their allegiance to Hitler, whom, (D) they see as the big planner of their little lives.

Now this is somewhat tangled, although ordering it into these four assertions helps some. We have set ourselves quite some work, in translating and interpreting molecularly each of the four parts of the hypothesis. To short-cut it: for (A) we develop an index for "inability to plan life-ways." Perhaps we ask each individual about details of his daily routine and his weekly and yearly cycle, scoring each detail as to its indication of ability or inability to plan. We also ask directly about the images or lack of them that they have about the future and their future, etc. Then we carefully relate these scores, and come out again with a scale of types: at one end are those most able to plan their life-ways, at the other end those least able.

Then we go to segment (B) of the hypothesis, building indices to work and leisure within bureaucracies. And so on, with (C) and (D).

Finally, we interrelate our molecular indices to all four features of our hypothesis, reduce them, and emerge with a master scale: at its top are people who seem unable to plan their own lives, have been duly exposed to and "trained" by bureaucracies,[8] who began to be pro-Hitler in the major crises in Weimar society, and who have an image of Hitler as an omnipotent regulator and giver of satisfactory life-plans.

Given the crude state of our empirical technique and the clumsiness of our index building, we would probably finish with five cases in our extreme types, but that in itself has no logical meaning: what we are doing is translating an elaborate macroscopic explanation into molecular terms, and this must be done if we are serious about relating problematic observation to explanation. If we have other macroscopic explanations we must handle them in the same way; in our design we must think through their index structure.

---

[8] For simplicity of presentation, I skip here the causal links between, e.g., B and A implied in the hypothesis.

Now we run our observations to be explained against our explanation, and this is what we obtain:

Observation of Hitler Sentiment	Predisposition According to Bureaucratic Hypothesis		
	High	Intermediate	Low
Pro-Hitler	80%	20%	5%
Intermediate	15	60	15
Anti-Hitler	5	20-	80
Total	100%	100%	100%

Maybe. But if so—

After controlling all the possible other variables we can think of, the reader might agree that we have earned the right to discuss, on the macroscopic level, bureaucracy, dictatorship and the character traits of modern mass-man. That is, to shuttle between macroscopic observations and macroscopic explanations.[9]

VI

Even this brief discussion of this sketchy model suggests general rules of procedure for interpenetrating more neatly molecular terms and macroscopic concepts. We must build up molecular terms; we must break down macroscopic conceptions. For, as matters now stand, the propositional meaning of many macroscopic statements is ambiguous and unclear; the conceptual meaning of many molecular statements is often barren.

Any macroscopic statement that makes sense *can be* reduced to a set of molecular assertions—by untangling its dimensions and clarifying the index structure of each of them. Any molecular statement can presumably be built up to macroscopic levels of abstraction—by combining it with other molecular indices and elaborating it syntactically—although many of them are probably not worth it, except as a formal exercise in ingenuity.

Every macroscopic study runs the risk of being confused by the wealth of materials that come into its scope. In order to decrease the chance of ambiguity in the semantic dimension of macroscopic con-

[9] Of course, by the time we had gone through the three steps outlined, surely Hitler would have us in his clutches; but that is an irrelevant incident, and of no concern or consequence to the *designer* and methodologist of research, however inconvenient it might be to the research worker.

ceptions, we must strain towards a clarification of their index structure and, while making them as clear as possible, we must work towards an increased codification of how we are using them.

Every molecular study involves a series of guesses about the important variables that may characterize and explain a phenomena. In order to increase the chance that our focus will be upon key variables, we must strain towards possible levels of macroscopic concepts in our molecular work, but not stretch indices of explanatory variables, or at least do so only with an awareness of our speculative posture.

The sociological enterprise requires macroscopic researchers to imagineer more technically, as well as with scope and insight; it requires technicians to go about their work with more imaginative concern for macroscopic meaning, as well as with technical ingenuity. Perhaps we cannot hope, except in rare instances, to have combined in one man all the skills and capacities required. We must proceed by means of a division of labor that is self-guided, in each of its divisions, by an understanding of and a working agreement upon a grand model. When as individuals we specialize in one or the other phases of this model, we must do so with a clear consciousness of the place of that phase within the model, and thus perform our specialist role in a manner most likely to aid another specialist in the architectonic endeavor. The development of such clear consciousness, in fact, is the complete and healthy significance of discussions of the method of the social studies.

ROBERT REDFIELD[1]

THE ART OF SOCIAL SCIENCE*

A dozen years ago I was a member of a committee of social scientists on social science method charged to appraise some outstanding published works of social science research. Our task was to find some good publications of social science research and then to discover in what their methodological virtue consisted. The first part of our task we passed on to the communities of social scientists themselves. We asked economists to name some outstanding work in their field, sociologists to pick a work in sociology, etc. We limited the choice to publications by living social scientists. Of the books or monographs that received the greatest number of nominations, three were then subjected to analysis and discussion. I participated in the study of the methodological virtues of *The Polish Peasant* by Thomas and Znaniecki and of Webb's *The Great Plains*. These were books nominated by sociologists and historians, respectively, as outstanding in merit.

A curious thing happened. Herbert Blumer, who analyzed *The Polish Peasant* for the committee, came to the conclusion that the method in that book was really unsuccessful because the general propositions set forth in the work could not be established by the particular facts adduced. The committee had to agree. Yet it remained with the impression that this was a very distinguished and important work. Webb's history of cultural transformation in the American West fared no better at the hands of the young historian who analyzed that work. He pointed out many undeniable failures of the author of *The Great Plains* to use and to interpret fully some of the evidence. And yet again a majority of the committee persisted in the impression that Webb's book was truly stimulating, original, and praiseworthy.

[1] A lecture delivered at the University of Chicago in May, 1948.
*Reprinted by permission of The American Journal of Sociology, Vol. LIV, No. 3 (November 1948), pp. 181–190.

Of course one does not conclude from this experience that the failure of facts to support hypotheses, in whole or in part, is a virtue in social science or is to be recommended. No doubt these books would have been more highly praised had these defects been proved to be absent. But does not the experience suggest that there is something in social science which is good, perhaps essential, apart from success with formal method; that these works have virtues not wholly dependent on the degree of success demonstrated in performing specified and formalized operations on restricted and precisely identified data?

I recall a comment I heard made by a distinguished social scientist whom I shall call A, about another distinguished social scientist whom I shall call B. A said of B: "He is very successful in spite of his method." Now, A was one who laid great stress on the obedience of the research worker to precise methods of operation with limited data, whereas B was much less so concerned. Yet A admired B, and the success he recognized in B was not worldly success but success in advancing our understanding and our control of man in society. Perhaps A felt that B's success was troubling to A's own views as to the importance of formal method. But A, a generous and able man, recognized something of virtue in B as a great student of man in society—a something other than methodological excellence.

What is that something? In attempting an answer here, I do not propose a separation between two ways of working in the scientific study of society. Nor do I deny that social science is dependent upon formal method. I seek rather to direct attention to an aspect of fruitful work in social science which is called for, in addition to formal method, if social science is to be most productive.

Let us here try to find out something about the nature of this non-formal aspect of social science through a consideration of three books about society that have long been recognized as important, influential, and meritorious: De Tocqueville's *Democracy in America,* Sumner's *Folkways,* and Veblen's *The Theory of the Leisure Class.* For from almost fifty to a hundred years these books have interested and have influenced many kinds of social scientists. Veblen and Sumner were economists, but the books they wrote are important for sociologists, anthropologists, historians, and other kinds of social scientists. De Tocqueville's book is a work interesting to political scientists as well as to historians of America, but it is quite as much a work in sociology, for De Tocqueville was concerned not so much in reporting what went on in the United States in 1830 as he was in defining a sort of natural societal type: the democratic society, including in the type not merely its political institutions but also its moral, familial, and "cultural" institutions and attitudes, treated as a single whole.

None of these books tells very much about research method, in the sense of teaching special procedures of operation with certain kinds of data. There is nothing in any of them about kinship genealogies, or sampling, or guided interviews, or margins of error. There is nowhere in them any procedure, any kind of operation upon facts to reach conclusions which might not occur to any intelligent and generally educated person. Sumner made notes on the customs of exotic peoples as he read about them. Veblen's methods as represented in *The Theory of the Leisure Class*, are no more formal than Sumner's. The factual substance of De Tocqueville's book is the record of his own observations as he traveled about America looking at what there was about him and talking to the people he met. If these books have merit, it is not by reason of any inventions or devices of method, for they exhibit none. Yet these are books which have for many years profoundly affected the course of social science and have contributed to our understanding of man in society. They might be even more important if they also made contributions to or through formal method, but, as they do not, something may be learned from them about that part of the study of society which is not formal method.

Perhaps these are not works of research. Perhaps for some "research" always means special procedures of operation which have to be learned or means analysis of some small set of facts or very limited problem. If this is your view of research, I shall not dispute it. Then the three books are not works of research. But what is there in them that is admired and that is valuable in the study of man in society that is not dependent upon formal method?

If these three classic books are not books in social science, what are they? They are surely not novels, or journalism, or yet belles-lettres. That they have qualities of literary style is true—and is not to be deplored—even Sumner's book impresses with the effective iteration of its terse, stark sentences. But the value of these books for the student of society lies not in any appeal they make to aesthetic sensibilities but for the illumination they throw upon man's nature or upon the nature of society. It is true that great novels do that too. But there are, of course, important differences between the books named, on the one hand, and, let us say, *War and Peace* and *The Remembrance of Things Past,* on the other. These last are works for social scientists to know about and to learn from, but they are not works of social science. They are not because neither Proust's book nor Tolstoi's is a generalized description of the nature of society stated at some remove from the personal experiences of the writer. De Tocqueville made his own observations, but he stated his results objectively in generalized and analytical terms making comparisons with other observations and conclusions easy. Tolstoi wrote about a real Russia during the real Napoleonic Wars, but his Pierres and Natashas are imagined, individual, personal, intimate, and ungeneralized. It is not difficult to distinguish the great analyses of society, as objectively studied and presented in generalized conclusions, from the works of personal record and of freely creative imagination.

Are the three books "objective" descriptions of society? In varying degree, but all three to some degree. Probably De Tocqueville, who of the three writers was least a professional social scientist, impresses one most with an air of severe detachment, of willingness to look at this social being, a democratic society, without blame or praise. De Tocqueville's work seems as objective as a social scientist might wish. Sumner, too, is describing, not evaluating, yet there is in the *Folkways* an undertone of patient scorn for the irrationality of man, for man's obedience to whatever folly his tradition may decree. Veblen seems the least objective. Below the forms of scientific analysis lies, urbanely and ironically disguised, the condemnation of a moralist. As a recent writer on Veblen has put it, he used "the realistic paraphernalia of scholarship" to attack the morality of capitalistic society.[2] Nevertheless, even Veblen's book presents a fresh description of a part of modern society, and the description is not that of a creative artist but of one who is responsible to facts studied and facts verifiable.

The three books are works which are not novels, which do not have much to say about formal procedures of research, and which, nevertheless, throw light upon man in society through the more or less objective presentation of generalized conclusions from the study of particular societies. In these respects they correspond with what

---

[2] Daniel Aaron, "Thorstein Veblen—Moralist," *Antioch Review,* VII, No. 3 (fall, 1947), 390.

is by at least some people called "scientific." What did the authors do that constitutes their contribution to the understanding of man in society?

It is surely not that these writers have been proved to be invariably right. Indeed, in each case there are points in which in the later days they have been found wrong. Veblen's account overemphasizes competitiveness in terms of consumption and accepts a good deal of what was then current as to race and as to stages of social evolution which is not inacceptable today. Sumner's conception of the mores, immensely stimulating as it was, exaggerates the helplessness of men before tradition and is especially inadequate as a concept for understanding modern societies—as Myrdal has recently shown. And, although De Tocqueville's account of early American society is perceptive and revealing to a degree that is almost miraculous, there is certainly confusion in it between what is necessarily democratic and what is characteristic of the frontier and between what must be characteristic of any democracy and what happened to be in the Anglo-American tradition.

In three respects these books, which have nothing to teach about formal method, make great contributions to the understanding of man in society.

In the first place, each is an expression of some perception of human nature. In each case the writer has looked at people in a society, or in many societies, and has directly apprehended something about their ways of thinking and feeling which are characteristic of the human race under those particular circumstances. His central concern has not been some second- or third-hand index or sign of human nature, some check marks on a schedule or some numbered quantities of anything. He has looked at people with the vision of his own humanity.

Not all of what is called social science is concerned with human nature. The study of population is not concerned with it until matters of population policy are reached. Marginal analysis in economics is concerned with such a slender sliver of human nature, so artificially severed from the rest, that it, too, is unrepresentative of studies of human nature. And this is also of necessity true of much of the archeology of the North American Indian.

These last-mentioned kinds of investigation, worthy as they are, are the special or marginal cases that mark the outskirts of the study of man in society. The essential nature of man in society is his human nature and the expressions of that human nature in particular institutions. To find out the nature and significance of human nature there is no substitute for the human nature of the student himself. He must use his own humanity to understand humanity. To understand alien institutions, he must try to see in them the correspondences and the divergences they exhibit in relation to the institutions with which he is more closely familiar. To understand an alien culture, it is not, first of all, necessary to learn how to interview or how to make schedules for a house-to-house canvass, useful as these skills are. It is first needful to have experienced some culture—some culture which will serve as the touchstone in apprehending this new one.

One aspect of the great merit of the three works mentioned lies in the central attention directed by Sumner, Veblen, and De Tocqueville to the humanity of their subject matter and in the success each had in apprehending the particular facet of that humanity as it was shaped and conditioned by the surrounding circumstances. Sumner, looking especially at small, long-isolated societies or at the later little-changing societies derived from primitive conditions, saw the resulting creation, in each individual there born and reared, of motives and designs of life that were there, in the customs of that society, before him. He saw in human nature the extraordinary malleability of human nature and the precedence of custom over habit. Veblen looked freshly at the behavior of consumers, saw them as people who actually do buy and consume, in their families and their communities, and recognized theretofore insufficiently recognized aspects of human nature in society. De Tocqueville touched Americans in their age of self-confidence and in a great number of true perceptions saw what their behavior meant to them and why. Just compare his success in using his own humanity with imagination, and yet with detachment, with Mrs. Trollope's failure to achieve understanding of these same people.

It is at this point that the methods of the social sciences—now using "method" in its broadest sense to include all the ways of thinking and even feeling about subject matter—approach the methods of the creative artist. Like the novelist, the scientific student of society must project the sympathetic understanding which he has of people with motives, desires, and moral judgments into the subject he is treating. Neither the one nor the other can get along without this gift, this means of understanding. But whereas the novelist may let his imagination run freely, once it is stimulated by personal experience and reading, the scientific student must constantly return to the particular men, the particular societies, he has chosen to investigate, test his insights by these, and report these particular facts with such specificity that his successor may repeat the testing. In spite of this all-important difference, the territories of the humanities and of the scientific study of man in society are in part the same. The subject matter of both is, centrally, man as a human being. Human beings are not the subject matter of physics and chemistry. So it would be error to build a social science upon the image of physics or chemistry. Social science is neither the same as the humanities nor the same as the physical sciences. It is a way of learning about man in society which uses the precise procedures and the objectivity characteristic of physics as far as these will helpfully go in studying human beings but no further; and which uses, indispensably, that personal direct apprehension of the human qualities of behavior and of institutions which is shared by the novelist.

A second observation may be made about the three books chosen. Each brings forward significant generalizations. In the case of Veblen's book, the general conceptions that are known by the phrases "pecuniary emulation," "vicarious consumption," etc., are, like the concepts in *Folkways*, names for new insights into persistent and widely inclusive aspects of man's nature in society. In reading these books, we catch a glimpse of the eternal in the light of the ephemeral. We see ourselves as exemplifications of patterns in nature. Social science is concerned with uniformities. The uniformities are exaggerated; they transcend the particularity of real experience and historic event; they claim more than each fact by itself would allow; they say: "If it were really like this, this would be the pattern." De Tocqueville, too, offers such patterns that go beyond the particular facts. Indeed, the case of De Tocqueville is particularly plain in this connection, for so interested is he in presenting a system of coherent generalizations as to the necessary nature of democratic society that in many passages he makes no reference at all to what he saw in the United States but derives one generalization as to the democratic society he conceives from some other generalization already brought forward. He is not, therefore, to be rejected as a contributor to the scientific understanding of society, for these deductions are tied to generalizations that in turn rest upon many particular observations of many particular men and events. The concept, like the novel, is a work of creative imagination but a work more closely and publicly bound to particular facts of observation and record.

Like the apprehension of the humanly significant, the making of the generalization is a work of imagination. Sumner did not find out that there is such a thing as the mores by learning and applying some method of research. He discovered it by watching the people around him and by using the observations recorded by other men and then by making a leap of thought across many diversities to apprehend the degree of uniformity that deserves the term "mores." In the reaching of a significant generalization as to man in society there is an exercise of a gift of apprehension so personal and so subtly creative that it cannot be expected to result merely from application of some formal method of research.

The three books show thinkers about man in society who have had some new and generalized apprehension of human nature or of human institutions. They have succeeded in communicating this apprehension in such a way as to show it to be both important and true. It is true in the sense that there are facts accessible that support it. It is not, of course, all the truth, and it may be that some other apprehension will come to appear "more true," that is, even more illuminating, as applied to some set of circumstances.

There is another quality in the thinking and the creating of the three writers that deserves recognition by itself: the freshness and independence of viewpoint with which each looked at his subject matter. One feels, in reading any one of the three books, how the writer saw what he saw with his own eyes, as if the previous views of it were suspect, just because they were previous. One feels in the case of each writer a discontent with the way some aspect of man in society was then being regarded, a clear-headed willfulness to take another look for himself. There is a disposition to make the thing looked at a true part of the viewer's own being, to go beyond obedience to the existing writings on the subject. De Tocqueville was dissatisfied with the views of democracy current in his time: the passionate condemnations or the equally passionate espousals. He would go to the country where the angel or the monster was actually in course of development, and he would, he resolved coolly, look for neither monster nor angel; he would look at what he should find, and grasp it, in its whole and natural condition, as one would look at a newly arrived class of animal. He could weigh the good and the bad, then, after he had come to understand the natural circumstances that would produce the creature. Sumner's book is in one way a reaffirmation of a viewpoint then current and in another way a reaction against it. As the folkways come about by no man's planning but through the accidental interactions of men and the competition of alternative solutions, they are consistent with that conception of unrestrained individualistic competition which Sumner supported in the economic sphere. On the other hand, the *Folkways* reads as a reaction against the Age of Reason. It seems to say that men do not, after all, solve their problems by rational calculation of utilities. Looked at anew, the ways of men appear not reasonable but unreasonable and determined by pre-existing customs and moral judgments which make the calculation of utilities seem absurd. From this point of view the book is an act of rebellion. An economist looks for himself at the whole human scene and says, too emphatically, no doubt, what needs to be said to correct the preceding vision. Something not so different could be said about the fresh look that Veblen took.

It may be objected that the qualities in these three works are qualities one may expect to find only in an occasional book written by some unusual mind. These books have passed beyond social science, or they fall short of it; and the humbler toiler in the vineyard cannot expect to learn from them anything that would help him in tending the vines of his more limited hypotheses or in pressing the wine of his more restricted conclusions.

Yet all three of the qualities found in these works may be emulated by the student of any human aspect of man in society. It is not only in good major works that there is found that human sympathy which is needful in apprehending a human reality. The exercise of this capacity is demanded in every study of a community; it is exacted in every consideration of an institution in which men with motives and desires like our own fulfil the roles and offices that make it up; it is required in every interview. One may be taught how to pursue a course of questioning, how to map a neighborhood, or how to tabulate and treat statistically the votes cast in an election; but to know how to do these things is not to be assured of meaningful conclusions. Besides these skills, one needs also the ability to enter imaginatively, boldly, and, at the same time, self-critically into that little fraction of the human comedy with which one has become scientifically concerned. One must become a part of the human relations one studies, while holding one's self also a little to one side, so as to suspend judgment as to the worth of one's first insight. Then one looks at the scene again; perhaps, guided by something one has known or read of human beings in some comparable situation, in some other place or age, one may get a second insight that better withstands reëxamination and the test of particular observations. This procedure, call it method, non-method, or what you will, is an essential part of most of social science, great and small.

As for the exercise of the ability to see the general in the particular, is this not also demanded of anyone who takes a scientific attitude toward anything in human nature or society? We are not freed from the obligation to look for what may be widely true by the narrowness, in time and space, of the facts before us. Surely Sumner did not wait to conceive of the mores until he had piled up those five hundred pages of examples. Malinowski provided a clearer understanding of the nature of myth, in its resemblance to and its difference from folk tale, from the view he had of the stories told and the ways they were told in a small community in the South Seas. Webb, a historian rather than one of those students of society who more easily announce generalizations thought to be widely applicable, does not, in his *The Great Plains,* announce any; but the value of the work lies for many in the fact that it is easily read as an exemplification of the tendency of institutions adjusted to one environment to undergo change when imported into a new and of the effects of changes in technology upon human relations. The social scientist is always called upon to use his imagination as to the general that may lie within the immediate particulars. The formal method may lead him to these generalizations; after he has added up the cases, or completed the tests, he may for the first time see some correspondences that suggest a generalization. But it happens at least as often that he sees the generalization long before the formal methods have been carried out; the exercise of the formal method may then test the worth of his insight. And a significant generalization may appear without formal method. The conceptions of marginal utility in economics and of the marginal man in sociology perhaps illustrate the development of a concept, on the one hand, with close dependence upon formal method and, on the other, without such dependence. In the latter case Park was struck by resemblances in the conduct of particular men and women whom he met, American Negroes, mission-educated Orientals, and second-generation immigrants: humane insight, guided by scientific imagination, then created the concept.

The third quality of good social science in its less formal aspects is freshness of vision. It is the looking at what one is studying as if the world's comprehension of it depended solely on one's own look. In taking such a look, one does not ignore the views that other men have taken of the subject matter or of similar subject matter. But these earlier views are challenged. Maybe, one says, it is not as my teachers told me I should find it. I will look for myself. One has perhaps heard something about folk society. But at this particular society with which I am concerned I will look for myself. Perhaps there is no folk society there. Perhaps there is something else, much nearer the truth.

It is difficult for teachers who have expounded their own views of some aspect of man in society to teach their successors to take some other view of it. Perhaps it cannot be taught. Yet somehow each generation of social scientists must rear a following generation of rebels. Now rebellion is not well inculcated in the teaching of formal procedure. Indeed, an exclusive emphasis on formal procedure may cause atrophy of the scientific imagination. To train a man to perform a technique may result in making him satisfied with mastery of the technique. Having learned so much about field procedure, or statistics, or the situations in which interviews are held and recorded, or the criticism of documents, the new social scientist may come to feel that he has accomplished all the learning he needs. He may rest content in proficiency. Proficiency is excellent, but it must be combined with an imaginative dissatisfaction. In little investigations as in large ones, the situation studied demands a whole look and a free look.

It is equally doubtful whether one can give instruction in the exercise of humane insight or in recognizing the general in the particular when the generality is not thrust upon the student by a marked statistical predominance. These are qualities of the social science investigator that perhaps depend upon the accidents of natural endowment. Humane insight is a gift. The concept is a work of creative imagination; apprehension is a gift. In stressing the necessity, in good social science, for the investigator to think and to speculate independently and freely, in emphasizing the reliance of good social science upon the personal and human qualities of the investigator, one seems to be talking not about a science but about an art and to be saying that social science is also an art. It is an art in that the social scientist creates imaginatively out of his own human qualities brought into connection with the facts before him. It is an art in degree much greater than that in which physics and chemistry are arts, for the student of the atom or of the element is not required, when he confronts his subject matter, to become a person among persons, a creature of tradition and attitude in a community that exists in tradition and in attitude. With half his being the social scientist approaches his subject matter with a detachment he shares with the physicist. With the other half he approaches it with a human sympathy which he shares with the novelist. And it is an art to a greater degree than is physics or chemistry for the further reason that the relationships among the parts of a person or of a society are, as compared with physical relationships, much less susceptible of definitions, clear and machine precise. In spite of the great advances in formal method in social science, much of the understanding of persisting and general relationships depends upon a grasp that is intuitive and that is independent of or not fully dependent on some formal method. In advancing social science, we invent and practice techniques, and we also cultivate a humanistic art.

The nature of social science is double. In the circle of learning, its place adjoins the natural sciences, on the one hand, and the humanities, on the other. It is not a result of exceptional political ambition that political scientists and anthropologists are to be found included both in the Social Science Research Council and in the American Council of Learned Societies; it is a recognition of the double nature of social science. On the one hand, the student of society is called upon to apprehend the significant general characteristics of human beings with something of the same human insight which is practiced by a novelist or a dramatist. On the other hand, he is obliged to make his observations and his inferences as precise and as testable, and his generalizations as explicit and as compendious, as the examples of the natural sciences suggest and as his own different materials allow.

It is the example of the natural sciences which social scientists have on the whole striven to imitate. In the short history of social science its practitioners have turned their admiring gazes toward their neighbors on the scientific side. They have looked that way, perhaps, because the natural sciences were the current success. They have looked that way, surely, because when the students of human nature in society came to think of themselves as representing one or more disciplines, with professors and places in universities and in national councils, social science was not very scientific: it was speculative and imprecise. To achieve identity, it had to grow away from the making of personally conceived systems of abstract thought. It had to learn to build, a brick at a time, and to develop procedures that would make the building public and subject to testing. But now the invention and the teaching of special procedures have received too exclusive an emphasis in the doing of social science and in the making of social scientists. In places the invention and the teaching of special procedures have gone ahead of the possibility of finding out anything very significant with their aid. It is certainly desirable to be precise, but it is quite as needful to be precise about something worth knowing. It is good to teach men and women who are to be social scientists how to use the instruments of observation and analysis that have been developed in their disciplines. But it is not good to neglect that other equally important side of social science.

To identify social science very closely with the physical sciences is to take one view of the education of social scientists: to think of that education chiefly in terms of formal method and formal knowledge of society already achieved and to be taught. Then programs for making social scientists will be made up of training in techniques and the opportunity to take part in some kind of research in which the procedures are already determined and the problems set by some established master. Then the holder of a fellowship will go to a school, where a way of working is well known and well fixed, and he will acquire the procedural competences taught at that school.

If this is all we do for young students of society, we are likely to have proficient technicians, but we are not likely to have great social scientists or to have many books written that are as illuminating and as influential as those by Sumner, Veblen, and De Tocqueville.

It would be well to give some attention to the humanistic aspect of social science. Part of the preparation of good social scientists is humanistic education. As what is called general education, or liberal education, is largely humanistic, it follows that the social scientist has two interests in liberal education. Like the physicist, like everybody else, the social scientist needs liberal education in his role as a citizen. But, in addition, he needs liberal humanistic education in his role as a social scientist.

The art of social science cannot be inculcated, but, like other arts, it can be encouraged to develop. The exercise of that art can be favored by humanistic education. If the social scientist is to apprehend, deeply and widely and correctly, persons and societies and cultures, then he needs experience, direct or vicarious, with persons, societies, and cultures. This experience is partly had through acquaintance with history, literature, biography, and ethnography. And if philosophy gives some experience in the art of formulating and in thinking about widely inclusive generalizations, then the social scientist needs acquaintance with philosophy. There is no longer any need to be fearful about philosophy. The time when young social science was struggling to make itself something different from philosophy is past. Now social science is something different. Now social scientists need to learn from philosophy, not to become philosophers, but to become better social scientists. The acquaintance with literature, biography, ethnography, and philosophy which is gained in that general education given in high schools and colleges is probably not rich enough or deep enough for some of those who are to become social scientists. The opportunities for advanced education given to some who appear to have exceptional gifts as students of man in society may well consist of the study of Chinese or East Indian culture, or of the novel in Western literature, or of the history of democracy.

The humanistic aspect of social science is the aspect of it that is today not well appreciated. Social science is essentially scientific in that its propositions describe, in general terms, natural phenomena; in that it returns again and again to special experience to verify and to modify these propositions. It tells what is, not what ought to be. It investigates nature. It strives for objectivity, accuracy, compendency. It employs hypotheses and formal evidence; it values negative cases; and, when it finds a hypothesis to be unsupported by the facts, it drops it for some other which is. But these are all aspects of social science so well known that it is tedious to list them again. What is less familiar, but equally true, is that to create the hypothesis, to reach the conclusion, to get, often, the very first real datum as to what are A's motives or what is the meaning of this odd custom or that too-familiar institution, requires on the part of one who studies persons and societies, and not rocks or proteins, a truly humanistic and freely imaginative insight into people, their conventions and interests and motives, and that this requirement in the social scientist calls for gifts and for a kind of education different from that required of any physicist and very similar to what is called for in a creative artist.

If this be seen, it may also be seen that the function of social science in our society is a double function. Social science is customarily explained and justified by reason of what social science contributes to the solution of particular problems that arise in the management of our society, as a help in getting particular things done. As social scientists we take satisfaction in the fact that today, as compared with thirty years ago, social scientists are employed because their employers think that their social science is applicable to some practical necessity. Some knowledge of techniques developed in social science may be used: to select taxicab drivers that are not likely to have accidents; to give vocational guidance; to discover why one business enterprise has labor troubles while a similar enterprise does not; to make more effective some governmental program carried into farming communities; to help the War Relocation Authority carry out its difficult task with Japanese-Americans.

All these contributions to efficiency and adjustment may be claimed with justice by social scientists. What is also to be claimed, and is less commonly stressed, is that social science contributes to that general understanding of the world around us which, as we say, "liberalizes," or "enriches." The relation of social science to humanistic learning is reciprocal. Social scientists need humanistic learning the better to be social scientists. And the understanding of society, personality, and human nature which is achieved by scientific methods returns to enrich that humanistic understanding without which none can become human and with which some few may become wise. Because its subject matter is humanity, the contribution of social science to general, liberal education is greater than is the contribution of those sciences with subject matter that is physical. In this respect also, creative artist and social scientist find themselves side by side. The artist may reveal something of universal human or social nature. So too may the social scientist. No one has ever applied, as a key to a lock, Sumner's *Folkways* or Tawney's *Religion and the Rise of Capitalism* or James's *The Varieties of Religious Experience*. These are not the works of social science that can be directly consulted and applied when a government office or a business concern has an immediate problem. But they are the books of lasting influence. Besides what influence they have upon those social scientists who come to work in the government office, or the business concern, in so far as they are read and understood and thought about by men and women who are not social scientists, or even as they are communicated indirectly by those who have read them to others, they are part of humanistic education, in the broad sense. Releasing us from our imprisonment in the particular, we are freed by seeing how we are exemplifications of the general. For how many young people has not Sumner's book, or Veblen's book, or some work by Freud, come as a swift widening of the doors of vision, truly a liberation, a seeing of one's self, perhaps for the first time, as sharing the experiences, the nature, of many other men and women? So I say that social science, as practiced, is something of an art and that, as its best works are communicated, it has something of the personal and social values of all the arts.

EARL S. JOHNSON

HUMANISM AND SCIENCE IN THE SOCIAL STUDIES*

The social studies are the middle studies, beholden to the humanities for their subject-matter and to the natural sciences for their methods. My fear is that they stand in some danger of losing their middle position by leaning too much in the direction of the natural sciences.

The humanities and the social sciences have a common subject matter, namely humanity: feelings, sentiments, opinions, standards and ideals. As Robert Redfield has said, the humanities bring particular men and women to our direct acquaintance through a swift and intimate understanding of them. The social sciences, however, seek to convert such understandings into formal generalizations.

For Redfield's term "the social sciences" I now wish to substitute the term "the social studies." The social studies are not concerned to maintain the classic and quite disparate structures of the social sciences. Rather, they seek to draw from and draw together the substance of the social sciences but without loss of "their habits of mind." Redfield's way of knowing as an anthropologist can thus be used as a way of knowing in the social studies. He wrote: "I think now that what I see men do, and understand as something that human beings do, is seen often with a valuing of it. I like and dislike as I go. This is how I reach my understanding of it." This process he termed "feeling-knowing."

From this same compound of senses comes my concern with the bivalences of the social studies. These bivalences are at once natural and legitimate but are seen darkly, if at all, by many teachers. If taken as harmful dualisms they confront the social studies with two equally frightening consequences: propaganda on one hand and purposeless scientism on the other.

*Reprinted by permission of *American Behavioral Scientist,* Vol. VII, No. 8 (April 1964), pp. 3–7.

The focus of this article is thus the humanistic-scientific nature of the social studies, which may be viewed from such paired perspectives as belief and knowledge; value and fact; the non-rational and the rational; and impulse and reason. All are variations on the theme of the affective and the cognitive. All report man as a conscience and a mind. These dichotomies or bivalences must be clarified so that they are not mistaken for dualism. For this clarification I shall report the counsel of reliable scholars in the social sciences.

THE NATURE OF PERCEPTION

I begin with the nature of perception but find myself immediately in difficulty. I cannot treat it "neat and clean" because it is much more than an optical mechanism. When I look, especially at social objects, I look *with* as well as *at*—that is, with my interests and biases. Hence, I cannot do what Bacon asked, namely divest my mind of all preconceptions— "lay them by" as his words have it.

Whitehead's counsel I find much more reasonable: "No prehension can be divested of its affective tone [for] concernedness is of the essence of perception." And there is Darwin's older and equally reliable counsel that "all observation must be for or against some view, if it is to be of any service." Thus I find perception implicated with just those issues which I noted in my brief list of paired perspectives on the social studies.

I know, of course, that the possibility of pure objectivity to which nineteenth century science was committed must now be abandoned. The scientist has never looked at his world with a blank mind and an empty stare. All scientific work, as Michael Polanyi tells us, has about it a quality of *connoisseurship* which makes complete detachment of knower from the object of his study impossible. In the area of the natural sciences, however, interest and bias intrude only upon the knower while, in the area of the social sciences, they intrude upon both knower and known.

THE NATURE OF SOCIAL FACTS

Just as perception is not "neat and clean," so I find that I cannot treat, with *seriatim* precision, any of the paired perspectives of my concern. I look now into the nature of social facts. But, as facts, they do not lie about ready to be espied and possessed by me. They are made through their being consequences of my discriminating awareness. That such awareness is less heavily laden with interest, bias and purpose than would be the case if the facts were in the realm of physical nature is attested by the relative ease with which consensus may be reached concerning the nature of factness of a crystal, and the relative difficulty with which consensus may be reached concerning the nature of factness of an urban slum.

The reason for the difference is not far to seek. Facts about social and animate things—willful things—are more highly personal than facts about physical and inanimate things—unwillful things. Around the former Justice Holmes' "penumbra of doubt" hovers closer and less apt to disappear than around the latter.

Michael Polanyi confirms what insight tells us in his observation that we have to exercise "more personal faculties—involving more far-reaching participation of the knower in the known—in order to understand life," especially in what he calls its "higher manifestations." Among such manifestations are the elaboration of various forms of socio-political policy in which, to use Polanyi's language, "our subject matter will tend to include more and more of the very faculties on which we rely for understanding of it," Among these, I suggest, are desire and judgment.

It is thus clear that "facts of human nature" are much more controversial than "the facts of Nature." But it would be a mistake to regard to co-efficients of "the facts of human Nature" as imperfections. They are, rather, the necessary components of all knowledge, especially social knowledge.

THE RELATION OF KNOWLEDGE TO FEELING

It has been suggested that the only way to get facts of any kind, independent of concepts and theories, is "merely to look . . . and forthwith remain perpetually dumb, never uttering a word or describing what one sees, after the manner of a calf looking at the moon." But this is a commentary on gaping, not perceiving! This brings me to some observations about belief and knowledge hardly to be distinguished from the phenomena of value and fact. The data to which belief most readily attaches are social—but not to the exclusion of physical data. (Perhaps the pairing with which I am now concerned were better named, feeling and knowing.)

The relation between knowledge and feeling is well illustrated in a study of the meaning of certain terms, social facts. To the question, "Are all men equal?," 79 per cent of Northern respondents said, "yes," while 61 per cent of the respondents from the South gave the same reply. But, when the question, "Are Negroes equal to whites?," was posed, the responses were 21 per cent and 4 per cent from the Northern and Southern respondents, respectively. Erich Fromm's explanatory comment is that "the person who assented only to the first question undoubtedly remembered it as a thought learned in class and retained because it is still a part of a generally recognized, respectable ideology, but it has no relation to what the person really feels; it is, as it were, in his head, without any connection with his heart and hence without any power to influence action."

Archibald MacLeish, poet rather than scientist, asks with deep concern if we feel our knowledge. He goes on to remark that "knowledge without feeling is not knowledge and can lead only to public irresponsibility and indifference, and conceivably to ruin [for] when the fact is disassociated from the feel of the fact . . . civilization is in danger." It would be novel but interesting and perhaps even effective if, once in a while, teachers of the social studies would ask students how they feel about some facts, particularly those whose factuality the students doubt or deny because they run counter to their beliefs.

What MacLeish is saying, if expressed in terms of the Negro problem, is this: if the only ground on which teachers stand in dealing with that problem is science, by which for instance they may expose the error of the belief in the Negro's inborn inferiority, they still do not lay hold of the moral principle. Our students may thus have awareness of a reliable fact but they do not, by that means alone, have command over a principle which the fact helps to illuminate. I wonder how many social studies teachers are aware of their involvement in an unavoidable indoctrination—unavoidable because the facts they teach are the facts about the social values which they have *chosen* to teach.

Teachers of the social studies need to understand the implications of Ernst Cassirer's observation that "ignorance is not so far from the truth as prejudice." They need also to understand that students' heads may be in error because their hearts are, and *vice versa*. But neither of these errors is sensibly affected by propaganda, and scientism neither admits their presence nor cares a whit about them.

John Dewey would resolve the dilemma by insisting on the conversion of beliefs into examined beliefs, or "goods *de facto* into goods *de jure*." So would I. The issue is not that it ought to be done, but how it may be done. Would that the conversion were as simple as a matter of fact and logic; the statistics I have just cited do not permit me to believe so. It may be that we shall have to take account not only of Dewey but also of St. Augustine: admit that belief should rest on knowledge, but also that knowledge may stand on belief.

THE PURPOSE OF HISTORY

The writing and teaching of history afford further confirmation of the complexities of social knowledge. Just as the writing of history is conditioned by what one age finds worthy of note in an earlier one, so the teaching of history ought to be conditioned by what an account of the past may be worth to the present generation of students. Teachers need to ask of history such questions as these: What ought its study do for my students? What have facts about the past to offer youth now? What ideas and ideals does the past afford which will help them relieve some anxiety, satisfy some curiosity, resolve some doubt, or clarify some issue? In this view I am greatly encouraged by Santayana's remark that "facts are nothing until they become symbols."

If these are the proper canons by which the past may be made relevant and significant for the present and the emerging future, the teaching of history like the writing of it must be selective. Whitehead has suggested what ought to discipline this selective process: ". . . the main danger is the lack of discrimination between details which are now irrelevant and the main principles which urge forward human existence, ever renewing vitality by incarnation in novel detail." The same philosophy of selection is implicit in the last chapter of Dewey's *The School and Society:* "Social life we have always with us: the distinction of past and present is indifferent to it. . . It is life for all that; it shows the motives which draw men together and push them apart, and depicts what is desirable and what is hurtful."

The only alternative to the conception of history which I thus share with you is that which Toynbee characterizes as "one damned fact after another."

THE TELEOLOGY OF THE SOCIAL STUDIES

From my concern with the purposes of history I now must ra͏ͅ the question as to whether the social studies admit of purpos͏ͅ problem of purpose, or teleology, must be met head-on. If it issue of purpose it would appear to raise the issue of mechanism and to what end men employ it. Thus the issue of ends and means if joined.

In this matter, the social studies present no difficulty. The term *social* connotes teleology or purpose; the term *studies* connotes mechanism or means. Implicit in these terms are all the paired perspectives which identify the humanistic or purposeful, and the scientific or implemental.

We may, with no difficulty, find the teleology of the social studies in "a firmer purpose" and its mechanism in the means by which "a wider knowledge" is had. To these two terms, Whitehead adds his third, "resonance from the teacher's personality," which seems to me to suggest that *it* is both end and means. Leaving aside now the role of the teacher, he suggests the same possibility of joint ends and means in the social studies in his belief that "the task of reason is to promote the art of life." The counsel of Whitehead in these matters is affirmed by George Herbert Mead: "Thinking is not a realm which can be taken outside its possible social uses." Thus the mechanism called *thought* is joined with the purpose called *social action,* the ultimate concern of the social studies.

Discussion of teleology leads me to a concept which I seldom find in the social studies or in discussions about them. This is the concept *spiritual,* and its identification with such humanly attainable virtues as intellectual excellence, devotion to duty, and reverence for truth and human dignity. So conceived, it lies in the realm of the natural and is attainable outside and beyond the realm of creeds and dogmas. It is that attribute of man which empowers him to command science to work for good and wise purposes. Thus he responds to the lure of an ideal.

THE RATIONAL–NON-RATIONAL BIVALENCE

This brings me to consider the remaining paired perspectives of the social studies: the non-rational and the rational, or their equivalents, impulse and reason.

Here I inherit an embarrassment of riches. I think of Dewey's "there is no thought unless it be enkindled by an emotion," and his view that "rationality . . . is not a force to evoke against impulse and habit [but] the attainment of a working harmony among desires." These are needed correctives to the notion all too prevalent among students, that the task of reason is to dismiss emotion. But I like best the thought of Graham Wallas in these matters: "Men will not take up the intolerable disease of thought unless their feelings are first stirred, and the strength of the idea of science has been that it does touch men's feelings, and draws motive power for thought from the passions of reverence of curiosity and of limitless hope."

Despite the mutuality and balance which is struck between the non-rational and the rational in these scholarly testaments, the prestige of the *rational* is hard to match, and even more difficult to deny and allay. How it came by that prestige and sustains it one finds in William James' remark that "it has the loquacity, it can challenge your proofs, and chop logic and put you down with words."

For the classic representation of the relationship between the non-rational and the rational I turn to Max Weber's "ethics of conviction" (or absolute ends) and "ethics of responsibility." Weber was not, as I understand him, recommending politics without passion or conviction. Quite to the contrary. But in order to discipline that passion he was recommending that it be held to accountability. Weber pointed up the danger of living only by an ethic of conviction which, historically, has been expressed in the axiom: "Do right, though the heavens fall." But Weber, perceiving perhaps that the heavens are still in their place, counseled the practice of an ethic of responsibility to keep them there. Thus his ethics complement and re-enforce the role of the non-rational and the rational, or of impulse and reason.

I believe that it is not necessary that passion or reason reign. What is required is something akin to the rule of goodness under the regency of wisdom. This does not require that the passions be dismissed, rather that they be disciplined and instructed by reason and, paradoxical as it may sound, that reason be informed by passion.

SOME ISSUES OF METHOD

I have surveyed the counsel of scholars on the natural and legitimate bivalences of the humanistic and the scientific as they are joined in the social studies. Their counsel and mine has been to help us keep these bivalences from becoming fatal dualisms. As a senior clerk in the court of the social studies I should like to make some *obiter dicta* on methodological implications.

For methodology, I wish to substitute "ways of knowing." These are three: the way of fact, the way of logic by which facts are ordered and related, and the way of imagination. They are not separated or fixed in their order; they *are* common to each of the three great bodies of knowledge—the humanities, the social studies, and the natural studies. There is, however, a significant difference in the valences assigned to them within these great bodies of knowledge. As befits the subject matter of the natural studies the heavier valence falls to fact and logic; as befits the subject matter of the humanities the heavier valence falls to imagination; but in the social studies their valences should be equal.

For heuristic purposes these three ways of knowing may be located along the continua of a series of polar constructs. The first of these is Pascal's spirit of geometry and his spirit of finesse, a continuum from "knowledge about men" gained through statistical methods, to "acquaintance with men" gained through the methods of participation, or sympathetic introspection—Einfuhlung—thus incorporating skill and a quality of experience. These would result, respectively, in the mastery of the tools of inquiry and informed passion, both of which I believe to be proper and powerful agents making for the transfer of understanding.

Second, are the poles of MacIver's spatial knowledge and social knowledge, giving us ecological man on the one hand, and, on the other, consensual or political man.

Third is the polarity which we owe to Wilhelm Dilthey's method of *Anschauen,* literally looking at man as a physical object, and his *nach erleben,* literally re-living the experience of another and through empathy making it one's own.

IMAGINATION IN THE SOCIAL STUDIES

I fear that there has been a neglect of the imaginative way of knowing in the social studies, and thus wish to consider it in relation to the equal claims and valences of fact and logic.

I do not find imagination lying at a pole opposite that of fact and logic, cold and rational inquiry. Rather I find them meeting and mixing as Dewey's metaphor permits: the compatibility of warm emotion and cool reason. If I wish to treat imagination as somewhat removed from fact and logic I may do so by assigning it the role of the making of hypotheses, the "ifs" of social study later to be tested by fact and logic to produce the "then" of reliable knowledge. It provides the

HUMANISM AND SCIENCE

mystique to be investigated later by fact and logic as technique. But lest we delude ourselves we must keep in mind that "the growth of what is known increases the scope of what may be imagined and hoped for." Furthermore, imagination is the way insight is both had and spent, and insight must, insofar as possible, be brought before the court of fact and logic.

Thus imagination not only brings images worthy of submission to inquiry but helps us to form them. It also helps us express our thoughts, for without it teaching is uninspired and uninspiring. To stifle it is to stifle the creativity of our students. To increase its range and set it free is one of the grand purposes of education. Its function is to provoke, to motivate and give intent and purpose to both thought and action. To make these functions finally effective it requires, of course, the means and method of facts and logic.

In both historical and contemporary social study we can bring persons and events to mind through imagination, when to bring them into our physical presence is impossible by reason of the factors of time and distance. Although there may be some doubt that we can, in our time, *think* as men once did or now do in far-away places, we can come to *feel* as they did and do and thus come to an understanding of them. The demand that we develop, in our students, a knowledge about and a sensitivity to the conditions of mankind in our crowded and worried world is an insistent one. This cannot be honored without great drafts on their imagination. Thus what they may not know as reliable and verified knowledge, they may appreciate through the way of knowing which I call imagination.

Whether the severest test of imagination as a way of knowing lies in the field of history or in such contemporary studies as civics and social problems is less important than that we understand how imagination complements and is complemented by fact and logic.

In writing about the historian's "scientific conscience" as it manifests itself in the nineteenth century, the philosopher Hocking remarks that it "became a vast technique for sifting evidence and the exclusion of all but the verifiable facts. The only difficulty with this procedure," he tells us, "is that the important facts of history are never verifiable, for they take place in the mind. They have to do with the passions and motives of men which no one ever sees. The real historical deeds are decisions, not the consequent movements of arms and legs; but the historian can only verify the movements. The decision and its precious tempest of inner debate remains inaccessible"—except, as Hocking adds, through the ability of the historian to *infer*. That this is a talent and skill which rests heavily on the imaginative way of knowing, Hocking well knows and says so: "Now a powerful induction is no result of following logical rules—*pace* the textbooks, [that is, by their leave] there are no rules. It comes as a stroke of insight, after long mulling over the data, which—under new light from God knows where, probably an intimation of necessity—re-conceives those data."

Surely, imagination is involved in this process. But imagination works on the future as well as on the past. It may be used to construct the future as well as reconstruct the past—to bring to mind not only what might be, what could be, but what ought to be. So conceived, it is part of the moral dimension of the mind, and thus of the "ought capacity" which gives man his place in "the great chain of being."

THE PEDAGOGICAL MORAL

In conclusion, I recall Redfield's image of the common subject matter of the humanities and the social sciences: feelings, sentiments, opinions, standards, and ideals. Are not these strange, even forbidding nouns to all but the rarest of social studies teachers? Does not an understanding of them require the rediscovery of imagination as a way of knowing? My intention is not to put the social studies out of balance but rather, through renewing our concern with imagination, to put them in better balance.

I come now to the pedagogical moral of my account. It is this: we ought to make our students aware of the *ways* they know if we would make them more fully aware of *what* they know. In this view, the ways of knowing with which I have been concerned and which are mandated by the bivalent nature of man and the social studies would become quite as much the substance of their study as its method. Thus, it seems to me, the controversial nature of the social studies would be seen as native to their humanistic and scientific make-up and, hence, not as a problem to be solved but a lesson to be learned. So, too, would we serve Quintillian's conception of our task: "So teach that your students will not always have to be taught."

BIBLIOGRAPHY

Becker, Ernest. *The Structure of Evil: An Essay on the Unification of the Science of Man.* New York: George Braziller, 1968.

Horowitz, Irving L., ed. *The New Sociology: Essays in Social Science and Social Theory.* New York: Oxford University Press, 1964.

──────. "Mainliners and Marginals: The Human Shape of Sociological Theory," in Llewelyn Gross, ed. *Sociological Theory: Inquiries and Paradigms.* New York: Harper and Row, 1967, pp. 358–383.

Johnson, Earl S. *The Theory and Practice of the Social Studies.* New York: Macmillan, 1956.

Kapp, K. William. *Toward a Science of Man in Society.* The Hague: Martinus Nijhoff, 1961.

Lynd, Robert S. *Knowledge for What?* Princeton, N.J.: Princeton University Press, 1939.

Mills, C. Wright, ed. *Images of Man.* New York: George Braziller, 1960.

──────. *The Sociological Imagination.* New York: Oxford University Press, 1959.

Myrdal, Gunnar. *Value in Social Theory.* New York: Harper & Row, 1959.

Polanyi, Michael. *Personal Knowledge.* Chicago: University of Chicago Press, 1958.

Redfield, Robert. *Human Nature and the Study of Society.* Chicago: University of Chicago Press, 1962.

──────. *The Social Uses of Social Science.* Chicago: University of Chicago Press, 1962.

Sorokin, Pitirim A. *Fads and Foibles in Modern Sociology.* Chicago, Ill.: Henry Regnery Co., 1956.

Znaniecki, Florian. *The Cultural Sciences.* Urbana, Ill.: University of Illinois Press, 1952.